THE GREAT DAYS
SUNDERLA

THE GREAT DAYS OF
SUNDERLAND

Six League Titles and Two FA Cups

David Potter

First published by Pitch Publishing, 2023

Pitch Publishing
9 Donnington Park,
85 Birdham Road,
Chichester,
West Sussex,
PO20 7AJ
www.pitchpublishing.co.uk
info@pitchpublishing.co.uk

A CIP catalogue record is available for this book
from the British Library.

ISBN 978 1 80150 432 4

Typesetting and origination by Pitch Publishing
Printed and bound in Great Britain by TJ Books, Padstow

Contents

Introduction

IT IS extremely sad to see Sunderland where they are. It was a throwaway remark by a commentator at the League One play-off final of May 2022 that woke me up to just how big a team Sunderland are – or could be – when he said something to the effect that about 20,000 season tickets had already been sold for the 2022/23 season. And this was for a team who were endeavouring to get out of the third tier of English football. Fortunately they won through to earn a spot in the Championship but when one looks at their support and the passion that they can engender, it is hard to provide an answer to the question, 'Why are they not in the top tier – and near the top of it?'

The Mackems have been champions of England on six occasions. Sadly their last triumph was in 1936 – the year of the Berlin Olympics, the Spanish Civil War, the abdication of King Edward VIII and poignantly for the local area, the Jarrow Crusade when the local unemployed walked to London to protest about not having a job. The previous five occasions were all before the First World War, so it would be fair to say that there has been no recent league success.

But there was a spectacular winning of the FA Cup on 5 May 1973 when Sunderland, in the old Second Division, beat the highly successful but never popular Leeds United through Ian Porterfield and Jim Montgomery, mainly, but another nine heroes as well – and Bob Stokoe's hat became an icon on Wearside. Change 1973 to 1937 and you will find Sunderland's only other success in the FA Cup. This time it was against Preston North End – Proud Preston – another fine team with all sorts of fine players like Bill Shankly and the two O'Donnell brothers, but Sunderland then had Bobby Gurney and Horatio Carter, who preferred to be called Raich.

So six leagues and two cups make up the total of their achievements. Many people will remember 1973, and there will still be a dwindling few who recall 1937 and 1936, but sadly there is not a Mackem left who can remember being able to say, 'We are the champions of England.' No League Cups. There have been near misses, some of them unlucky ones, but you get nothing for bad luck. There have also been championships of the lower divisions as well, but these are always faded glories, for most people in the British Isles are of the opinion that Sunderland is a big enough town and there is a big enough support for the club to be in the top tier.

Sadly the decline of Sunderland and the decline of the British Empire are remarkably parallel. Sunderland (the very name seems to be onomatopoeic in that it sounds like iron girders being thrown about, does it not?) was a vital cog in the massive structure of Great Britain in Victorian and Edwardian days. Changed days! Maybe the slow death of the empire was to be deplored, maybe not; but the fact that there is no strong Sunderland AFC is surely a bad thing.

Naturally there are other reasons as well. It would not be difficult, throughout the past century and a bit, to point the finger at inefficient stewarding of the club, incompetent managers, and players who underperformed after almost bankrupting the club with ludicrous wages and transfer fees. But that happens elsewhere as well. The point about Sunderland is that it was once very different and could of course be different again in the future. Pandora released all sorts of evils on the world out of her box, but she also released hope. 'Walk on, walk on with hope in your hearts' is the line from a song beloved of many football fans. Sunderland need more hope than most clubs. It doesn't need to be like this.

One will not get very far in a conversation with a Sunderland supporter without hearing the words

'Newcastle United', followed by an expletive not very far away either. There does seem to be a complex here, not least because a traveller to Sunderland, certainly by train, usually has to go through Newcastle first. Local rivalry is of course healthy and even the lifeblood of football, and it is sad that the two sleeping giants of the north-east often miss each other by being in different divisions, with the Mackems, sadly more often than not, lower down than the Geordies.

But although local rivalry is both healthy and indeed inevitable, this one can obfuscate things. There is the real danger of this one getting out of hand, to the detriment of both clubs. Violence is not unheard of among those whom the educational system has failed to reach, but there is too much social intercourse between the two cities to allow the situation to develop further than footballing rivalry. They are basically the same people with the same outlook on life, the same aspirations, the same deprivations and the same general DNA. There is the Bob Stokoe example. He won the FA Cup with Newcastle as a player in 1955, and with Sunderland as a manager in 1973. He is therefore much loved in both places.

We must always remember that football is all important. Shankly's much quoted aphorism that football is 'much, much more important' than life or death is clear rubbish, but football still comes quite high. It always has in this area, but one finds that a given year is defined not only by how well our team has done, but whether 'we' have done better than 'them'. In other words, Sunderland ninth in the Premier league and Newcastle tenth would be a good season. Never mind that Liverpool, Manchester United and London giants like Chelsea, Spurs and Arsenal are 20 points ahead, the fact the 'we' have beaten 'them' is paramount. Sunderland's (and Newcastle's) aspirations should be higher than that. They once were. It's just a pity that it is all so long ago now.

Unless otherwise stated, quotes are from the *Sunderland Daily Echo*.

1

League Champions 1891/92

THE FOOTBALL League was formed in 1888, and Sunderland were elected to join at the AGM in May 1890. Thus they played their first season in the competition in 1890/91 and achieved only moderate success that year, the title being won by Everton, having been won by Preston North End in the first two seasons of its existence.

The league (a fairly revolutionary idea whereby every team played each other twice, home and away for points) was centred in Lancashire and the Midlands. Sunderland were clearly the geographical outsiders, and there had been doubts about whether it was wise to include them, but their acceptance was probably due to several reasons. One was that they were good, already referred to as 'the team of all the talents'; another reason was that they were well supported and they could bring a certain amount of finance; and further was the political one that the Football League wanted to be seen as the 'English' league, rather than just a local one. They had not yet made any overtures to southern clubs, but it was good to have a northern club, particularly one full of Scotsmen. Perhaps one day, they might even be called 'The British League'.

Rail links to Sunderland were good, and there was a certain excitement, even a bit of missionary zeal, as the clubs decided to welcome the Wearsiders, and to enjoy the chance to see the north of the country. Sunderland for their part took the opportunity to represent the north-east. They were one step ahead of teams like Newcastle East End and Middlesbrough Ironopolis in this respect.

Replacing Stoke, who had transferred their allegiances to another organisation called the Football Alliance, Sunderland performed creditably in 1890/91, finishing seventh, but suffering the embarrassing experience of having two points deducted for fielding an ineligible player. Everton were the champions, Sunderland's jousts with them ending up 1-0 for the home team on both occasions. It was in every sense a learning experience for Sunderland.

As in every summer, there were changes in 1891 as far as the Football League was concerned. The number of clubs was increased from 12 to 14. The bottom four clubs – Accrington, Aston Villa, Derby

County and West Bromwich Albion – were all re-elected, and they were joined by Darwen and Stoke, Stoke having thought better of their dalliance with the Football Alliance. Two of the teams who were not admitted were Newton Heath (who in later years would become Manchester United but no one seemed to think they were a viable concern in 1891), and Sunderland Albion who earned only one vote, presumably that of Sunderland Association Football Club, the organisation that we are primarily concerned with.

Thus the 14 teams in 1891/92 were seven from Lancashire: Preston North End, Burnley, Blackburn Rovers, Accrington, Everton, Darwen and Bolton Wanderers; six from the Midlands: Aston Villa, West Bromwich Albion, Wolverhampton Wanderers, Notts County, Derby County and Stoke; and one from the north-east in Sunderland. There were moves afoot to form a Second Division as well, but as yet there was nothing from the London area. Those who objected to the inclusion of Sunderland on the grounds that they were too distant would find there was an added reason to be unhappy, for Sunderland won the league that year.

Sunderland's squad for 1891/92 consisted of 17 players, only three of whom were Englishmen, the rest having come from Scotland in search of professional wages. Theoretically at least Scotland was all amateur, although it was a rule honoured more in its breach than its observance – and sometimes blatantly so. But in England professionalism was all legal and above board, even though there was a certain horror in some parts of polite society about the idea of people earning their living by playing sport.

Their Englishmen were Tom Porteous, John Oliver and David Hannah, while Scotland supplied Ned Doig (the goalkeeper from Arbroath), John Murray, John Auld, Donald Gow (recently signed from Rangers), Willie Gibson, James Hannah, John Harvey, Hugh Wilson, John Smith, Jimmy Millar, Jimmy Logan, Jimmy Gillespie, John Campbell (the prolific goalscorer) and Johnny Scott. Doig was quite a character. Born in Letham near Forfar in 1866 and christened Edward Doig, he was sometimes referred to as Ed, Jed or Ted, but most often as Ned. He has a great claim to be looked upon as the best Sunderland player of all time.

The person in charge was a local man called Tom Watson. He would be destined to have a great managerial career and this was the start of it. One is wary of using the word 'manager' in the context of the 1890s; the role was nothing like that of our 21st-century concept of supremo. In theory he was little more than a 'match secretary' with no authority over team selection, for example. But he would of course advise the committee and the directors, and he could, without seeming to choose the team and decide tactics as well. Watson did that, and with conspicuous success.

Sunderland's 1891/92 season opened with a home game at Newcastle Road against Wolverhampton Wanderers on Saturday, 5 September. The *Sunderland Daily Echo* was optimistic and upbeat about the new season, and told readers that there would be about 100 junior teams in the area starting their season, as well, such was the passion for this game. The visitors arrived on the Friday night along with a few supporters (following one's team to away fixtures was an increasing habit in the 1890s, albeit confined to the more affluent) and jokes were made about packs of 'wolves' hanging about the centre of the town, with even a reference in the singular about a local girl being paid attention to and courted by a charming 'wolf'. There were three new Sunderland players – James Logan, Donald Gow and James Hannah – for the season. Hannah was already well known, for he had played for Sunderland Albion, but the other two were Scottish and needed some introduction.

The reporter for the *Sunderland Daily Echo* was very impressed with Logan, who was 'fine, able-bodied … single and very abstemious in his habits'. 'Abstemiousness' or the abstention from alcohol was a great (and rare) habit to possess in Victorian society, for drink was a terrible problem. He was also very affable, lived in 'diggings' in Zetland Street, Monkwearmouth, and was only 22 years old. He came from Troon in Ayrshire, a county which 'not only gave a poet to Scotland, but was the nursery of some of the very best of players now before the public' and already loved Sunderland and the area. Gow, from Blair Athol in Perthshire, was slightly more experienced having played for Rangers, who shared the inaugural Scottish championship with Dumbarton in 1891. He had also developed a liking for Sunderland, but had been unwell recently and was expected to be unavailable for the opening fixtures. In the event, Logan didn't play in the first game either.

Sunderland's team in the 5-2 defeat of Wolves was Doig, Porteous, Oliver, Murray, Auld, Gibson, Smith, Millar, Campbell, Scott and Hannah. It was 2-2 at half-time, but Sunderland really turned on the style and after Millar scored the fifth goal just before full time 'the enthusiasm of the crowd now knew no bounds and a perfect din prevailed until the referee blew the final whistle'. Millar had scored a hat-trick and Campbell the other two. It was a good start to the season in reasonable weather.

But then came a stumble. Three in fact. The first was at the famous ground of Deepdale, home of Preston North End, the club who had won the Football League in the first two years of its existence in 1889

GREAT DAYS OF SUNDERLAND

and 1890 (and the FA Cup into the bargain in 1889) and were generally known as 'Proud Preston'. It was a game that many looked forward to, even though North End had not started the season well. They had never yet defeated Sunderland at Deepdale and it was a much-anticipated event.

Sunderland travelled down to Lancashire on the Friday night, spent the night in a hotel and then on Saturday morning visited the ground (for the first time in the case of many of their players) and then had a walk around the town, followed by quite a few of the locals who had been told who they were. Being football players they were instantly recognised by being better dressed than most and by their athletic appearance. It was all good-natured stuff, though, and the players were under orders to talk to fans, even those who were supporting the other side.

A crowd of 7,000 – a huge attendance for this infant game of football – appeared at Deepdale for a game which the *Echo* told us was played on a day 'totally unfit for football'. And why was that? The afternoon was 'brilliantly fine' and 'without a breath of air', and the reporter clearly believed that football was meant to be played in worse conditions than this, and that they should still have been playing cricket. Indeed, that very day, Sunderland Cricket Club were in action, losing to Norton – a result that meant

Norton were the champions of the Durham County Cricket League.

The report of the game also made an astonishing gaffe when it gave the final score as Preston North End 3 Sunderland 4. This seems to be a bit of wishful thinking (later analysts would talk about a Freudian slip) for the report made it plain that Preston won 3-1. It is a sad fact about Victorian sports reporting that mistakes were frequent, for proofreading was a science very much in its infancy, and once the reporter filed his report and gave it to the compositor it was not really looked at much before it appeared on the streets.

Sunderland fielded the same team as had won against Wolves the previous week, their only goal coming before half-time. Millar was the scorer 'when a scrimmage was in progress' but he did not have a good game overall. Doig was singled out for his fine goalkeeping near the end, and the game was described as 'splendid' with *Athletic News* of the view that it would be good to see a team 'equal to Sunderland' at Deepdale every Saturday.

As the team returned north that evening, the atmosphere was still upbeat. A defeat to the famous Preston team was not exactly a huge disaster. Excuses could be made – the heat was excessive, the opposition were generally agreed to be one of the best in England – and in any case, it might be an idea to try out some other players, particularly the new ones, when Sunderland went back to Lancashire the following week to play Bolton Wanderers. Besides, the team hadn't really played badly, and it was early days yet.

It was a slightly changed side chosen for the trip to Bolton. They met at the Central Station at 1.30pm on the Friday, being booked in to the Douglas Hotel, Manchester. The fact that the *Sunderland Daily Echo* reported this meant that there was a fairly large crowd of well-wishers to see them off; the main emotion of the crowd, one imagines, would have been sheer jealousy and envy at the lot of a professional football player who was able to travel on trains and to stay in hotels. Although the life of a footballer was as precarious in 1891 as it is now with the constant risk of injury and the fear of losing your job after a bad run of form, nevertheless it was better than working down the mines or in the shipyards.

A team of Doig, Porteous, Gow, Wilson, Auld, Murray, Smith, Millar, Campbell, Hannah and Scott took the field at Pike Lane to take on the 'Trotters', as Bolton Wanderers were called. Bolton, a cotton manufacturing town and in 1891 reasonably prosperous, had already developed a love of football, and the Wearsiders were given a good reception by the non-partisan locals.

It was, of course, long before the days in which supporters could travel in any great numbers to watch their team in away games, but one of the great advances of the early 1890s had been the telegraph system which meant that a report of the game could be sent almost immediately to the office of the *Sunderland Daily Echo* which duly produced its evening 'pink' edition, and had it on the streets promptly, on sale at the usual points of outside the railway station, theatres and music halls, and although newspaper vendors were sometimes discouraged from entering public houses, they nevertheless did so, selling their papers for a penny to the avid readers. Thus shortly after the 'pink' was issued at 7.15pm, most people knew that Sunderland had sustained another defeat in Lancashire when going down 4-3 to Bolton.

It was generally agreed that Sunderland had bad luck. They scored first and last in the first half, but conceded four in between to make it 4-2 for Bolton at half-time. The pace was fierce but slowed in the second half, the only addition to the score coming from a penalty by Hugh Wilson. The first-half goals had been scored by Johnny Campbell and Jimmy Millar. But it was a dispirited bunch of Mackems who made their way home from Lancashire. There was another away fixture to come the following week as well.

This one was at Aston Villa, the famous team from Birmingham who had already won the FA Cup in 1887 and were generally regarded as one of the best around. They played at a stadium called Perry Barr, and had arranged this game for Monday, 28 September to take advantage of a large crowd likely to assemble on a local holiday. Meanwhile, Sunderland played on the Saturday against Newcastle East End, for there was as yet no Newcastle United, although things were certainly moving in that direction with rumours of secret talks between the directors of the city's West End and East End clubs.

The crowd at Perry Barr was a large one of 10,000, and the weather was good, but they saw a very poor performance from Sunderland who were 4-2 down at half-time and although they rallied a little in the second half, they still lost 5-3. It was agreed to have been a good game, and Sunderland earned a little praise for their performance, but this now meant that they had lost three away matches in a row, admittedly against possibly the three toughest teams in the league. It did not look like championship-winning form, and yet no one could say that they were playing badly, and as the wiser supporters would say, 'There is a long way to go yet.'

Had this happened in the 21st century, of course, there would have been cries of 'sack the manager' and the TV stations and newspapers would have dug up ex-players and gnarled journalists to say what exactly was wrong at Newcastle Road. In the 1890s there was a resigned acceptance of what was happening, and wishes that things would improve. Tom Watson was aware that things could be better, but went around telling everyone that the three fixtures lost were all away from home, and that the team did not really play all that badly.

The rot was stopped on 3 October when Everton, the defending champions, came to town. Both teams had played friendlies against Scottish opposition in the previous midweek. Sunderland had lost 4-2 at Newcastle Road to Queen's Park (the club who refused to join the Scottish league because they feared it would lead to professionalism becoming legalised) whereas Everton were on their way back home, as it were, from Glasgow where 'in slashing form', they had defeated Rangers 4-1. They arrived in the north-east on the Friday and, clearly aware of the nuances of local rivalry, trained at the ground of Newcastle East End at Heaton, rather than anywhere in Sunderland.

Sunderland's team was Doig, Porteous, Gow, Murray, Auld, Gibson, James Hannah, Smith, Campbell, Scott and David Hannah. James Hannah was given his debut. He would very soon become a favourite of the Sunderland crowd, earning the nickname of

'Blood', presumably bestowed as a compliment for his whole-hearted approach to the game.

The weather was once again favourable, and about 8,000 fans appeared to see the tussle. It was a tough game, with Everton's centre-forward Fred Geary being injured several times (the local press reports did not say so, but one assumes because of a few hard tackles) and the home side eased home 2-1. The first goal came from Campbell and the second one was described quaintly – albeit obscurely – by the *Sunderland Daily Echo* in the following terms, 'The outcome of a fierce onslaught, the ball went past Jardine [Everton's goalkeeper] and number two was chalked up for Sunderland amid tremendous enthusiasm which broke forth afresh when, after some little demur by Everton, the ball was taken to the centre and restarted by Geary, a sign that they had conceded the point.' Other highlights included an invasion by 'the inevitable dog which caused some amusement until recalled by its owner'. Geary was eventually taken off late in the game after he came off second best in a shoulder-charging joust with Ned Doig, and Sunderland finished narrow but deserved winners.

The defeat of the champions was a cause for celebration and from now on, Sunderland's season took off, just as the days began to get shorter and the weather began to deteriorate. The following Saturday saw a friendly against Middlesbrough – a good 4-1 win over opposition that were 'not of the strongest' – and then came the next two league encounters, a double-header with West Bromwich Albion starting at their Stoney Lane ground on 17 October and at Newcastle Road seven days later. Both games were comfortable victories, 5-2 and 4-0.

The away fixture was played in poor weather of wind and rain, and West Brom, playing with the benefit of such conditions, led 2-1 at half-time, but Sunderland turned things around brilliantly after the changeover and won 5-2 with two goals from John 'Jock' Scott, two from Johnny Campbell and one from Jimmy Millar. The success, and the impressive form, was repeated the following week when Campbell scored three and Hugh Wilson scored the fourth with a penalty, something that was still unusual in football, for it had only been introduced recently. The crowd of 7,000 left Newcastle Road that afternoon very pleased with what they had seen. The 'Throstles' had no reply to offer and the *Sunderland Daily Echo* was pleased to say that the result had been Sunderland's best performance of the season so far.

A week later on Hallowe'en, when Sunderland beat Accrington 4-1 in another fine performance, the press described their fans as 'on thoroughly good terms with themselves and the players' as they left the ground, having seen some fine goals, and their newspapers over the rest of the weekend were able to tell them that their team had now climbed to fifth in the league, having been at the bottom after their three successive defeats in September.

The first week in November saw 'another spoke in the wheel of the Sunderland train' (as it was well described by the local press), which came at Ewood Park, the ground of Blackburn Rovers, one of the truly great teams of the Victorian era. Blackburn had slipped a little of late but they were still the FA Cup holders for the past two years, having won it five times in all. Sunderland travelled to Lancashire without Donald Gow who had stayed behind with an injured ankle, and conceded a goal within the first 30 seconds.

This need not, of course, have proved to be fatal, and Sunderland did indeed fight back, but they still lost 3-1 in a good game. Still, there was no shame in losing to Blackburn with Campbell in particular having hard luck on several occasions. Goalkeeper Doig was also a busy man but for some reason fortune was with Blackburn. Sunderland, however, were far from despondent, and from now on they rallied and went on a glorious unbeaten run which became the talk of the British Isles.

It all started when Derby County visited Newcastle Road on 14 November. As was often the case in

Victorian times, the two teams, along with Sunderland Albion who were playing an exhibition match against a Canadian side, were given free tickets to the theatre on the Friday night, in this case the People's Palace, where they were applauded as they took their seats before the show.

The Saturday was a dull, dry and windless day at Newcastle Road and Derby won the toss to choose to defend 'the lower end' of the ground. The referee was given a strange description in the *Sunderland Daily Echo*, 'A favourite referee with Sunderland spectators as shown by his cordial reception never granted to his predecessors.' Whether this was the reporter being sarcastic or not, we cannot say, but the referee was Fitzroy Norris of Bolton, and presumably a well-known and frequent visitor to the ground.

Sunderland fielded Doig, Porteous, Murray, Wilson, Auld, Gibson, Hannah, Smith, Campbell, Scott and Millar. Derby were a reasonable team with one or two internationals, but they were simply swept aside by a rampant Sunderland, clearly hurting after that defeat at Blackburn. The score was 5-0 at half-time with some extra entertainment supplied by Jimmy Millar who at one stage ripped his pants, and had to retire to have them repaired lest he offend Victorian sensibilities, for there were some (albeit, admittedly, only a few) ladies in attendance.

On a more serious note the goals were scored by Campbell (two), Hannah, Scott and Millar, and the team left the field at half-time to the cheers of the 8,000 crowd, for each of the goals had been well worked and a feature of the game had been the teamwork of the red and whites. However, the 'Peakites', as Derby were described, stayed on the field to have a 'council of war' but it did them little good other than a consolation goal after Campbell scored another two. In the second half the weather was described as 'thick' which seems to indicate a typical November mist descending, and the value of the early start (2.40pm although it should have been 2.30) was seen before darkness descended. Sunderland eased off late on, and although their never-happy supporters were heard to shout 'Play Up', the game finished quietly with Doig dealing more than competently with whatever came his way.

The 7-1 scoreline raised eyebrows throughout the footballing word, and it 'was only in a very dark blue moon' that Derby were on the wrong end of such a thrashing, although one feels that *Empire News and the Umpire* was guilty of an understatement when it said, 'Sunderland had the better of the game and won.' Sunderland were now fourth in the league with six wins and four defeats, but still some way behind pacesetters Bolton Wanderers.

From then on, Sunderland never really looked back. Burnley were the next visitors to Newcastle Road on 21 November for what was a far tighter game. The press reported that the local MP Samuel Storey was in attendance and that there was a cold wind which 'threatened toothache' to the players and spectators. Burnley scored first but Sunderland equalised through a penalty by Hugh Wilson, after Hannah had been fouled. 'Lalty', as Wilson was called (for no apparent reason), converted the penalty by sending it all along the ground, and the teams reached half-time at 1-1. Some of the Burnley play was not above reproach in the view of some of the Sunderland supporters and the visitors were 'hooted at' as they left the field.

Play continued to be tough in the second half, and it was from a free kick that John Smith, another scion of Ayrshire, scored and 'the music of the onlooker was given full tongue'. What that phrase of the *Sunderland Daily Echo* meant we cannot be sure, but it could be that the Sunderland supporters all burst into song. There were no partisan songs on those days but it was not unknown for strains of music hall favourites like 'Sweet Caroline' or 'Daisy Bell' to be heard when things were going well.

Presumably they were still singing at full time, for, although Sunderland got another penalty which was well saved by the goalkeeper this time, Doig,

Porteous and Oliver were in fine form to keep out the determined attacks of the Lancastrians and Sunderland had now won two games in a row. It was a good day for the team in other respects as well, as Bolton lost to Blackburn, and Sunderland would now be within one point of the leaders if they won their game in hand.

Away form had not been so good in 1891 and that was why Sunderland's 3-1 victory at Stoke on 28 November was all the more welcome. The pitch was dreadful, the conditions were poor with wind and rain and the crowd was little more than 1,000, but Sunderland took advantage of the conditions in the first half and scored three times, then restricted Stoke to just the one in the second half. Millar, Scott and Hannah were the scorers in a result which further consolidated their challenge.

Thus Sunderland reached the month of December in a strong position. The days were dark, the weather was cold and wintry but the football was good, and attendances remained respectable with the town in general (including councillors and ladies whom one would not immediately class as football fans) gradually beginning to take more of an interest in how the team were doing. The first match in December was against Notts County at home. The 'Lambs' as they were called were of course one of the pioneers in the game, going back to the early 1860s, but were far from being one of the strongest teams in the league in 1891. They were not expected to do well against Sunderland and they didn't, for the hosts, with both Hannahs in the team and Donald Gow back from injury, swept them aside.

Hugh 'Lalty' Wilson played in the forward line, and the half-back line read Murray, Auld and Gibson. 'The Lambs were in for a close shearing,' said the *Sunderland Daily Echo* and at one point Notts were reduced to nine men, one of their injured being the man with the unlikely name of Harold Daft, who was a renowned England international. Notts were 3-0 down at half-time and finally lost 4-0 to goals from Wilson, John Hannah and Campbell (with a penalty) in the first half and Wilson again in the second half. As often happened in December when floodlights were only a pipe dream in the minds of a few eccentrics, the game finished in darkness and may even have been cut short by referee Omerod of Accrington. No one complained, though, and once again the Mackems left the ground in a great state of happiness.

Darwen came next. They were in their first season in the Football League, and not doing particularly well, but they could not really have expected the hammering that 'the team of all the talents' handed them. 12 December 1891 was a very cold and unpleasant day

31

with low clouds and constant drizzle. The game, which kicked off at 2.15pm, would have finished in total darkness had not the rain turned to sleet and then to snow in the second half, something which at least brightened things up, and allowed referee Mr Norris of Bolton to keep it going.

It was still an unpleasant experience and the *Sunderland Daily Echo* revealed that 'the fall of the flag' (a signal that there were only ten minutes of the game to go) came 'to the great satisfaction of the spectators', but they would already have been quite happy with what they saw on the field for the result was 7-0, David Hannah, Millar and Campbell scoring two each and Wilson another with Darwen 'unable to break their egg' and totally outclassed whether the conditions were good or not.

This result was a good one for Sunderland because they were now join third in the table alongside Aston Villa, but they had played fewer games than the two teams above them, Bolton Wanderers and Preston North End. They had now played 14 out of their 26 for the season. No league match was scheduled for 19 December, so Sunderland played a friendly against Middlesbrough Ironopolis (a 7-1 win) and prepared themselves for their festive tour of Everton on Christmas Day and Wolverhampton Wanderers on Boxing Day.

It is of course very tempting to think that Christmas in Victorian times was all about cards, snow, bowls of punch and jolly red-faced mothers bringing in turkeys for pleasant, well-behaved children to enjoy. The contrast between that and the reality of Christmas in a working-class town like Sunderland could hardly have been more stark, although everyone did at least make an effort to enjoy the few days of holiday.

Football was played on Christmas Day, in Sunderland's case a trip to Liverpool to play Everton. The growing impression that Sunderland were the best team in England was confirmed by their 4-0 win before a bumper crowd of 16,000 at the ground of the 1891 champions whom they had now beaten twice. Millar, David Hannah and Auld (with a long-range shot from outside the penalty area) scored in the first half and then John Hannah scored in the second. Sunderland also managed to miss a penalty, and the game did not go down well among the Everton supporters, at least two of whom managed to get on to the park to remonstrate with the referee before being apprehended by the constabulary 'to learn the folly of their ways'.

It was a great result for Sunderland, and the *Daily Echo* told how the result was received in the town on Christmas Day, 'The utmost interest was evinced in the match and the result was anxiously waited for in

Sunderland. The half-time and final results were given out at the music halls before crowded audiences who cheered vociferously. A number of the business men in town also managed to obtain the result of the game by private wire and their "flimsies" were conspicuously pasted up in their places of business. Much satisfaction was expressed on all sides when it became known that Sunderland had beaten last season's champions.'

There was more cause for happiness the following day. The game was played with a morning kick-off, so by mid-afternoon everyone knew that Sunderland had beaten Wolves 3-1 with goals from Wilson, Smith and Millar at Molineux. This match was a lot less clear-cut, for Wolves fought hard and the pitch was a lot softer after a recent thaw, but it was another fine success for Sunderland, although celebrations were severely curtailed by the news of ten people being killed in a panic in a theatre at Gateshead after a very minor fire.

Sunderland played another few friendlies before the turn of the year, and finished 1891 still third but handily placed, and in the opinion of many a good bet for the championship in 1892. It so happened that the next league game was not played until 1 March, but the intervening months were far from uninteresting.

The new year was spent playing various friendlies against Scottish and local teams, and business resumed properly on 16 January. This was when the FA Cup began with Notts County drawn at Newcastle Road. A certain interest was shown in this tournament and there were even a few who suggested that Sunderland could emulate the feat of Preston, who had managed to win both the Football League and the FA Cup in 1889.

The FA Cup was undeniably considered to be more important than the Football League. It was older, having started in 1871, and it covered a wider geographical area than the Football League did. There was something very exciting about it as well in that one bad game and you were out. Sunderland had been in the FA Cup before but had never really done well, for the trophy was very much in the possession of Lancashire, having been won for the past three years by Preston and then Blackburn Rovers twice.

One of the problems about this competition, however, in the early years was that it always seemed to be bedevilled by protests. This was what happened here. Sunderland beat Notts County 3-0 but County immediately indicated that they were going to protest against the conditions. They had a point here, for it had been a cold and frosty day and several players had been seen to slip about, but the referee (and there were two neutral linesmen as well) said that the game could go ahead. The rumour that the 'Lambs' (Notts County enjoyed a certain reputation for being litigious and serial protesters, if they didn't get their own way) were also going to complain about Donald Gow not being eligible proved unfounded, but the Football Association met on the Wednesday night and decided that Sunderland v Notts County and several other games were to be replayed on the following Saturday. The replay would be at Newcastle Road.

This last point sweetened the pill 'more than somewhat' because it did mean another big gate and as Sunderland had thumped Notts County on a poor pitch first time around, there was no reason to believe that they couldn't do so again. So Sunderland, although there was a lot of moaning and mumping in the town along with unsubstantiated claims of favouritism and bribery, went along with it and were duly rewarded with a big crowd and another victory. And of course the cynics were not slow to claim that it was all about another game and another big pay day.

But in the meantime, a major issue had developed in the royal family with the death on 14 January of Prince Albert – or Eddy, as he was known – the eldest son of the Prince of Wales and second in line to the throne. Contemporary sources are united in saying that the death, apparently of influenza, of this young man was no great loss to the world. He is usually described as dull, anti-social and like so many members of the royal family, unable to cope with his sexuality, although it possibly went too far to say that he was Jack the Ripper, the terror of London prostitutes. His fiancée Princess Mary of Teck may have been devastated by the news, but she did not give up easily and was soon paired with his younger brother George, becoming Queen after all in 1910.

Possibly the death of the louche and amoral Eddy did not cause as much distress in Sunderland as the newspapers would have liked us to believe, and it certainly took second place in conversation to the outrage against the cheats of Notts County. But be that as it may, the second game went ahead in slightly better conditions in front of another big crowd who 'hissed and hooted' at some of the County players, and this time Sunderland won comfortably 4-0 with two goals from John Campbell, one from John Smith and another from David Hannah. They all came in the first half with Campbell receiving 'a regular tornado of applause' for his efforts amid cries of 'They're not in it' directed at the futile efforts of the visitors.

Sunderland then faced a trip to Accrington for the next round, on 30 January. Once again we had frustration about the game not being able to be played at the first attempt, this time because of 'pitiless' rain and an added complication of the referee not turning up, and a replacement having to be sent for. It was decided that play was impossible, but illogically, the teams decided to play a friendly instead. It was back to Accrington on 6 February.

This time Sunderland got a fright for Accrington scored first and were 1-0 up at half-time. But to the accompaniment of 'frantic applause from the small knot of Sunderland supporters', Campbell scored, then Millar, then finally Campbell again just at the very end. It was a tough game, though, and credit was paid to the half-back line of Murray, Auld and Gibson for their efforts in 'crumpling up' the Accrington attacks.

The quarter-final paired Sunderland against Stoke. Sunderland were now looked upon as one of the favourites to lift the trophy, but on 13 February at Stoke in front of a large crowd of about 10,000 on a bright but cold day, they were held to a 2-2 draw even though the game went to extra time. All the goals came in the first half of normal time, and the pace visibly slowed during the rest of the match with Sunderland probably glad to hear the final whistle for it meant another home tie at Newcastle Road – even though they were aware that there were increasing rumours circulating about how there seemed to be a cup fixture every week, and how the finances of the club, consequently, seemed to be doing rather well.

The replay on 20 February 1892 was one of the great days of that season as Sunderland, playing superbly, beat Stoke 4-0. The crowd was given as 9,000, with the weather dry and bright enough albeit with rather too much of a wind blowing from the 'bottom' end. Stoke chose to play with the wind in the first half, but it did not seem to make too much of a difference, for goals from Jimmy Millar and David Hannah saw Sunderland lead 2-0 at half-time. Millar's goal was a beauty, coming after he trapped the ball then teed it up before driving between the sticks, and then Hannah's goal came at the end of the half after a sustained spell of Sunderland pressure. Goalkeeper Rowley saved his first shot, then his second, and eventually Hannah scored.

Hannah then scored again at the start of the second half, and with the wind now behind them, Sunderland pressed but could not add to their total until John Campbell headed home a fourth near the call of full time. The 'referential whistle' which signalled the end of the game was greeted with great enthusiasm, for it meant that Sunderland were in the semi-finals of the FA Cup and only a game away from the final.

Aston Villa, the winners of 1887, awaited them in the semi-final, which was to be played at the neutral venue of Bramall Lane, the home of Sheffield United. It would be fair to say that this was the biggest single game in Sunderland's history so far. They had been in a semi-final in 1891, but this was now a lot bigger with far more interest. A special train was run by the North Eastern Railway Company to convey spectators. It would leave at 7.25am and hope to arrive in the 'cutlery town' by midday, thus allowing fans time to refresh themselves before the game. For so many Sunderland supporters it gave them the opportunity to go to another town to watch their favourites. Very few would have ever seen a game other than at Newcastle Road or some local ground like Newcastle East End, Sunderland Albion or perhaps Middlesbrough Ironopolis. Sheffield was a long way away in 1892. Even though the railways had narrowed the gap geographically, there was still a huge financial cost to getting there. That many managed to do so was remarkable.

Sadly it was all a huge disappointment. One can almost sense the tears in the eyes of the *Sunderland Daily Echo* reporter on the Monday morning as he recorded the sad events of Bramall Lane. The crowd was huge and there was a problem with encroachment on the field from time to time, but that does not really explain how the Wearsiders, having held their own and more in the first half, collapsed so catastrophically in the second half to lose 4-1 to a Villa side who would then go on to lose to West Bromwich Albion in the final. Sunderland scored first through Scott 'in a scrimmage' (some sources say it was Campbell) but then Villa equalised with a shoulder charge on Ned Doig which reportedly looked somewhat unfair. The second half was basically all about Aston Villa, who took over and the *Daily Echo* was sadly forced to conclude, 'The Wearsiders were having the worst of the exchanges and some of their supporters even said that they had never seen them play so ill. The attack lacked sting and Porteous at the back seemed unable to cope with Villa's left.'

The train journey home that night was a sad and becalmed experience. There seemed to be no rhyme or reason in the result, and it was a performance out of character with the rest of the season. In modern parlance Sunderland 'never turned up'. It was also true that Villa, always a good cup team under George Ramsay, raised their game. *Empire News and the Umpire*, a newspaper much respected in the 1890s for its lack of a partisan approach to the game, was at a loss to describe how Sunderland collapsed so totally in the second half. But it said, tellingly, that only Auld and Gow played up to reputation.

So there was no trip to the Kennington Oval for the final for Sunderland and their fans that year, but the season was far from over. There were still ten league games to be played because Sunderland had spent all January and February playing FA Cup ties. They were now actually in a stronger position to win the championship because their rivals had all played 20 matches to their 16, and if they could win their games in hand, they could be top.

But the FA Cup defeat was not easily got over. The whole town was mystified at how easily the players had been rolled over in the second half, and people wondered whether there was 'bickering' in the camp. A few injuries had been sustained, notably to Johnny Campbell, the centre-forward, who was not expected to be back for a few weeks.

Sunderland did not have long to lick their wounds or to feel sorry for themselves as there was a game to be played on Tuesday, 1 March against Bolton Wanderers at Newcastle Road. It was a vital game in the title race for Bolton were one of the teams ahead of Sunderland, but for all sorts of reasons the fixture was poorly attended. The weather was bad with wind and hail, Tuesday was not the best of afternoons to attract a crowd, many people had spent all their money going to Sheffield, and more had decided to shun their favourites for that dire performance in that semi-final in which so many fans had placed so many hopes.

The meagre crowd were nevertheless quite vocal in their support, with cries of 'good old Sunderland' heard often, although there was also the occasional snide reminder that they should and could have done that at Bramall Lane. The game turned out to be almost a mirror image of the semi-final with a 1-1 draw at half-time being converted into a 4-1 win at full time. The Trotters scored first, but Jimmy Millar equalised and then in the second half Smith scored twice and Scott once. The change of ends meant that although Sunderland were now playing up the slope, they had the advantage of the wind and the sleet, and although we may put down the description of Bolton being 'blinded by the snow' to a certain amount of rhetorical exaggeration perhaps, there seems to have been little doubt that the Mackems were enjoying the better of the conditions.

In any case the weather had abated a little by the time the game finished and Sunderland had now consolidated their position in third with 26 points from 17 matches, whereas Bolton were only two points ahead but had played 21 times, and still top were Preston North End with 31 points from 20, meaning that Sunderland could overtake them by winning their games in hand. In any case, the vital fixture now appearing fast on the horizon was the visit of 'Proud Preston' on 12 March.

But before that, there was a visit to Accrington's ground, described, a little unhelpfully perhaps, as being 'off the Burnley road'. The *Sunderland Daily Echo* reporter was a little hard on Accrington when he described it as 'not a very pleasant place to visit at the best of times', although he did concede that the nice weather was a great help. But very few people would have considered Sunderland at the height of the industrial age (as 1892 undeniably was) as a place of great beauty either.

Sunderland had already beaten Accrington twice in 1891/92, in the FA Cup and in the league, and were confidently expected to do so again. It seems that the people of Accrington thought so as well, for in spite of the splendid weather and the pitch being in capital condition the spectators were 'not as numerous as expected'. That was a pity for they missed a splendid game. Sunderland duly won, but eight goals were scored, and there was at least one major controversial incident.

With Campbell still being unavailable to play, Sunderland's forward line read John Hannah, David Hannah, Smith, Millar and Scott, and they had a splendid first half culminating in going in at half-time leading 3-0. It was Sunderland's first goal that caused the trouble. David Hannah was injured in a tackle, and the Accrington players 'stopped playing' under the impression that referee Mr Lewis of Blackburn would stop the game to allow treatment, but Sunderland continued and duly scored. 'For several minutes the hooting was loud and vigorous' and there were even cries for the Accrington players to walk off, but wisely, they stayed on under protest.

More booing was heard as the players left the field, but in the second half it was a far more determined

Accrington who came out. They scored in the first minute to cheer up their support, but then had the mortification of conceding an own goal. In spite of this they kept pressing hard, and Doig was called upon more than once to save the day. The key moment, however, came when Millar scored for Sunderland, this goal being 'received in dead silence', for presumably Millar was the man being blamed for scoring that strange goal in the first half. That made it 5-1, and the game looked over, as indeed it was, even though Accrington then scored two late goals to make the scoreline the more respectable 5-3. Indeed, they probably did enough to deserve a draw. Mr Lewis was far from a popular man in Accrington that night.

On Monday Sunderland returned to Sheffield to play The Wednesday (later Sheffield Wednesday) in a friendly at their ground, Olive Green, and won comfortably 3-0. This showed that they were still in good form, but more importantly, rumours began to spread around the town that Johnny Campbell might be back in the side for the vital game against Preston.

This proved to be the case as football fever rose in the town (a huge crowd assembled at the station just to see the arrival of the Preston players) and indeed the country over the weekend in both England and Scotland. It was the Scottish Cup Final at Ibrox between Celtic and Queen's Park as well as 'the game that all England was looking to' at Newcastle Road. In the event the Scottish Cup Final had to be played as a friendly because of overcrowding and serious encroachment, but the Sunderland game proved to be decisive.

A crowd of 14,000 were there including quite a few who had travelled up from Preston, and they saw Sunderland at their best. Oddly enough for March (but by no means an unprecedented occurrence) the pitch had to be cleared of snow, but as it was mainly wet snow with no ice the match was able to go ahead, and indeed the conditions were conducive to good football, particularly of the sort that Sunderland were playing. Snow fell intermittently, at the start and again in the second half, but as it did not settle it did not cause any real problems. Centre-half John Auld scored twice – something that was not perhaps as unusual as it might have been, because an attacking centre-half was common – and the other goals were scored by John Campbell and David Hannah.

This result now put Sunderland in a very strong position – three points behind Preston but with three games in hand, and having also played three fewer than Bolton who were on the same points, Aston Villa now having dropped out of the race in spite of a 12-2 defeat of Accrington. There now followed, however, a very tricky trip to Derby.

This was 19 March, and Sunderland faced a change
of venue. It was played at Ley's Ground (which in time
became known as the Baseball Ground) because the
County Ground was being used for horse-racing. The
game should have been played earlier, but had to be
postponed. This day was also the day of the FA Cup
Final – a rather easy win for West Bromwich Albion
over Aston Villa – but for Sunderland supporters their
match was incredibly tight.

And once again, it was Auld who came to the
rescue. After nearly 90 minutes of somewhat sterile
football played by two exhausted teams, Sunderland
forced a corner on the right. The ball came across and
found the Ayrshire cobbler (he had been a shoemaker
and shoe repairer before becoming a professional
footballer) who hammered home for his third goal in
two games. Auld was no apparent relative of Bertie
Auld, the hero of Celtic several generations later, nor
to 'Daddy' Auld, the Minister of Mauchline Church in
Ayrshire who tried so hard and with so little success to
deter Robert Burns from his life of sexual extravagance.

It was one of those games that a team just has to
win in order to become champions. Not all league
titles are won by champagne football. More are won
by the 'grinding out of results', and this was an excellent
example of that. As no other team at the top of the
table was playing that day, Sunderland gained ground,

and were now only one point behind Preston with two games in hand.

There may have been a certain element of 'grudge' in the game of 26 March, for the visitors were Aston Villa, the team who had removed Sunderland from the FA Cup but who had themselves been defeated in the final. Once again it was a tough match with the issue in doubt until the very end and 10,000 there to watch it, even though there was still snow around. After a goalless first half, 'Lalty' Wilson put the Wearsiders ahead, but then Villa equalised, and it looked as if Sunderland were heading for their first draw of the season when, with two minutes to go, John Hannah headed the winner from a Gibson cross. The *Sunderland Daily Echo* reported graphically, 'Hats went off and a startling roar burst from the throng at the unexpected success of the Wearsiders.'

The table at the end of March made happy reading for the Sunderland fans. They were one point ahead of Preston and had five games left whereas North End only had four. This was the time for 'nerves' and 'bottle'. They were in the lead. It would be a crime to throw it all away now.

April dawned with the Scotland v England international at Ibrox. Many of Sunderland's Scotsmen might have felt entitled to be considered for a cap in this game – Auld, Campbell, Wilson, Doig and a few others had cause to feel that they might have done better than the Scotsmen chosen, but the Scotland selectors opted for an all-Tartan XI (as it was called) of men who played for Scottish clubs. It was Scotland's loss in more ways than one, for England won comfortably, 4-1.

The issue at stake was amateurism v professionalism. Scotland was still technically an amateur country, and had Sunderland players been chosen, they might have expected to be paid officially. As it was, everyone knew well that Scotland's players were paid with money placed surreptitiously in their shoes. It was 1893 before professionalism was officially legalised in the country, but by then many Scotsmen had decided to play professional football in England anyway.

It was Scotland's loss but Sunderland's gain as progress to the league title continued. Stoke returned to Newcastle Road (they had been there in the FA Cup in the winter) and for a long time put up a good performance before Sunderland took control in the second half and ran out 4-1 winners with two goals each from John Hannah and John Campbell. Campbell's first earned the admiration of the press. He had his back to the goal but 'swung round and with a lightning-like shot, spun the leather into the net'.

On the bank holiday Monday after that, Sunderland travelled to Scotland to play Rangers at Ibrox. They attracted a large crowd and won 1-0, leading people to wonder why these Sunderland players hadn't been playing for Scotland. Saturday, 9 April was a significant day in Scotland because Celtic won the Scottish Cup for the first time, but it was not a day that will be looked back upon with any great satisfaction in Sunderland circles, for the team went to Notts County, lost 1-0 and Hugh Wilson, to his own horror, missed a penalty. This game might have put Sunderland virtually out of sight, but as it was, they had now caught up with Preston in terms of games played, were three points ahead and there were three matches to go. Basically, they needed only three more points.

It was Black Saturday (the Saturday between Good Friday and Easter Monday), 16 April, that saw Sunderland home. They won the title in emphatic style by beating Blackburn Rovers 6-1 before a large crowd of 10,000. The *Sunderland Daily Echo* made a comment about the mood of the Sunderland weather being not dissimilar to the complexities of the mood of a woman because that Easter weekend there was both snow and lovely warm weather as well as the normal outbreaks of rain. There was no doubt about the mood of the Sunderland team, however, as they dismissed Blackburn with a degree of contempt. Johnny Campbell got four goals and Jimmy Millar and John Hannah one each, and the press reported how 'applause resounded all round the ground' at the splendid play of the Sunderland side.

Curiously, very little was made of the fact that this performance meant Sunderland had won the title. Admittedly they had to wait a little for a 'wire' concerning the Preston result to the effect that Aston Villa had beaten them to make absolutely sure, but by Saturday night the good people of Sunderland knew that their football team were the champions of the Football League.

One is immediately struck by the lack of fuss there seems to have been about the Sunderland team winning the championship. The trophy was due to be presented at the AGM of the Football League on 13 May, but there was no great celebration, no parading through the streets in open-top brakes or tramcars, just a simple acknowledgement that Sunderland were the champions. On 18 April, Easter Monday, the Wearsiders beat their local rivals Sunderland Albion 6-1 in a friendly, and that seemed to be as important as anything else. Two other league fixtures needed to be played – away trips to Burnley and Darwen – and they were both comfortable wins, meaning Sunderland finished their league programme with 21 wins out of 26, five defeats and amazingly no draws.

They deserved to be call 'the team of all the talents' for it was hard to spot a weakness. They set down a marker for themselves, and it is also no coincidence that almost immediately after the Sunderland triumph,

Newcastle East End and Newcastle West End got together and formed a team called Newcastle United. It was as if the city of Newcastle felt that it could not let Sunderland get off with all that. The rivalry of the north-east had now begun.

2

League Champions 1892/93

CHANGES WERE made to the Football League in 1892. In the first place a Second Division was formed. This was more or less a takeover of a pre-existing competition called the Football Alliance, but it was an important step forward in the advancement of the Football League, even though it did not as yet contain southern or London teams.

This meant the top tier was renamed as the First Division, and it was also expanded to 16 teams, arguably a better number. Darwen were not re-elected and joined the Second Division, while three teams moved in at the highest level, all significantly from big cities and with a large support, and all fated to make a huge impact on English football. They were Nottingham Forest, The Wednesday, and a team called Newton Heath who would become arguably the most famous club in the world when they became Manchester United.

There were thus seven teams from Lancashire: Accrington, Bolton Wanderers, Everton, Blackburn Rovers, Newton Heath, Preston North End and Burnley; seven from the Midlands in Nottingham Forest, Notts County, Wolverhampton Wanderers, West Bromwich Albion, Stoke, Derby County and Aston Villa; one from Yorkshire in The Wednesday, and of course Sunderland in the distant north.

There was a general election in the summer of 1892. Sunderland, a two-member constituency, voted Liberal for Samuel Storey and Edward Gourley, but the subsequent parliament was a hung one. The Marquess of Salisbury's Conservatives were the biggest single party with 314 seats as distinct from the Liberals' 272, but the Irish Nationalists more or less won all of Ireland and with the support of their 72 seats, the Liberals could outvote the Conservatives. This was in fact what happened, and thus William Ewart Gladstone became prime minister for the fourth time, again under Queen Victoria – who could not stand him. Gladstone was 82 and most of his ministry would be dominated by the vexatious issue of Irish Home Rule, which, had it been granted and had the House of Lords not stood in the way, would have saved a lot of trouble in the 20th century.

Of more concern to the establishment was the election of three members of the Independent Labour

Party, something that perhaps began to show that the working classes were becoming a little impatient with the Liberals, who promised much but delivered little in terms of social progress. Even more concerning was the appearance of one of these Labour MPs, Keir Hardie, wearing a cloth cap, a symbol of working-class life and indicating that life for the privileged was soon to be under threat.

All this was of great interest to Sunderland supporters, but the really interesting thing was the start of the football season in August, and the big question of whether 'the lads' could repeat their success of the previous season and win the championship again with 'the team of all the talents'. Some even felt that they could do what Preston North End did in 1889 by winning both the First Division and the FA Cup.

The season opened with a pre-season game against 'Nops', the nickname of Middlesbrough Ironopolis, and then the league season began on Saturday, 3 September with a trip to Accrington. On the campaign's eve the *Sunderland Daily Echo* printed a list of players with drawings of them and a short paragraph about them. A new import from Scotland was the man from Queen's Park with the unfortunate name of Bob Smellie. He arrived with a high reputation as a defender and would replace Donald Gow, who had returned to Scotland to play for Rangers.

The *Sunderland Daily Echo*'s reporter appeared to have had some unhappy memories of the Lancashire town, for he continued the vendetta he began in the 1891/92 season and wrote, 'As is usually the case when the Wearsiders visit Accrington, the weather was of the most miserable description, rain falling heavily while there was a strong west wind.' A crowd of only 3,000 turned up – which was disappointing for the first day of the season when the opposition were the league champions – but there was little shelter at the ground. The Accrington supporters who stayed at home probably made the right decision, but it was a shame there were no (or very few) Sunderland fans there, for they would have seen their team lay down a great marker for the new season by winning 6-0. News travelled quickly in 1892, and by 'chucking out' time at the pubs all over England, everyone knew that Sunderland were not likely to surrender their crown very easily.

The Sunderland team was Doig, Porteous, Smellie, Wilson, Auld, Gibson, John Hannah, David Hannah, Campbell, Scott and Millar. Johnny Campbell had the honour of scoring the first goal of the season and he went on to notch a hat-trick with Jimmy Millar, John Scott and David Hannah scoring the others, while at the other end, the only shots that Accrington could muster were comfortably dealt with by Ned Doig.

Then on Monday, 5 September at Newcastle Road, Sunderland played a friendly against Celtic who were on tour in the north of England. Someone described this game as Scotsmen now living in England v Irishmen now living in Scotland. It was a rough-house match tactfully described as 'feisty and competitive', and 'characterised by a great deal of roughness' for a great deal was at stake, Celtic having won the Scottish Cup last year and Sunderland the Football League. The winner would have a reasonable right to call themselves the champions of Britain. Both teams had a Johnny Campbell in the forward line, and it was the Sunderland one who scored the only goal of the game.

A reasonable crowd turned up but more would have been expected on the following Saturday to see the arrival at Newcastle Road of the great Notts County side, reputed to be the oldest surviving club in the world as they had been founded in 1863. They were certainly the first to have kept records, accounts and so on. They hadn't had any great success in recent seasons, but a good team now seemed to be emerging from the shadows. Indeed, in 1894 they would win the FA Cup.

The *Nottingham Evening Post* was initially very pessimistic about County's trip to Sunderland. It went as far as to say that 'Abandon Hope All Ye Who Enter Here' should have been written on the gateposts of Newcastle Road because everyone had lost there in 1891/92, and

Notts County themselves were on the wrong end of rather severe 4-0 hammerings in both league and FA Cup. But the County players performed 'vigorously' and were even leading 2-1 at half-time, something that caused great joy back home in Nottingham with the prospect of a famous victory in sight, but Sunderland equalised. Nevertheless, the Nottingham journalist enjoyed the sight of his men pressing in the last ten minutes and reported, 'The Sunderland spectators were treated to the unusual spectacle of seeing their men penned in the goal and kicking anywhere to prevent the ball from going through.'

The *Sunderland Daily Echo* was broadly in agreement with this assessment of the way that the game went, but stressed far more the unpleasant nature of the play. There was a hint of 'previous' or bad blood between the teams when apparently the two captains, Oswald and Porteous, 'advanced towards each other without shaking hands' before the coin was tossed, and there were a few reports of referee Mr Hardisty of Middlesbrough having to make 'timeous interventions'. For example, James Hannah went for a ball with Hendry of Notts County, but the visiting man 'using his hands shoved Hannah down amidst cries of execrations from the onlookers' and was 'heartily hissed' by the crowd.

Notts County thus did little to deserve their nickname of 'the Lambs', but they went in at the interval 2-1 up, and the Sunderland supporters, 6,000 of them, were discussing the game in a 'half-hearted, disgusted sort of way' for rarely did their team win after going behind, and now they had to face both the wind and the sun. But the pessimism of the Wearsiders was premature and unjustified, for the match resumed with the home team taking a grip. The game was characterised with quite a lot of 'rough and tumble' before Millar scored from a distance late on to equalise.

Thus the return of league football to Newcastle Road may have been a little disappointing as far as Sunderland and their supporters were concerned, but there was also a certain happiness that the football season was back. It was felt that maybe Sunderland were allowing themselves to become too involved in the 'rough and tumble' of games, and that if they just concentrated on the pure playing of football as they had done the previous season, they might have got on a great deal better.

The following week, however, saw Sunderland at their best. This was a trip to Perry Barr to play Aston Villa, who under manager George Ramsay were generally regarded as one of the better teams in the game. A huge crowd of 12,000 arrived with the opinion expressed that if Villa were to have any chance of winning the Football League, they would certainly have to beat Sunderland.

Travelling from Sunderland to Birmingham in 1892 would have been a reasonably simple, albeit expensive, journey, and some away fans made their way to the game. The weather was pleasant and the *Birmingham Daily Post* wrote, 'This huge gathering made heavy demands on the vehicular accommodation of the city and for some hours the route to the match presented a lively scene.'

Sunderland won the toss and chose to play with the benefit of the wind and the sun, and to the stunned admiration of the home crowd they totally dominated proceedings. By 20 minutes they were well ahead with two goals from Campbell and one from Wilson. The home support, 'while applauding Sunderland's performance, urged their pets to play up' but although Doig was occasionally drawn into action, the first half finished with Sunderland 3-0 ahead.

The second half saw a little more effort from the home side, but no sooner had they pulled one back than James Hannah ran up and made it 4-1, then John Harvey (described as a 'little terrier') scored to make it 5-1 before late in the game Hannah scored again. The final score was thus 6-1 and it was a result that made all Britain sit up and take notice for it was not all that often that a team like Aston Villa were put to the sword to that extent on their home ground. And before September was out, another great side, Blackburn

Rovers, who had almost made the FA Cup their own in the last decade, had experienced the quality of Sunderland at their best.

This time a large crowd of 12,000 appeared, buoyed by news of what had happened at Aston Villa, and they enjoyed another good performance from Sunderland in fine autumn sunshine. Doig was a virtual spectator for large parts of the game from which Sunderland emerged with great credit and the 5-0 scoreline did not flatter them. Two goals came from Campbell, and one each from Millar, Harvey and James Hannah. Jimmy Gillespie on the right wing was the only forward who did not score, but he was arguably the best man on the park.

The home crowd had now seen Sunderland at their best, and the city was totally animated with the football being played by this fine team. Already they were beginning to talk about the possibility of the league being won for a second year in a row. The writer from *Empire News and the Umpire*, one of the few newspapers that appeared on a Sunday in 1892, was confident that there would be an exciting title race in 1892/93 between Sunderland and Preston North End, but favoured Sunderland after he had seen them 'run the legs off Blackburn Rovers' and their only stutter had been when they 'faltered but did not fail' against Notts County.

Stoke put up some fierce resistance at Newcastle Road on 3 October, and for a while 'anxiety was noticeable around the ropes' lest Stoke equalise the 2-1 lead that Sunderland held at half-time, but Doig was at his best once again and managed to keep them out. On one occasion Schofield of Stoke was through the defence and looking likely to score until 'a loud thump' announced (for the benefit, presumably, of those of a nervous disposition who had closed their eyes) that Doig had managed to fist the ball clear.

In spite of various attempts by a grimly determined Stoke side, the score stayed at 2-1 to Sunderland until late on when James Hannah settled the issue when he picked up a pass from Millar and 'sent the ball through at one side clean out of reach' of goalkeeper Rowley. The *Sunderland Daily Echo* made one of its rare misprints when it said that the score was 5-1, whereas in fact it was only 3-1. The first-half goals had been scored by Johnny Campbell and James Hannah.

Next came a trip to Everton, who in 1892 were somewhat complicated for they had just moved from their home at Anfield to a new ground not far away called Goodison Park. Back at Anfield, the owner of the ground, who had been a director of Everton but disagreed with their decision to move, stayed put and formed his own team – which he called Liverpool Football Club.

There was, however, nothing complicated about the way that Sunderland demolished Everton. The weather was miserable but that did not deter a crowd of 18,000 to 20,000 from attending, and they saw some fine football from both sides with Johnny Campbell scoring twice, and Jimmy Gillespie and Hugh Wilson once each. Sunderland's team of Doig, Porteous, Smellie, Wilson, Auld, Gibson, Gillespie, Harvey, Campbell, Millar and Hannah confirmed to a journalist from the *Liverpool Echo* that they were indeed the team of all the talents, and 'left a great impression on the Liverpudlian mind'. They were now second in the league, one point behind Preston North End who had played a game more.

It is always true that the making of a great team is the half-back line and in the all-Scots line of Hugh Wilson, John Auld and Willie Gibson, Sunderland had one of the best you could imagine with Wilson one of the top players around. Not only could he play, he could also inspire as a captain. He had been born in Mauchline in Ayrshire, not far from a few other great Scottish players like Dr John Smith of the 1880s, not to mention the famous poet Robert Burns.

Two home games followed the successful trip to the new Goodison Park, the first being the return of Accrington, still sore, one presumes, from the dreadful 6-0 walloping that they received on their own ground on the first day of the season. This time they put up a better performance but were severely outclassed. The weather was dreadful with wind and rain, and this was something of a leveller. The match followed, to an extent, the pattern of earlier games with Sunderland 2-1 up at half-time but unable to add the killer goal. This one, however, was different in that the Reds of Accrington managed to get an equaliser 'after the flag had fallen' – an indication that there were only ten minutes remaining – with a shot that had deflected off Porteous. It was then that Sunderland rallied, Gibson putting them back in front and finally Campbell made it 4-2 from a penalty awarded after an Accrington player had fisted the ball out. This completed a hat-trick for Campbell who had scored twice in the first half, and it was another fine win for Sunderland.

The following week saw one of the truly great names of English football arrive on Wearside. This was West Bromwich Albion, holders of the FA Cup. They had also won the cup in 1888 and had been runners-up on two previous occasions, so this fixture produced a chance to see the cup winners take on the league champions.

West Brom arrived at 9pm on the Friday to stay at the Queen's Hotel in Fawcett Street, and proved to be very sociable to journalists with their secretary prepared to hold court in the lounge where presumably a few drinks loosened the tongue. The weather proved to be a bit of an issue with an early fall of sleet, but that stopped at about noon on the Saturday and there was no problem with the conditions, although it was still very cold.

The game itself was remarkable as the Throstles were simply swept aside by a mighty Sunderland for whom Jocky Scott had returned after a suspension. Once again the score at half-time was 2-1, but this time in the second half Sunderland simply went berserk and scored another six goals, driving past the Brummie defence as if it did not exist. Hannah, Harvey, Campbell, Millar and Scott, arguably the best available Sunderland forward line, took total charge of the game with Campbell scoring a hat-trick, Millar two and Scott and the two wing-halves Wilson and Gibson one each. It was described as 'devastating' and 'giddy' and attracted the attention of the national press.

But Preston kept winning as well. Sooner or later, however, all good things must come to an end and on the last day of October Preston drew with Blackburn, but that was also the day that Sunderland suffered their first loss of the season. This event took place at Olive Grove, the home of The Wednesday, and Sunderland had every reason to complain about bad luck for it was late in the game before Wednesday managed to get their winner, and they had to play for most of the match without the services of Jimmy Millar, who was injured after bruising his kneecap in an accidental collision with a Wednesday player near the end of the first half.

Scott and Campbell had scored for Sunderland in the 3-2 defeat, but the league table that night showed that Preston were two points ahead, but having played one game more – ten to the Wearsiders' nine.

November had arrived, that month when the days shorten and the romance of football has usually gone. Phrases like 'nitty-gritty' are common to describe November fixtures, but it is usually the period when trends begin to emerge, and it becomes plain just which clubs are likely to be involved in the race for the title. A club can have a few impressive performances in the good weather in September. November often involves rain, mud, frost and fog – all these things being a severe test of a footballer's temperament rather than his ability.

On Guy Fawkes Day, Sunderland entertained Burnley and won 2-0. It was a bizarre occasion. The game kicked off quarter of an hour late to the impatience of the home crowd of 6,000 who soon, however, found out the reason for the delay, in that Nicol and Chambers of Burnley had failed to put in an appearance having apparently missed their train, and the visitors were obliged to play with only nine men, not having any reserves with them. But what they lacked in numbers they made up for in aggression, and the game was frequently stopped by Mr Hardisty of Middlesbrough for fouls. In spite of that, Campbell (in the first minute) and Scott scored twice before half-time.

The second half saw the appearance of the 'Burnley truants', and the game was slightly more even, but still rough with the Sunderland supporters expressing the wish that their opponents should either play football or depart the field. Sunderland's forwards, several of whom – Gillespie in particular – received a severe kicking, were unable to add to the score and a thoroughly unsatisfactory match finished 2-0 to Sunderland. Sunderland had 'nothing to reproach themselves for', according to the local press, and were lucky to emerge without serious injury. Preston, however, also won, so it was status quo at the top.

There was a brilliant quote in the *London Star* of Friday, 11 November. Sunderland had no league game the following day but a friendly had been organised against the famous London amateur side Corinthians, and the writer was clearly looking forward to a rare visit of the Wearsiders to The Oval: 'Several times this week I have asked myself why I feel so happy, and then I remember that Sunderland are to be at The Oval on Saturday. Hip! Hip! Hurrah! A cleverer set of men probably never took the football field, for they have neither the height, weight nor more than the average speed to assist them. They play with their heads rather than their feet, or to be more correct they use their brains to control their feet … In a word the match will be a battle of the giants and those who miss it will be sorry afterwards. Teams often come to London with a great reputation and leave it behind them, but on this occasion I am quite convinced that Sunderland will prove equal to the task they have set themselves.'

Unfortunately Sunderland couldn't quite live up to this somewhat extravagant build-up and lost 4-2, but that wasn't entirely their fault for the game was played in an archetypal London November fog of the type that Charles Dickens and Arthur Conan Doyle loved to describe with such relish, and in which Jack the Ripper would have been able to practise his trade with impunity. Thousands turned up, but even if Sunderland had been at their best, their talents would not have been clearly visible. It was a disappointing experience, but it was an experience nevertheless, and it did not really do the players all that much harm, particularly as it involved a trip to the capital.

The next three weeks involved the city of Nottingham. The way that fixtures were arranged in the Victorian era was sometimes quixotic, but it meant that Nottingham Forest were at Newcastle Road on 19 November and then two weeks later the venues were reversed. In between, Sunderland had a trip to the other Nottingham club, Notts County, who had a deserved reputation of being their bogey team.

The 1-0 win over Nottingham Forest on 19 November was more emphatic than it seemed. The weather was frosty and cold, and Sunderland scored through a fine Campbell shot midway through the first half. They should have scored more goals, and although some of the forwards had an off-day Doig was seldom troubled, such was the grip that the half-back line of Wilson, Auld and Gibson held over the game. The reported attendance caused a few problems; 4,000 were there at the start, but by the time the second half began it had risen to 8,000. Did the club reduce admission prices?

The following Saturday was a less happy experience at the Trent Bridge home of Notts County. The weather was described as 'boisterous', and the match was really a tale of two goalkeepers with County's Toone being very influential in keeping out Sunderland while Ned Doig had one of his rare off-days. The first goal in the 2-1 defeat came when Doig came out to punch a ball away but 'mulled' it, which seems to mean that he punched it the wrong way into his own net. Then after James Hannah had equalised, Harry Daft headed a winner for Notts.

That was the end of November, and 3 December saw Sunderland back in Nottingham. It was as if the Wearsiders were going out of their way to take revenge for their defeat at Trent Bridge because, more or less across the road at the Town Ground, they won 5-0 with a hat-trick from Campbell, one from Gillespie and another from Wilson, although the *Sunderland Daily Echo* did admit that there was not really a five-goal difference between the sides. Nevertheless, it was a fine performance from Sunderland with both Hannahs outstanding in the unremitting December rain. Preston North End also won 5-0 that day, as it happened, and the table now stood with Preston on 23 points from 15 games, and Sunderland on 21 from 13.

Sunderland did not have a league match on 10 December. They instead took part in a friendly against Middlesbrough which was lucky to be finished, having been played in snow throughout, while Preston beat West Bromwich Albion to move four points ahead while Sunderland had three games in hand. But the match of the season was now approaching with Preston at Newcastle Road on 17 December. It was highly anticipated, and hardly surprisingly, for the Football League had been in existence for four years, and between the two of them Preston and Sunderland had won it three times, with Preston still a source of admiration of all England for having won the league and FA Cup double in 1889.

The game was much talked about locally and no fewer than six special trains brought people from Preston. The team themselves proved less than totally co-operative. Tom Watson, helpful and courteous as always, offered his services to arrange hotel accommodation but Preston chose to keep their movements in the dark, presumably fearing some attempt to 'nobble' their players, such things being by no means unusual in Victorian football. That move did, however, betray a lack of trust in their own players from the Preston management.

Midwinter or not, it was a fine day which would 'not have been out of place in September', and an attendance of nearly 20,000 appeared, probably a record for Newcastle Road with many supporters 'unable to find a foothold on the timbers' and having to follow the game by the shouts of the crowd and the occasional glimpse of a red and white strip of Sunderland or a white shirt of Preston who were 'a powerful, well-built set of athletes'. Certainly the receipts of £600 – an astonishing amount of money for 1892 – were by some distance a record.

The match itself was disappointingly rough with 'loud hissing' being directed at several Preston players, Russell in particular, for being too reckless in his behaviour to Doig and some Sunderland supporters being described as 'beside themselves with rage'. David Hannah was also described as being 'kicked in the face' by a Preston player called Ross.

It was goalless at half-time but the longer the game went on, the more it became apparent that Sunderland were the better team, and that the mighty half-back line of Wilson, Auld and Gibson were ignoring all provocation and winning the day. But it was seven minutes from time before Sunderland scored. It was Johnny Campbell 'in a throng' in the Preston penalty area who managed to drive a ball home, then with 'hats being raised and flung frantically' and then almost at the call of time, James Hannah sent another one 'clean between the posts' to finish the game at 2-0 and to put Sunderland in a very strong position, only two points behind leaders Preston but with three games in hand.

The noise was intense as the crowd 'marched back' into town to their homes and to the various destinations, for not only had there been supporters from Preston at this game, there had also been trains from Newcastle, Darlington, Yorkshire and even Scotland. But Sunderland were now the talk of the whole United Kingdom, and everyone agreed that they were indeed 'the team of all the talents'.

The euphoria on Wearside would last for a long time, and possibly even encouraged a few to take the trip to at least one of the games of the 'Christmas Tour of the Midlands', as it was somewhat grandiosely put. The first port of call was Stoney Lane on Christmas Eve. There had been some frost (although nothing too severe) but the pitch was in fine condition. West Bromwich Albion were of course very anxious to repeat another 8-1 thrashing of the kind they received at Newcastle Road early in the season, and were probably quite happy to get off with a 3-1 defeat. On the other hand the *Birmingham Daily Gazette* stated quite unequivocally, 'The Albion were simply outclassed throughout the whole game. Nothing could possibly be finer than the Sunderland play in the first 45 minutes, when they took a lead by three goals to one. With a bit of luck the Albion might have drawn even in the last half, for Sunderland appeared to play rather careless, while the Throstles kept pluckily at it till the last.' This seems to have been quite a fair summing up.

Both the Hannahs (erroneously called brothers in some of the Midlands papers) scored, then Albion pulled one back with what looked like a foul on Doig before a deflection from a free kick earned Sunderland an own goal. That was the score at half-time and it stayed that way until full time as well, when Sunderland eased off a little and might have conceded on one or two occasions. The 8,000 crowd, however, departed satisfied with what they had seen, turning festive and singing 'Christmas and other songs of a cheerful nature' as they departed into the midwinter darkness.

This result meant that Sunderland enjoyed their Christmas dinner at their Wolverhampton hotel knowing that they were now equal on points with Preston, but having played two games fewer. They had every reason to feel confident as they moved to Molineux to take on Wolverhampton Wanderers on Boxing Day. But this was a bad day for the Wearsiders with the flatness that had been apparent in the second half against West Brom becoming even more pronounced. The forwards were distinctly off-colour in what was a dull game and a great disappointment for the large holiday crowd of 15,000 until their favourites scored twice in the later stages.

This result was greeted with despair on Wearside, but it was simply one of those games that happens from time to time. Wolves were not a bad team and raised their game whereas Sunderland sagged a little. Sunderland then defeated Rotherham in a friendly on the way home, and then on Hogmanay, not having a league match they took on Scottish visitors in Rangers whom they defeated 4-0 on a difficult pitch. Sadly on the same day, Preston beat Stoke 2-1 which meant that once again they were four points ahead with Sunderland having played three games fewer.

And thus ended the remarkable year of 1892 in which Sunderland had won the title in the spring and were challenging hard for it in the winter. Occasional mistakes had to be balanced by some really fine performances, and there could be no denying that in

Ned Doig in goal, Hugh Wilson at right-half and John Campbell at centre-forward, they had players who were as good as any.

In the outside world, William Gladstone was back as prime minister, something that inevitably meant that Irish Home Rule dominated the headlines. It was no secret that Gladstone and Queen Victoria did not enjoy a good relationship. Both were now old and more than a little cantankerous, both being used to getting their own way, and many music hall performances would feature sketches of two 'love birds' Billy and Vicky who kept falling out with each other.

The favourite song seemed to be 'Daddy Wouldn't Buy Me a Bow Wow', but trade remained constant with reasonably full employment in Sunderland and Newcastle, although health, housing and education remained absolutely shocking. It was often felt that the Liberals might now do more about it, but the criticism was increasingly made that Gladstone was far too obsessed with Ireland, and people were turning more and more to the various socialist or Labour parties that were beginning to spring up, particularly in industrial areas like Sunderland.

It was the month of January 1893 that saw Sunderland really assert themselves with six wins out of six, one of them being the vital one against Preston at Deepdale, and one – in the FA Cup – against the team with the pompous and portentous name of Royal Arsenal. By the end of the month they were clear leaders of the First Division and would not be seriously challenged until the end of the season. The month of January is often like that. It regularly, in midwinter conditions, sorts out the men from the boys.

New Year's Day was a Sunday in 1893 so games were scheduled for the following two days, and they could hardly have been more attractive than Wolves and Everton. The Wolves game was described by a reporter in the *Sunderland Daily Echo*, who clearly had some knowledge of Shakespeare, referring to *A Winter's Tale* for the snow was so heavy at one point that the players agreed to leave the field in the first half. The snow was not consistently heavy, however, and they were able to come back. The underfoot conditions were satisfactory, according to the referee Mr Lewis of Blackburn, but the high number of goals scored in Sunderland's 5-2 win indicated that the ground was possibly not as ideal as some would have liked.

Nevertheless, it was great for the Wearsiders to get some revenge for Boxing Day. Campbell was out with an ulcerated throat for this game and also missed the meeting with Everton, but the forward line of Gillespie, Harvey, Millar, David Hannah and James Hannah performed splendidly with James Hannah scoring a hat-trick, David Hannah scoring one and

Jimmy Millar the other goal. Four came in the first half and the big fear in the second half was not so much Wolves fighting back as the game being abandoned. Fortunately the conditions did not deteriorate too much, and it was played to a finish.

Snow was also around for the visit of Everton. The wind, however, was more of a factor as was always likely to be the case in the primitive stadia of the Victorian era where there was a lot less protection than there is today with the high surrounding walls. The combination of wind and rain played a disproportionate part against Everton, but it was to the credit of the Sunderland men that they managed to win, especially when it was noticed that little Johnny Harvey had sustained a bad injury to his arm which turned out to be broken. To his credit he played on to the finish, but he would be out for a couple of months after that.

Playing with the wind and the intermittent snow behind them, Sunderland were 3-0 up at half-time. Millar scored twice, once off the underside of the bar and the second when he hit the ball 'with a tremendous bang', and the team's third was one of dubious legality when both Hannahs appeared to shoulder-charge the goalkeeper into the net.

The second half saw Everton on the rampage with the advantage of the elements. They scored three goals and might have added more but for the brilliance of

Doig who denied them many times, but Sunderland got a key goal when Gillespie scored with a header from a Gibson free kick, and then were able to sustain tremendous pressure from the 'terrier Toffees' as they were called. Full time came to a 'grateful cheer when the whistle went'.

All this meant that Sunderland were level with Preston with one game fewer played, and the pair were due to meet the following Saturday at Deepdale with Sunderland now worried about injuries to key players. In the event, Johnny Campbell was back and Jimmy Millar was able to move to inside-right to make a forward line of Gillespie, Millar, Campbell, David Hannah and James Hannah. It was 'the wee Scotch terrier' Jimmy Gillespie (who also rejoiced in the unlikely name of 'Taffy' for some obscure reason) who was the hero of the hour with two early headed goals in the 2-1 win, which saw Sunderland now two points ahead of Preston with a game in hand.

Accounts of the game varied. The *Sunderland Daily Echo* was naturally very upbeat about the Sunderland performance, and stressed the dirty fouls of the Preston players and the injuries sustained by Wearside men like Campbell and Gillespie who limped painfully after the game, whereas the more neutral *Empire News and the Umpire* said that although the match was rough, Sunderland were by no means always the injured innocents. The consensus of opinion was that Preston were unlucky not to get an equaliser, something that came across in the extravagant praise given by everyone to Ned Doig.

What everyone did agree about, however, was that the crowd was a huge one with a great many 'excursionists' from Sunderland, but also quite a few 'football-minded' people from as far away as London and even Bristol. The crowd was given as 18,000 and as the cheapest amount charged was one shilling, so it was not difficult to work out that the receipts were by no means inconsiderable.

The ground was packed (such was the craze for football in the 1890s) and seats were at a premium with those less lucky lining the side of the park, encroaching occasionally and having to be pushed back by the police and soldiers who were on duty there. The crowd, though animated and occasionally critical of the Sunderland players, were not hostile to the visiting supporters, and the afternoon was peaceful, albeit noisy. Occasionally, there were odd turns of phrase like 'the excitement was terrible'.

The *Sunderland Daily Echo* gave two interesting comments on the arrangements for the press. One was that although the local journalists were under cover, the 'strange pencillers' (i.e. the reporters from the north) had to sit near the touchline 'exposed to a bitter wind and intermittent showers of hail' while to the amazement of the writer and in an almost iconoclastic move for the times, two female journalists 'descriptive and artistic' were present, presumably working for a magazine which was interested in crowds who attended football matches.

Such were the wonders of the modern telegraph system that the result reached Sunderland at 4.15pm and editions of the 'pink' were on sale a few minutes later with a report on the first half and the full-time result in the 'Stop Press' section. 'The utmost satisfaction prevailed at the result and congratulation were indulged in on all sides,' the newspaper wrote. But that was nothing compared to the reception that awaited the Sunderland players when they arrived at the station at 20 minutes to midnight. There were some 'excursionists' on that train with them, but the main body arrived on a later train which got in a few minutes later.

The *Daily Echo* also told a remarkable story of how before they left Preston (a trim and pleasant station which contrasted well with the Sunderland station which was not nearly as clean), secretary-manager Tom Watson and captain Hugh Wilson called upon the singers to assemble, and they sang to the amused Preston public as they waited for their train to arrive. Given the amount of Scottish players, it is not surprising to read that they entertained their hosts by singing:

'We're no awa tae bide awa
We're no awa tae leave you
We're no awa tae bide awa
We'll aye come back and see you!'

It was one of the favourites of the Glasgow music halls and a number with which the Scottish players would have been familiar. It was an excellent piece of public relations.

The next three weeks saw Sunderland, in spite of the cold weather, in a permanent state of happiness and excitement as far as football was concerned. Three home games were played – two in the league and one in the FA Cup – and they were all won with a degree of ease, so it was now very difficult to believe that this team, the conquerors of 'Proud Preston' on their home patch, was not now going to emulate the Lancashire club's achievements of 1889. The supporters were happy and just for a while, they walked tall. At least as far as football was concerned, they could forget, for a time, the squalor and degradation of the slums in which so many of them were compelled to live and breed children. Such can be the power of football and a successful team.

Aston Villa were the visitors on 14 January. Villa were a long way adrift of Preston but they were still third in the table with an outside chance of winning it

GREAT DAYS OF SUNDERLAND

if both Preston and Sunderland suffered a collapse. A good game was expected, and 8,000 were at Newcastle Road even in spite of the wintry conditions. Not a single spectator could have predicted that the score would be Sunderland 6 Aston Villa 0. Villa were simply taken apart by the rampant Wearsiders for whom Gillespie scored twice, Campbell and both Hannahs one each, and there was a rare goalscoring contribution from Bob Smellie. It was a marvellous display of sustained attacking football from a very fine Sunderland side.

The following Saturday brought the special tingle of the FA Cup. Curiosity was the man emotion on Wearside when the draw paired Sunderland at home with the team called Royal Arsenal, whom they had never come across before. In 1893 Arsenal – as they later became – lacked the worldwide renown that is theirs today, but they had been heard of in the north-east. There was a certain perception of them being just a little above themselves since they added the word 'Royal' to their title after they had started off in 1886 as merely a group of lads who worked in the factory in Woolwich which made cannons. To describe a football team as 'Royal' did seem to be a little presumptious.

They had turned professional in 1891 and did not hide their pretensions to be, among other things, the first southern team to win the FA Cup, but they were dismayed to discover that their first trip in 1893 was to the ground of the men who were top of the Football League and who were capable of wiping the floor with famous teams like Aston Villa. They arrived in Sunderland on the Friday night to be met with a reception which was not so much hostile as simply interested to see these men from the wealthy south. They looked remarkably like any other set of football players as they talked to the fans, although it was interesting to hear their somewhat unusual accents. They stayed at the Roker Hotel overnight, and were seen early in the morning doing some light training on the beach, but without over-exerting themselves.

Sunderland and their supporters approached this tie very warily, not really knowing what to expect, for no one had any great experience of London football. It was generally believed that Sunderland were the best team in the country, so there really should be no bother, but this was the FA Cup, a competition in which Sunderland had so far failed to distinguish themselves and which they desired and coveted so much. Neither London nor the north-east had ever won the FA Cup, so there was a great deal at stake.

The apprehensions of the local fans were hardly justified. In wet conditions with the occasional heavy downpour, Royal Arsenal, after an initial show of strength, were simply overwhelmed by a Sunderland team on song in the same way as they had been the previous week. It was 5-0 at half-time with a goal from David Hannah and two each from Millar and Campbell, and in the second half Sunderland eased off a little until Millar completed his hat-trick near the end.

Arsenal were not without their chances in the second half, testing Doig on a few occasions, and unlike some other visitors to Newcastle Road that season they won the respect of the fans for their 'plucky play' and their refusal to 'dish out the raw meat' as a few other sides had done. The mood changed from hostility to even a little sympathy and a wish expressed that they could score at least one goal, and the few London supporters that they had brought with them were wished a safe journey home with unlikely questions asked about whether the Queen and old Gladstone were 'at it'. Such badinage was greeted with good humour, and the Londoners left Sunderland with a high opinion of north-east football and hospitality.

The bottom line for Sunderland was that they were in the next round of the FA Cup. It would be a difficult trip to Bramall Lane to play Sheffield United on 4 February, but first there was a visit from the other team from the town where all the knives were made – The Wednesday, who had been the first side to beat Sunderland that season, back in October.

Revenge was duly meted out to the tune of 4-2 on that dull, but not entirely unpleasant day of 28 January.

The game saw the debut of Willie Dunlop, yet another man from Ayrshire, playing at centre-half in place of the injured John Auld, and was notable for a hat-trick by James Hannah. The 8,000 crowd departed happy and their evening papers made pleasant reading, for although Preston also won, Sunderland were now four points in front with both teams having played 21 games and therefore having only nine left. The title looked as if it were Sunderland's to throw away, but the way that the team were playing gave no one any reason to believe that this was going to happen.

But now attention turned to the FA Cup (or as it was more commonly called at the time the 'English Cup', or in the vernacular, 'Ta Coop'). The team left Sunderland station once again to a great send-off on the Friday night, and some supporters travelled to Yorkshire on the Saturday morning with a great deal of optimism. Once again that feeling was justified by a 3-1 victory with two goals from Millar and one from Campbell. The crowd was a mighty one of 10,000, but by half-time they were mostly hushed into silence because of Sunderland's dominance with only the small pocket of visiting supporters being seen to smile. It was well into the second half before Sheffield United scored, and that was because of an uncharacteristic mistake by Doig, but there was seldom any strong challenge after that, with the goalkeeper atoning for his error with a few fine saves, including one near the end of the game when he was, apparently, lying on his back.

Nothing seemed like stopping Sunderland now, even though the quarter-final draw paired them against Blackburn Rovers, a club who were known to be an FA Cup team having won it on five occasions in 1884, 1885, 1886, 1890 and 1891. It would not be easy as Sunderland had to travel there on 18 February.

But there was a league match first, four days before the Blackburn tie. In fact they were due on 11 February to make a rare appearance at Hampden Park to play Queen's Park, but the Scottish amateurs were involved in a cup replay against Hearts so Sunderland played a light-hearted friendly at Leith Athletic instead.

The return to league business was a rather sobering and chastening experience against Bolton Wanderers. Possibly taking things rather too lightly, Sunderland found themselves 3-0 down soon after half-time. They also had the most unfortunate experience of discovering just how fickle football fans can be. The third goal was quite clearly an error by Doig, and the fans turned on him with 'sarcasm' and laughter at his subsequent attempts, and some of the other players were also the subject of some scorn and derision.

But then again, just when things looked as if they were irredeemable, Sunderland fought back. A goal from each of the Hannahs, and then just at the end, a header from the unlikely source of left-half Willie Gibson saved the day. The fans, as was their way, now turned again, and although disappointed that a win could not be achieved, they felt that a point was at least something.

But the draw was not achieved without some adverse concomitant effects. The first-half performance in itself gave a great deal of cause for concern, and there were several injuries. Millar, who had been scoring prolifically, was out but he seemed to be adequately covered. The problem was the injury to Bob Smellie. Sunderland made the questionable decision to bring Porteous across to the left-back position, and to give a debut to John Gillespie (no relative of Jimmy), and this was not a success.

As far as the FA Cup tie was concerned, the weather saw constant rain but that did not seem to affect the attendance at Ewood Park, which was given as a huge 28,000. It was not one of Sunderland's better days. Indeed it was a disaster with Blackburn more or less in charge throughout and so many Sunderland players out of touch. The famous half-back line was frequently overrun and the makeshift full-back combination was woefully inadequate. There had been a comeback on the Tuesday but there was nothing at Blackburn, and long before full time the telegraph was sending the baleful tidings back to Sunderland that the FA Cup was not likely to come to the north-east for another year. The Lancashire crowd was exultant with joy, while the 'excursionists' put a brave face on it as they headed back for their train in the unremitting Lancashire rain.

It was one of the saddest days for Sunderland in these times – but there was still some potential balm in Gilead. Before league fixtures resumed in March, Sunderland had a significant friendly fixture which they won 6-1. It was against the newly formed Newcastle United. The word 'United' was appropriate in these circumstances for the new team was an amalgamation of Newcastle East End and Newcastle West End; basically most of the players coming from East End but playing on West End's ground at St James' Park. Sunderland had played against East End on several occasions, but this game is often looked upon by some historians as being the start of the fierce rivalry which would dominate north-east thinking for the next century and more.

It was 4 March before serious league business began again, and while the FA Cup semi-finals were taking place (Wolves beat Blackburn while Everton needed three games to beat Preston), Sunderland made steady progress towards the championship by beating Newton Heath 5-0 before a record Manchester attendance of 15,000. This team played in yellow and green and would in time become known as Manchester United, but on this day they showed little signs of future greatness, and both they and supporters were quite clearly dismissed by the mighty men from the north.

Campbell scored two, and Harvie, Gillespie and Scott one each as the Heathens, after a spirited opening in which they might have gone ahead, were totally overrun. It being Manchester and spring time (nominally) there was rain, but the Sunderland men were impressed by the enthusiasm of the crowd, and certainly felt that there was a future for this club which had grown out of a group of lads working on the railway. Manchester was a very new city having sprung up virtually out of nothing and very much a child of the Industrial Revolution.

Seven games now remained, and all that Sunderland really had to do was to keep winning. But the FA Cup defeat still rankled and enthusiasm back home was lacking. Winning championships is all about grinding out results when life seems to have turned against you, and Sunderland now simply had to buckle down and do so, while admiring from a distance as Everton and Wolves would be gearing themselves up for the FA Cup Final on 25 March.

By that time Sunderland had made more progress towards the title with victories over Derby County and Stoke. The game against Derby at Newcastle Road was played in a ferocious gale, which funnily enough seemed easier to play against than with. The wind was described as 'capricious', but it did not stop Johnny Campbell scoring twice against it, as Sunderland, with Hugh Wilson now back from injury, adapted their tactics brilliantly and kept the ball on the ground. Derby pulled one back just before half-time, but it was confidently expected that a 'train carriage load of goals' would follow once Sunderland had the wind on their backs.

The *Sunderland Daily Echo* described the 6,000 crowd as using 'entreaty, command, invective, sarcasm and abuse' to encourage their 'pets' to add to the lead, but to no avail. But then, long after the ten-minute flag had fallen to warn everyone of how little time was left, Jimmy Gillespie at last got one past Robinson and the crowd could go home in a more relaxed frame of mind.

Sunderland were then at Stoke on 18 March. In marvellous warm weather before a good crowd of 10,000, Wilson scored the only goal of the game, and it was only through some rugged Stoke defending that Sunderland did not add to the total and the neutral press were in unanimous admiration of their passing ability and ball control. Two other results went down well with the Sunderland players that day too; Scotland beat Wales 8-0, and Burnley beat Preston 4-2.

It was this last result that made Sunderland realise just how close they were to the league title. They had 42 points from 25 games, well clear of Preston who had 31 from 23. Preston had seven games left, so their maximum potential was 45, meaning that if Preston suffered just one defeat combined with Sunderland winning one more match, the race was over.

It didn't work out like that. Sunderland didn't have a game on FA Cup Final Saturday when Wolves beat Everton 1-0 at a very overcrowded Fallowfield in Manchester. Sunderland made one of their frequent trips to Scotland and beat Third Lanark 4-0 while their next league game was on Good Friday at Blackburn, where a crowd of 12,000 saw a well-fought 2-2 draw which the Wearsiders looked as if they were going to win until the home side scored from a late free kick. They then stayed in Lancashire overnight for they were playing Bolton Wanderers on the Saturday. The day after Good Friday is frequently called 'Black Saturday' in Christian circles, and it was not a great game for Sunderland because they went down 2-1. Indeed, they were 2-0 down for most of the game and it was only when Campbell pulled one back in the later stages that they looked anything like their normal selves.

However, it was a good Saturday after all. Newton Heath amazed the world by beating Preston 2-1, a result which meant that Sunderland needed only one point from three games to become champions for the second year in a row. In fact they probably were already champions because their goal average was so superior, but they made absolutely sure when Newton Heath paid their first visit to Sunderland on Tuesday, 4 April.

On Easter Monday they had had famous guests at Newcastle Road in Queen's Park who had a few weeks earlier won the Scottish Cup. Sunderland won 4-2 before a large crowd. Queen's Park, strictly amateur, had made the decision NOT to join the Scottish league because they feared (correctly as it turned out) that it might accelerate the arrival of professionalism, but they still played in and had now won the Scottish Cup for the tenth time. The Scottish league was won for the first time by Celtic in 1893.

Sunderland finally settled matters with a somewhat anti-climactic 6-0 defeat of Newton Heath on the Tuesday afternoon, Campbell and Millar scoring twice each while the other goals were scored by James Hannah and Hugh Wilson, the latter playing at left-half to allow Dunlop to play at right-half while Gibson moved to left-back to cover for the still-injured Smellie. The Mancunians, now holders of the 'wooden spoon' at the bottom of the table, were clearly overwhelmed by it all, but they were still learning and were gracious in defeat.

Congratulations poured in to Sunderland from all over the United Kingdom. They still had to play a friendly against Middlesbrough Ironopolis and two league matches, against Derby and Burnley, and the phrase of 'the team of all the talents' became shortened to simply 'the talents' in the thousands of words of paeans of praise that were poured out about their exploits, with newspapers in Scotland and London (and even Newcastle!) particularly effusive in their encomia.

It had been a marvellous season with 100 goals scored in 30 league games. Sunderland had probably been lucky with injuries, but they had used only 15 players, something that perhaps says much about team selection and the willingness to stick with players even though they were having a rough spell. Doig had been superb in goal, but the mainstay had been the half-back line of Wilson, Auld and Gibson. Up front, as well as the obvious and already well-known successes of Campbell and Millar, both Hannahs had enjoyed magnificent seasons, and Gillespie and Harvey had emerged, often making telling contributions to the cause.

Sunderland's success was celebrated in Scotland as much as on the Wear itself, for so many of their players were Scottish, particularly from Ayrshire, and the men went home to be feted as heroes. In Sunderland itself, once the football season ended there was a certain feeling of emptiness, something that was not exactly filled by the royal wedding of Prince George, the Duke of York, to Princess Mary of Teck on 6 July. It was a public holiday and a chance to celebrate, but what was really wanted was the return of the football season.

For the past two years, Sunderland had enjoyed glory. The people now wanted and craved more and although there was a lot of cricket played in the district, it was football which gave them the chance to forget the appalling conditions in which they were compelled to live in the north-east in 1893.

3

League Champions 1894/95

SUNDERLAND, AS it were, took a rest from being league champions in 1894 – Aston Villa won it that year – but the Wearsiders returned to take over again in 1894/95. There were now 16 teams in the First Division with Sunderland still the only one in the north. There were two from Yorkshire: Sheffield United and The Wednesday; six from Lancashire in Preston North End, Blackburn Rovers, Burnley, Bolton Wanderers, Liverpool and Everton; while the other seven were Midlands teams in Nottingham Forest, Derby County, Stoke, Wolverhampton Wanderers and the three Birmingham teams of Small Heath, Aston Villa and West Bromwich Albion. The new team of the north-east, Newcastle United, the amalgamation of Newcastle West End and Newcastle East End, were in the Second Division. They did not do particularly well; despite playing acceptably well at home they were poor travellers.

Queen Victoria was still on the throne where she had sat for almost 60 years. The current prime minister was a strange man, Archibald Primrose, the 5th Earl of Rosebery. He had taken over after the retirement of William Gladstone. Rosebery was approved by the Queen, but a man who frankly was simply not cut out to be prime minister. He could not cope with Cabinet meetings where he had many opponents, he was frequently ill with various complaints – either physical or depressive – and he was far more interested in his racehorses. It was also no great secret that, although he was married, he was very interested in men and boys. He frankly had too much money and he symbolised all that was wrong in the way that Victorian society operated. He lasted little more than a year as prime minister but he was in Downing Street (or rather, he should have been) for all of the 1894/95 football season.

When things got boring, you could always rely on the Prince of Wales to have a scandal or two. Drink, gluttony, women, gambling debts – it was all there, and although the Church of England and the Establishment tried to pretend it didn't go on, everyone knew it did. He was in line to take over from his odious mother one day – but would he last as long as that?

Locally, things were much as usual with a great deal of poverty and deprivation but business was still booming in the shipyards and the coalmines.

The Industrial Revolution even seemed to be gathering pace.

The start of the season on 1 September 1894 could hardly have been more bizarre. The weather was fine for football enthusiasts who had been looking forward to this day since April. The visitors to Newcastle Road were attractive ones in Derby County. The teams were:

Sunderland: Doig, Meechan, Gow, Wilson, McCreadie, Johnston, Gillespie, Millar, Campbell, Hyslop, James Hannah.

Derby County: Robinson, Staley, Methven, Docherty, Archie Goodall, Cox, Bloomer, McMillan, John Goodall, Fletcher, Allen.

The referee? Ah, well there lay the problem! A telegram had been received from Mr Kirkham of Burslem saying that he had missed his connection at York and that he wouldn't arrive before five o'clock. But the game was meant to start at 3.15pm and the players were already out limbering up – a complicating factor being that Derby had now changed their side, Leiper having injured himself and been replaced by Staley.

In the meantime a spectator, a man on holiday from Southwick in Sussex by the unlikely name of J. Conqueror who had refereed games at junior level, offered his services. No doubt in Sussex, his nickname would have been William or perhaps Norman, but after a great deal of humming and hawing between both sets of directors, with the crowd becoming very impatient, it was agreed to accept Mr Conqueror.

The game started at last and after 45 minutes, Sunderland were winning 3-0 with Mr Conqueror in charge and everyone agreeing that he was having a good game. The players trotted off but took a long time to come out again after their interval, and when they did, there was no referee. It transpired that Mr Kirkham had arrived and insisted that the game should be restarted, that what had been played so far should be declared invalid, and that Mr Conqueror should be thanked for his services and dismissed. Not surprisingly Sunderland objected to this, but Derby saw it as a way of getting themselves off a rather uncomfortable hook. The crowd had had enough, and began to go home, but Mr Kirkham won his point and the game started again.

Half-time came and the score was once again 3-0. In the second half with both sets of players thoroughly cheesed off by all this, and in front of empty terraces and bleachers (the crowd had been present since about 2pm and it was now well after 6pm), Sunderland scored another five goals, to make the final score 8-0, although 11 goals had been scored since the original kick-off. All the forwards scored at least once, and Gillespie, Millar and Hyslop scored twice. It was beginning to get dark by the time the match eventually finished. You could say it was a game of three halves.

It wasn't exactly good public relations for football and naturally the shenanigans of Newcastle Road were a subject of much discussion and not a little ridicule in the national press, but in fact it was actually quite a good start to the season for Sunderland and a very poor one for Derby, for whom the great Steve Bloomer was hardly noticed. Even with the result at 8-0 (rather than 11), the score was still a record for Sunderland in the league.

The next league game was also at Newcastle Road, this time against Burnley. There was no repetition of the fiasco for referee Mr Fox knew the way from Sheffield to Sunderland and was as 'punctual as the landlord for the rent' in the striking Victorian imagery of the *Sunderland Daily Echo*. But there was a delay for another reason in that Burnley were wearing virtually the same strip as Sunderland, except it looked as if their shirts had 'been to the wash a little oftener and had consequently lost colour'. As was the convention in those days, Sunderland – the home team – changed into black and white, of all colour combinations.

A couple of decades later this might have raised an eyebrow or two, but it was too early in the history of Newcastle United to make anyone feel uncomfortable, and in any case the reporter thought that they 'presented an extremely athletic appearance'. Sunderland had played two friendlies in midweek, drawing 1-1 with Rangers at Ibrox and defeating Newcastle United 4-1 at St James' Park, and had picked up a few injuries, so the team was quite different from the one that faced Derby and read Doig, Meechan, McNeil, McCreadie, Auld, Johnston, James Hannah, Harvie, Campbell, Hyslop and Scott.

The crowd was slow to turn up with only 'a nucleus on the timbers' at 3pm, but by kick-off half an hour later about 7,000 were there, and they saw a great Sunderland performance. Sunderland began with the wind and scored early through Tommy Hyslop with a thunderbolt which produced 'maddened cheers' for one of the best goals ever 'pedipulated' at Newcastle Road. That was his first goal of his hat-trick for he scored one with his head and another with his foot in the second half, and Sunderland won 3-0. There were a few deficiencies in the play, according to the *Sunderland Daily Echo*, but not even the team's fiercest critics could complain about 8-0 one week and 3-0 the next, with a radically different line-up in the second game compared with the first, thanks to injuries. The season had truly begun but a serious test was now looming on the horizon with the first away fixture, against the defending champions, Aston Villa.

A crowd of 20,000 appeared at Parry Barr to see this game, almost all of them favouring the Villa, but keen to see the encounter with 'the crack northern side' who seemed to attract so many people to the grounds to watch them. The fact that Sunderland were the most distant side in the Football League and that whenever they played, a great deal of travel was involved for one side or another, added in a way to their mystique. But this was the Victorian age and the railway was king. Indeed it was the only viable way of travelling, and sitting on a train, and then living in a hotel was seen very definitely as one of the perks of being a Victorian football player. Along with their president, Cllr Henderson, and a few others, the players stayed overnight at the Colonnade Hotel, Birmingham, their favourite haunt in the Midlands. They would stay there for the weekend and then play a friendly with Leicester Fosse on the Monday.

Sunderland were playing down the hill in the first half, but it was Villa who scored the first goal through Smith in a 'scrimmage' in front of the posts. Sunderland, however, rallied and 'in a very fine run with their vanguard' Johnny Campbell scored with a low shot. Then in the second half the Wearsiders, who were playing more strongly against the slope, began to dominate and a fine one-two between James Hannah and Hyslop saw Hannah put Sunderland ahead, and it was a position they never really looked like surrendering, even scoring again near the end but having the goal disallowed for offside.

It was generally agreed that at this stage Sunderland looked like returning to their status as the best team in England with men like Ned Doig in goal, Hugh Wilson at right-half and James Hannah up front singled out as great players, but it was also stressed that there was a 'unity' among them and that they all played for each other in a way that other sides didn't. There was, however, a long way to go, if Sunderland were going to win their third league title in four years.

They made it four wins out of four the following week when West Bromwich Albion came to Newcastle Road. The Throstles were another famous team who had won the FA Cup in 1888 and 1892, and could usually be guaranteed to provide great entertainment. They were second in the First Division and were given a sporting reception by the 10,000 Sunderland crowd as they appeared on the crisp autumn afternoon of 22 September, wearing their black and white vertical stripes and white pants. But that was nothing in comparison to the reception that had greeted Sunderland.

The supporters had been clearly impressed by the result at Aston Villa and gave Sunderland a 'royal' reception as they ran out; the players, for their part, 'looked trained to perfection and each man bounded over the springy turf as if he had steel springs for muscles'. Referee Strawson of Leicester produced a new ball for the occasion, and 'Hughie' (Hugh Wilson) won the toss and decided to play uphill in the first half.

A certain amount of hilarity was caused by the referee's 'tootle' which seemed to have a 'severe attack of bronchitis' and produced a very 'feeble wail', but there was nothing feeble about Sunderland's play which probably deserved a lot more than the 3-0 win that it got. It was Campbell who scored the first goal. He picked up a free kick from Wilson, then dodged a defender, made space and crashed home a brilliant shot which the goalkeeper did well to get a hand on, but the 'impetus' was too great and the 'sphere' fell into the net.

Tremendous cheers greeted this and from now on 'affairs were rolling pronouncedly in favour of Sunderland' and with Andy McCreadie now impressing at centre-half, it was no surprise that they went further ahead, the goal this time coming from Jimmy Gillespie, and it was he who scored again in the second half following a free kick from Wilson.

The Throstles were a well beaten side and did not always endear themselves to the Sunderland crowd by their hefty tackling. Right-back Williams seemed to aim a kick at Campbell and was well warned by Mr Strawson, and when he did it again, he was very lucky not to be sent off. At one point McLeod tried a 'downy' trick (sadly one that is all too common in the 21st century) of lying down and feigning an injury, alleging a foul by Bob McNeill. It mattered not. Sunderland won 3-0, and even at this early stage of the season, it did not look as if anyone was likely to catch them.

These confident assertions in the local and national press (there is nothing new about journalists sticking their heads out and then getting them chopped off) were given a rough jolt even before September was out when Sunderland went down to Bolton Wanderers and lost 4-1. There seems to be no real reason for it other than that Sunderland, heads having swollen to an unacceptable extent, underestimated their opponents or that Bolton raised their game.

Or perhaps, Sunderland allowed themselves to be upset about a strange affair about the eligibility or otherwise of Tommy Hyslop. The *Sunderland Daily Echo* revealed that Mr J.J. Bentley, the secretary of Bolton Wanderers, and also the chairman of the Football League, seems to have written a letter to himself enquiring whether Hyslop was allowed to play. Back came the reply that there was no objection to Hyslop playing. But 'other circumstances had intervened' and Sunderland decided to drop their man in favour of David Hannah.

So what was this all about? It seems to have something to do with Hyslop changing his name, and the *Sunderland Daily Echo* gave a clue when it referred to Hyslop as 'the ex-Guardsman'. Hyslop was really Bryce Scouller, but he had changed his name to Tommy Hyslop for some obscure reason, although it is a reasonable supposition that it was something to do with him wanting to hide his military past. Or perhaps there had been some criminal charge? Whatever the reason, it was a matter of some controversy.

But with all due respect to David Hannah, Hyslop was badly missed at Bolton. The day was described as 'much too fine for the game', and Sunderland did not cope very well with the excessive and unseasonal heat. Bolton were 1-0 up at half-time, and although Harry Johnston scored for the Wearsiders, the Trotters, showing more energy and commitment, scored another three and Sunderland were well beaten. The *Sunderland Daily Echo* thought that Sunderland were a 'bit too clever' and that Campbell was the only player 'who seemed to know where the goal really was'.

But it was a chastening experience and it is one of the sporting truisms that a defeat can very quickly become a victory if one learns from it. The Hyslop business was clearly unsettling, but the team learned quickly, and they were good enough to recover at pace. It was also early enough in the season and Tom Watson was able to work with the players along with captain

Hugh Wilson. It would be after Christmas before Sunderland lost again in the league.

Whatever problems there were about Hyslop being allowed to play seem to have evaporated very quickly before the arrival of Stoke – three decades away from being renamed Stoke City – on 6 October. The Potters had a reputation of unpredictability and in the same way as Sunderland were referred to as 'the team of all the talents', Stoke were sometimes called 'the team of all the surprises'. Having recently defeated Aston Villa – a great sensation in the Midlands – they felt that they could perhaps land another surprise on Wearside.

The game was rather one-sided, at least in the first half when, in spite of playing against the rain and up the slight slope that there was at Newcastle Road, Sunderland led 3-0. The first was a slightly fortuitous own goal, but then immediately after that Hyslop, clearly a man with a point to make, scored a cracker of an individual goal, and then was instrumental in Jimmy Millar scoring a third. The match was played in constant rain which caused 'umbrellas to be raised and topcoats to be produced' while the reporter of the *Sunderland Daily Echo* made the smug remark that 'the press box was the most comfortable place in the enclosure'.

Both the rain and Sunderland eased off in the second half, but the ground was very wet, falls were frequent and play was 'of a scrappy nature'. Stoke pulled a goal back but never really threatened to score again, and the game finished on a quiet note with the points comfortably in the bag, and most of the bedraggled spectators already on their way home to dry out.

Then Sunderland went off to Scotland to play Dundee at Carolina Port, the club's home before they moved to Dens Park. This was of course a great day locally, not least for the friends and family of Ned Doig, who appeared en masse to see him in a crowd of 7,000. Yet the locals, who might have been expecting a feast of football from this great English side with the massive reputation, must have been disappointed by what they saw, for there were one or two fringe players playing and Dundee won 1-0 with the *Dundee Courier* disappointed that the 'visitors were indulging in some rather shady tactics'.

Friendlies, of course, ultimately do not matter and Sunderland enjoyed some Scottish hospitality before returning home. A tour of London would follow the next week, but it also included the important business of a league match on the way south at Derby on the Saturday, and the press told how the players left Sunderland on Friday lunchtime wearing silk ties in the club's colours, a silk tie in the 1890s being looked upon as a particularly ostentatious sign of luxury, but the directors were clearly keen to make the players feel important, particularly in London.

But Derby came first. *Empire News and the Umpire* was very impressed with the standard of play, which was described as 'splendidly contested'. Sunderland won 2-1 before 8,000 spectators which would perhaps have been more if the weather had been brighter, and it was the man of the moment Hyslop who scored with a 'clinking ground shot' for the first goal. The second was a penalty sunk by McCreadie after Campbell had been brought down. It was a good victory, but elsewhere, Everton – by virtue of their 3-0 win over Liverpool – preserved their 100 per cent record.

Everton were Sunderland's next opponents in two weeks' time, and in the meantime the Wearsiders' supporters were left scratching their heads at the form of their favourites in the intervening friendlies. Their tour of London saw two rather disappointing 2-1 wins against Royal Arsenal and Casuals FC, but then, to the amazement of all Scotland and Wearside, they travelled to Glasgow and defeated Queen's Park 8-1. Queen's Park had of late been struggling against the professional teams of Scotland, but they were far from a spent force and the win was a remarkable one, particularly for Sunderland's Scottish players and their many Scottish supporters.

But all eyes now turned to Goodison Park for the visit to Everton. It was considered important enough for the North Eastern Railway Company to run an excursion train at the price of six shillings, travelling through the night after leaving Sunderland at 12.30am. Quite a few fans availed themselves of the opportunity, and their support was heard in the huge crowd of 30,000. Everton had lost a game between their victory over Liverpool and this date, and Sunderland were the stronger team with Jimmy Millar scoring two good goals as his side held on until late in the game.

But then disaster struck. Doig, who was – unusually for the times – wearing a white jersey to indicate that he was the goalkeeper, was having a great game and the Everton fans were heading for the exits in great numbers and even when McInnes pulled one back in a scrimmage, no one thought anything other than a Sunderland victory would occur. But then with the very last kick, and in the aftermath of a throw-in, Boyle managed to get his foot to a ball and guide it past Doig to the dismay of the Sunderland excursionists, and to a huge groan outside the office of the *Sunderland Daily Echo* when the news reached the people gathered there.

It was a very undeserved draw for Everton, and a very bad blow for Sunderland but it meant that Everton topped the table at the end of October with 17 points from ten games, whereas Sunderland had 13 from eight. It looked as it was going to be an interesting chase for the title.

But by the end of November, Sunderland had made such progress that, although Everton were a point ahead, the Wearsiders had a game in hand. Three games were won over Wolverhampton Wanderers, Bolton and Liverpool at Newcastle Road, and there was also an honourable draw at Blackburn Rovers. This was championship-winning form, and their crowds loved it as once again football became the talk of the town.

The wind was blowing across Newcastle Road, and rain was threatening when Wolves arrived on 3 November. Without playing brilliantly Sunderland were good enough to win with a crisp turn and shot from Campbell after some fine work from Peter Meechan, and then a strange goal near the end when Campbell charged a defender to allow Millar to score. It is doubtful whether this goal would have been allowed in the modern game but then again, Meechan had earlier scored from a free kick, but in 1894 all free kicks were indirect and the goal was not allowed. But the game finished with no further scoring and Sunderland won 2-0.

The players would therefore have enjoyed their dinner at the County Hotel, Westoe, given to them by Cllr Marshall to celebrate his recent re-election to South Shields Town Council and the team's great

2-2 draw at Everton. Various toasts were proposed for the health of some councillors and the continuing success of Sunderland AFC. The mood of everyone was improved considerably with the news that Everton had drawn again, this time 4-4 with Small Heath, and as was almost *de rigueur* in these days, some of the Sunderland players sang songs and did recitations for the benefit of other residents of the hotel, and a great time was had by all.

The following week saw a trip to Blackburn and a creditable 1-1 draw, but it was the second time in two weeks in Lancashire that Sunderland had conceded a goal in the last minute to deprive them of victory. The team were handicapped by the absence for a large part of the game of Bob McNeill, who received a severe but accidental 'kick in the loin' and when he was off being treated Sunderland were obliged to bring Hyslop back to help the defence, something which severely impaired the effectiveness of the attack. All the same, the problem seemed to have been solved and the game over when Hall suddenly popped up to score in the last minute.

All this was very disappointing, but 17 November saw the visit to Newcastle Road of Bolton – whom Sunderland 'owed one' following the events of September. This time there seemed to be no objection to the fielding of Hyslop, and it was a particularly joyous occasion for the home supporters when their team won 4-0, with the reporter from the *Sunderland Daily Echo* summing things up when he said, 'I can well understand the football public throughout the country going on to ecstasies over Sunderland's play!'

Hannah scored twice in the first half when he breasted a ball over the line for the first one and scored in a 'ruck' for the second. On both occasions Bolton objected and threw tantrums when the referee gave the goals. They were roundly booed by the home crowd for such behaviour when Mr Stacey of Sheffield made his decisions, but this must be seen in the context of the rest of the game which was decidedly unpleasant with McGinn and Cassidy both guilty of bad fouls on Sunderland players while on the other hand, Peter Meechan was seen to be 'rushing like the bull of Basham' at Weir of Bolton.

In the second half, the limping Campbell scored a third and then towards the end Gillespie scored a fourth which the goalkeeper made a mess of, distracted by the onrushing Millar. It was a totally comprehensive victory and was greatly cheered by the Sunderland crowd who 'bounced with enthusiasm' on the way home, so delighted were they with the play of their team.

A week later the Sunderland faithful were 'wreathed in smiles' as they went home, and with good cause, for they had seen their team bounce back to win 3-2 after being two goals down with only quarter of an hour to go. This was against Liverpool, a club who had not yet made any kind of mark on English football and were quite clearly the inferiors to Everton in the city. It was Liverpool's first visit to Sunderland.

David Hannah had now joined Liverpool for he felt that he could not be guaranteed first-team football at Sunderland, and he was playing well enough to make the crowd wonder whether the Wearsiders shouldn't have tried a little harder to keep him. But the pressure was all Sunderland, but they kept missing chances while Liverpool took two – one by McVean, and then another right on the stroke of half-time when Bradshaw headed home a Curran free kick.

This had not gone down well with the 8,000 crowd who grew visibly and audibly a great deal more impatient as the chances continued to be missed and Liverpool defended well against the more or less constant Sunderland pressure. There was the feeling that this was simply not Sunderland's day, but there was always the feeling as well that one goal could bring another.

So it turned out. A long clearance from McCreadie found James Hannah, who beat his immediate opponent with an overhead kick, then ran past him and finished the move with a great goal. As often happens in such circumstances, it was an inspired piece of individual brilliance which broke the deadlock and great was the cheering. But quickly 'the flag fell' to indicate that there was less than ten minutes to go, and then immediately after that, Campbell hit the junction of the bar and the post but the ball rebounded to Hyslop who resisted the temptation to hammer it and passed instead to Campbell, who 'steered the pigskin into the net' for 2-2. The *Sunderland Daily Echo*'s reporter then said that it 'taxes language to depict', but 'there was more to come yet'.

More or less on time, Hannah 'shaped the ball beautifully' to Gillespie who 'hooked it past the goalkeeper in irresistible style'. Sunderland were ahead and the reporter now excelled himself, 'If the previous outbursts of enthusiasm had been remarkable, the tumultuous scenes that were here witnessed cast everybody's experiences of popular outbursts into the shade. Hats went off heads, hands heaved them into the darkling [sic] air, and the good old welkin [sic] pealed with the thunderous salvo of cheers. The staidest forgot themselves in such a situation and shook hands with each other as if they had been lifelong acquaintances.' Such was the rapture associated with supporting Sunderland in 1894.

The 'welkin' is usually only otherwise mentioned in 'Oh Come, All Ye Faithful!' and it may be that the reporter had been practising in his choir for Christmas, for the festive period was approaching. In fact many thought that it had come early. But the good form continued, and the season of Advent saw two further wins in the First Division.

The game at Nottingham Forest on 1 December was fogged off, but better luck was forthcoming four days later when Sunderland beat the Rest of the League 1-0 in a charity match at South Shields, and on Saturday, 8 December when Small Heath paid their first visit to Newcastle Road. They may have wished that they hadn't bothered for they went down 7-1 to a very strong Sunderland team, and one or two of the Heathens were very lucky to see the 90 minutes out with centre-half Jenkyns guilty of something that was more of an assault than a foul, but it went unpunished by the referee. 'The Heathens team is not a very brilliant one,' said the *Sunderland Daily Echo*. It is a wonderful piece of meiosis.

Sunderland had their crowd (a slightly disappointing one of about 5,000) purring with pleasure at some of the play with the forward line in particular of Gillespie, Millar, Campbell, Hannah and Scott 'passing and re-passing the ball with clock-like precision' – and that was without Tommy Hyslop. But four of the goals were scored by half-backs – McCreadie and Wilson had two each. Gillespie also had two and Millar one whereas the top scorer Campbell didn't score at all, but then again, he didn't need to.

And then on 15 December, Sunderland had more difficult opponents in Blackburn in the return fixture following their draw at Ewood Park in the autumn. The 3-2 scoreline was possibly a little deceptive for Sunderland were always on top of their illustrious Lancashire opponents, who were the only team in the league to have beaten the Wearsiders more than they had lost to them. The match had been billed as 'the game of the season'. It never came close to living up to that but Campbell and Scott were on target before half-time and then Gillespie scored the winner in the second half after Blackburn had equalised. It was an odd goal. Gillespie took a corner and the ball came over to Scott, who kicked it back in, and after the goalkeeper had parried it Gillespie hammered home to the relief of the home support, who were now getting very frustrated.

The game that was meant to be played at Preston on 22 December had to be postponed because of a gale, and thus the league table on Christmas Eve was a funny one. Everton were on top with 27 points from 16 games, while Sunderland were third with 24 from only 14 matches, and in between were Aston Villa with 25 points but they had played 19 times.

Things were looking good, but then Sunderland's directors made a mistake – two of them in fact – and the mid-season 'wobble' common to most good teams resulted. They agreed to play the postponed matches at Nottingham Forest and Preston in the week between Christmas and the end of the year – and lost them both.

There were sound reasons for their decision. The economic argument was, as always, a potent one in that there was always a lot of football played at this time of year, people were on holiday and big crowds usually appeared. The other was a desire to avoid a fixture pile-up, and it is here that one can, perhaps, detect an element of pressure being applied by the Football League's Management Committee. Sunderland were already behind with their matches, the FA Cup was appearing on the horizon and as the team was playing well, it seemed sensible to 'keep going'.

The problem was that Sunderland were already away to Newton Heath (in a friendly) on Christmas Day, and West Bromwich Albion on Boxing Day, and that fixtures against Forest on Wednesday, 27 December and Preston two days later would involve extending the 'tour'. Normally 'tours' involving living in hotels were very positive with the building up of camaraderie and team spirit, but this one, extended at short notice and at this time of year, did not seem to be a great success. It was also four games in five days, and that, even for football-mad people, is a bit excessive. It is quite possible that there may have been a 'falling out', something that is by no means unusual, but which can have disastrous and even deleterious effects on teams.

The sequence started well. The friendly with Newton Heath was won 3-1, and then on Boxing Day a fine win was registered against West Bromwich Albion. An even first half ended 0-0, but then Sunderland scored twice through Peter Meechan and Hugh Wilson, a full-back and a half-back, to prove the versatility of the team.

But next came the visit to Nottingham Forest. It was a tight game. Sunderland scored first through Millar, but Forest equalised just before half-time, and then with the play ebbing and flowing both ways, it was unfortunately the home side who scored through Rose with a shot that many people felt Doig should have saved. Sunderland then pressed and pressed but it was one of those days that the ball did not run for them, and the Wearsiders lost their first game since the end of September.

That was hard luck and could be easily recovered from, but things took a more serious turn on Saturday, 29 December when the team went to Deepdale and lost 1-0. The weather was not quite as bad as when the game had to be postponed, but it was still unsuitable with wind and hail, and little more than 3,000 spectators present. 'It was with the utmost difficulty that the players could keep their feet,' said *Empire News and the*

Umpire, and possible a more sensible referee might have abandoned the game for another and better day, but Preston scored just before half-time, and a now totally dispirited Sunderland side could make little impact on a determined North End. Good teams need good conditions to play good football, and Sunderland were thoroughly disadvantaged.

It was thus a dispirited Sunderland party that returned home. The second team had beaten Casuals 5-2 at home that day in a friendly that should have been fulfilled by the first team, and there were murmurings about the folly of agreeing to play Preston on that day. Everton had not played at all since before Christmas and stayed on 27 points with 16 matches played whereas Sunderland were now on 26 with 17 played. Aston Villa were also on 27 points but from 20 games. The programme had just reached the halfway stage, but the balance had begun to swing towards Everton.

And so ended 1894. The mood in the town as the new year was celebrated was one of general happiness about the team's performances, laced with a little anger at the club's directors for agreeing to such a crazy schedule at the end of the year. Things seemed to be slipping away, and yet the players had performed with such skill and panache up to those desperate last few days of the year that it was difficult to imagine them collapsing altogether. Doig, Campbell, Wilson and Hannah were great players and would remain so, and recently Meechan had shown a touch of class, and of course there was still the charismatic and ever-controversial Tommy Hyslop.

In any case, there was no time for introspective navel gazing. There was an immediate chance for revenge over Preston for they were the visitors to Newcastle Road on New Year's Day and there were then in the same week home games against Aston Villa and Nottingham Forest. It was crazy, frenetic stuff with high intensity all the time, and looking at it now, one wonders what would be the limit to how much football a professional player could stand.

What followed in 1895 would be a year that shocked Victorian Britain and made everyone acknowledge that there was something called homosexuality. I refer to the Oscar Wilde trial. The upper classes had probably all experienced it at public school, in the army and in the Church (and, as a general rule, the more widely it was practised the more vigorously it was denied and condemned), the working classes had probably seen it all as well (the place to learn about life was the back streets and slums of Sunderland), but the Wilde proceedings forced the middle classes to realise that such things did actually happen. All of that was for later in the year, however. The early part of the year in Sunderland was dominated by concern about the return of the league championship to Newcastle Road, and a possible capture of the FA Cup as well.

New Year's Day was cold and snowy, but the game against Preston was in no danger because the pitch had been protected by straw. Conditions were, however, far from ideal for the 10,000 spectators who were, nevertheless, rewarded with a victory. The Sunderland team for the first game of 1895 read Doig, McNeill, Johnston, Dunlop, Auld, McCreadie, Gillespie, Millar, Campbell, Hannah and Scott. Wilson, Meechan and Hyslop were all out, but Sunderland nevertheless rose to the occasion. The game was tight, a little feisty on occasion with a few vendettas being carried on from the previous Saturday's fixture but after a goalless first half, Campbell scored twice for Sunderland. Both goals were protested by Preston for offside (the first one more vigorously than the second) but referee Mr Tomlinson from Sheffield ruled in favour of the Wearsiders.

The year had begun well, but then champions Aston Villa appeared the following day. Another crowd of 10,000 saw a remarkable game which ended in a 4-4 draw, after Sunderland had appeared to be heading for a defeat when they were 3-2 down at half-time and facing the icy blast. Wilson was still out, but Meechan was back, and that was a help. Sunderland, however, showed their mettle, went 4-3 ahead and looked likely winners until Hodgetts equalised for Villa with a great individual goal.

But the excitement continued. Chances were missed, penalties were refused and the press reported, 'It became so hot that several staid supporters of the code could not stand it and had to leave the ground some minutes before the final whistle blew.' Fans were back in the centre of the town before the special evening edition of the *Echo* told them the final score. It was a tremendous match, but the general opinion was that Villa were unlucky not to force a win over a tired Sunderland side.

At last, on Saturday, 5 January, Sunderland's run of six games within the 12 days of Christmas came to an end. This was the visit of Nottingham Forest, and another attempt to avenge a recent defeat. There was by now a certain amount of what was called 'fatigue' in the size of the crowd, which was little more than 5,000, or more likely, people could not afford all these games. This was a shame, for the match was a fine one, and another draw in which Sunderland were two down in the first half but fought back with a goal from Millar before half-time, then one from Campbell late in the game. Just at the death, Campbell put the ball over the bar, and that was a great shame for a win for Sunderland would not have been undeserved.

Now that they were able to draw breath for a day or two, Sunderland and their fans were able to look at the league table which showed them at the top, but the advantage was with Everton because of their fewer games played. Sunderland and Aston Villa both had 30 points, earned from 20 and 22 matches respectively. But the men from Goodison had 27 points and had played only 18. On the other hand, Everton had to win those two matches, and as Sunderland had discovered, there were very few easy fixtures in this First Division.

That Sunderland had been in need of a rest was proved in the next game, on 12 January, one whole week later. It was a refreshed and energetic team that ran out at a snowy Molineux to defeat Wolverhampton Wanderers 4-1 in one of their better performances of the season. Hugh 'Lalty' Wilson was back and a feature of the play was his long throw-ins from which Sunderland derived such benefit. Hannah scored in the first half, as did Millar early in the second, followed by two goals in quick succession to ensure a deserved win and to reduce the Wolverhampton crowd to numbed acceptance and eventually admiration.

In *Athletic News*, for example, a journalist and self-confessed lover of Wolves who called himself 'The Wandering Wolf' stated quite categorically, 'The Wearsiders were altogether too sure, too speedy and too strong ... I am not going to trouble myself by attempting to name a weak spot in the team. How can you find fault with the shooting abilities of forwards who score four goals in one match ... I concluded last week by saying "Now for the Messieurs from Wearside!" Well, we've had 'em and we shall remember 'em.' Indeed they would, as indeed would other teams. It was a good day for Sunderland, and another piece of good news was Preston 2 Everton 2, which meant that even if the team from Goodison won their two games in hand, they could now only equal Sunderland.

The next week Sunderland had no league game, but played instead in a friendly against the impressive new side called Newcastle United at St James' Park, an equally impressive new ground on which money had recently been spent and which now dwarfed the old ground at Heaton where Newcastle East End used to play. Sunderland won this prestigious and psychologically very important game 4-1. Neither Everton nor Aston Villa played in the First Division that day either, so the title race stood still, but Sunderland now seemed to have the advantage with a great deal of 'feelgood factor'.

Once again, wintry conditions were a feature when Sunderland travelled to Stoke on 26 January, but once again they showed that they were a good 'bad-weather' team when they won 5-2. They were 3-0 up at half-time with goals from Hannah, McCreadie and Millar, and although Stoke made more of a game of it in the second half and scored twice, so too did Sunderland with counters from Jimmy Millar. The 5-2 scoreline is slightly misleading for Stoke's second goal came right at the end.

Amazingly, Stoke decided to protest about this game, claiming that short time was played and that they should have been allowed another goal which referee Mr Strawson disallowed. The grounds for the protest were flimsy to say the least and no more was heard about it, but Sunderland also heard the good news that Everton had drawn with Sheffield United, and now they were definitely in front of them, for Everton had played a couple of midweek games as well and they had both played 22 times. Sunderland now had 34 points and Everton had 33. Aston Villa also had 34 points, but had played 25 matches. Only eight league games were left but now something else appeared, the FA Cup, the tournament that everyone wanted to win.

Sunderland were drawn at home to Fairfield in the first round. Fairfield came from near Manchester and were one of the lesser-known Lancashire teams, it has to be said. The *Sunderland Daily Echo* likened it to a cat playing with a half-dead mouse, and in truth it was no bad analogy as Sunderland won 11-1. The crowd was described as the poorest ever at Newcastle Road for a cup tie with less than 2,000 people paying a total of £67. Fairfield received half of that and that would have been some sort of a pay day for them, but one can hardly expect that they would have been happy at some of the patronising comments of the *Sunderland Daily Echo* which said, 'The forwards seem to know how to combine, none of them playing selfishly. The halves were no use whatever, but the backs and the goalie were fairly good.'

This game clearly proved nothing and was little more than a training run for Sunderland, but the next round could hardly have thrown up a more demanding task against Preston, whom Sunderland would now be playing for the third time in the season, the previous two occasions being as recent as the new year, and on both occasions home advantage had been crucial. The cup tie was at Newcastle Road.

But before that came a trip to the Heathens of Small Heath in Birmingham on 9 February in the First Division. This match was, frankly, a disappointment and ended up in a 1-1 draw. The press pulled no punches by saying that Sunderland were content to play 'pretty' football and seemed to lack the necessary ruthless streak to kill off the opposition. No one seems to know who scored Sunderland's goal – 'Sunderland put through after a free kick', according to the report – but Hands equalised for Small Heath. Sunderland, whose 'passing was perfection' but their 'shooting was bad', could not get a winner and a point was lost. Everton, who weren't playing a league match that day, could now catch Sunderland if they won their game in hand.

It was a disappointment, but the FA Cup tie now pushed everything else to one side, and Sunderland took themselves off to their training centre at Gilsland. Some supporters were disappointed to read, however, that Sunderland had sold Tommy Hyslop to Stoke. It was indeed a strange transfer, for Hyslop had been a star for the club, but there was perhaps just too much baggage associated with him and his change of name. Stoke made an offer, it was accepted, and the Sunderland directors 'rather in the manner of a man handling a hot potato' let him go.

The weather in the lead-up to the game had been described as 'Arctic' but the pitch had been well protected by straw, and in any case, the day itself was fine and dry, almost as if it were the first day of spring. The Sunderland team caused a little concern because McCreadie and Hannah were injured. The announcement had been delayed to give the players time to recover, but they didn't make it, and the team read Doig, Meechan, McNeill, Wilson, Dunlop, Johnston, Gillespie, Harvey, Campbell, Miller and Scott.

The ground was full with very few vantage points left, and the crowd – which paid a combined £427 –

saw a very good game from which Sunderland emerged with a 2-0 victory, Johnny Campbell having scored both goals before half-time, one from close range and one from a rebound off the bar. The match lacked any kind of classy football, but once again Sunderland showed their ability to win important games, not least in the last ten minutes when Preston piled on the pressure and Ned Doig was called upon to make a few difficult saves.

The fine victory was the only piece of good news for the north-east, however, as Newcastle and Middlesbrough were on the wrong end of severe thrashings at the hands of Aston Villa and The Wednesday respectively, but speculation was growing that Sunderland might now win the First Division and FA Cup double, as Preston had done in 1889. The draw gave Sunderland another home tie, albeit against very difficult opposition in Bolton, news which was greeted with great joy and cheering on Wearside.

But returning to the league the following week, Sunderland now had to face the 'cutlery town' of Sheffield for the next four games – United at home then The Wednesday also at Newcastle Road in midweek followed by visits to Bramall Lane and Owlerton (as Hillsborough was known at the time), after the tie with Bolton. They won both home games – 2-0 over United and 3-1 over Wednesday. The match against United on Saturday, 23 February saw Sunderland obliged to wear white shirts because the visitors wore the same colours. It was a boisterously windy day, and both goals were scored by Campbell after the ball went over the head of Sheffield United's unfortunate reserve goalkeeper Wharton, who was playing only because the famous 'Fatty' Foulkes was injured. It was all the more creditable because John Scott had been carried off with a dislocated shoulder and Sunderland were forced to play with ten men.

Wednesday came on a Tuesday as it were, or, to expand it a little, The Wednesday visited Newcastle Road on Shrove Tuesday. Once again Sunderland showed their ability to play well against difficult opposition. Donald Gow, who had been out for some considerable time, was welcomed back to the team. The first goal was a remarkable one. After Wednesday's Allen saved a penalty the ball was thrown downfield, but Andrew McCreadie sent it back immediately and deceived the goalkeeper to put Sunderland 1-0 up to the sound of great cheering. Campbell scored the second goal with a deft swivel and shot, and then the third came after a charge on the goalkeeper which knocked him into the back of the net – a brutal but in 1895 still legal way of scoring.

So another two points for Sunderland, but even better news came when the wires buzzed with Sheffield United 4 Everton 2. Apparently Everton had a major problem with injuries to goalkeepers, but that was of little concern to anyone in Sunderland when they got their newspaper the following morning and saw that their team were now four points clear, albeit Everton had a game in hand. But the league (and Sunderland's dealings with the teams from Sheffield) had to take a back seat for the time being.

Sunderland now approached their quarter-final against Bolton with a considerable degree of optimism and confidence. Bolton were a team to whom Sunderland 'owed one' following events earlier in the season, but they were not the most difficult opponent left in the competition. Elsewhere, for example, The Wednesday played Everton, Aston Villa played Nottingham Forest and West Bromwich Albion played Wolves. It is an interesting comment on Sunderland's drawing power that their tie produced the poorest attendance of the day, and yielded the least money, although £457 was still a considerable amount.

A crowd of 14,000 were at Newcastle Road on a crisp, cold, bright, windy spring day to see the first FA Cup meeting between the two teams. Sunderland still had a few injury problems. Gow wasn't playing and Scott was still out with his injured shoulder, so the forward line read an unusual Gillespie, Millar, Campbell, Johnston and Hannah. Sunderland lost the toss and had to play from the road end against the sun and the wind.

The conditions seem to have been significant factors, for Bolton were on top in the first half and led 1-0, the goal coming from a major error by Doig, who simply missed the ball altogether when Henderson shot the Trotters ahead after about quarter of an hour. The rest of the first half was all about Bolton, and Doig on many occasions atoned for his previous blunder by saving hard 'shots and drives', and basically keeping his team in the game. Depression, however, filled the air as the players left the field.

But in a few recent matches Sunderland had come good late on, and the second half was a complete transformation, although their makeshift forward line made little impact on the defence and it was half-back and captain Hugh Wilson who won the day with two long-range strikes. The first one seemed to be controversial for some reason for there are reports of Bolton goalkeeper Sutcliffe running out 'with petitions' to referee Mr Strawson to disallow the goal, presumably on the grounds of Sutcliffe being impeded.

The ten-minute flag, that characteristic phenomenon of Newcastle Road, fell, and then 'Lalty' did it again, but this time there was no doubt about it. He received a ball from Johnston, teed it up and then with his back to the goal, scored with a remarkable overhead kick which left Sutcliffe static and everyone else amazed. As often happens in such circumstances, there was a split second's silence until everyone took it in, and then the excitement knew no bounds as the Sunderland players surrounded their captain to shower him with congratulations. But there was still work to do, and Sunderland had to battle hard to keep out the eager Bolton men, with Doig again proving his worth.

It was another great victory and within an hour or so – such were the marvels of modern telegraphy – everyone knew that Aston Villa, The Wednesday and West Brom were the other teams who had reached the semi-final, and the draw at the beginning of the week confirmed that Sunderland's opponents would be Villa. The news was hardly greeted with enthusiasm on Wearside for Villa had put Sunderland out of the FA Cup in two of the last three years, and were generally looked upon as one of the best cup tie sides of them all. The game was to be played at Ewood Park, Blackburn, on 16 April.

There then followed one of the most bizarre events of the decade, certainly of the season, when Sunderland on 9 March went down to Sheffield United and lost 4-0. The only possible excuse could have been the absence of Gillespie through injury, but even so, a 4-0 defeat for a team on the crest of a wave and heading for a possible league and cup double was pretty inexplicable. Naturally, this being Victorian football, involvement with illegal bookmakers was suspected, but no proof could ever be produced, and indeed a 'fix' really would need to be a little more subtle. The more likely explanation is simply that the Sunderland players took things too lightly, were keeping themselves for their semi-final, and all had a collective bad day, whereas United simply raised their game. Still, it was a serious blow to Sunderland's chances of the double. It meant that once again Everton, if they won their games in hand, could catch them at the top of the table.

The *Sunderland Daily Echo* was compelled to use the word 'sensational' to describe this game, but also reckoned that is often the mark of a good team if it can bounce back from such disasters. The Sunderland team decamped to Gilsland for special training and moved on to Lancashire on the Thursday in anticipation of the semi-final, while the North Eastern Railway Company announced that there would be a special excursion train leaving Sunderland at 6.42am on the Saturday and returning the same day. Coyly, the company did not mention the price, but admission to the ground would be from one shilling, although you could pay as much as 7s 6d for the centre stand. It was generally reckoned to be a very difficult result to predict, as indeed was the other semi-final at Derby between The Wednesday and West Brom.

It was not to be Sunderland's day. It was accepted that it was a great cup tie for the crowd of slightly less than 20,000 but Aston Villa were the better team on the day and deserved their 2-1 victory with fine goals from Smith and Hodgetts. Yet Sunderland were ahead at half-time after a long, trademark throw-in from Hugh Wilson found Hannah, but then Villa took command and, having scored twice, remained well on top, it being significant that *Empire News and the Umpire* gave praise to the Sunderland defenders like Donald Gow and in particular to goalkeeper Ned Doig, while saying very little about the forwards.

The *Sunderland Daily Echo* was, like the rest of the town, distraught. To a certain extent, excuses could be made about injuries, but then again a good side should have adequate reserves. The gate receipts were also disappointing at £781, and the question was asked whether too much had been charged to supporters. West Brom won the other semi-final, so it would be an all-Birmingham final and further distress was caused by the news that Everton won as well, so the gap at the top of the First Division was now only two points with chasers having a game in hand. Sunderland had four matches to play, three of which were away from home, but the home fixture was against Everton. It was due to be played on 6 April, but that was the day of the Scotland v England international at Goodison Park, and both teams were expecting to have players involved in that, so negotiations were under way to move it to 20 April. But first there was a somewhat ominous return to Sheffield, this time to take on The Wednesday at Olive Grove.

It was, of course, the game of the two defeated semi-finalists, but Sunderland at least still had something to play for, and there was certainly a little more urgency from them than there was from Wednesday, who gave all the signs of having given up for the season. Sunderland won 2-1, their first goal being a rare one from 'utility man' Willie Dunlop who shot from a distance and the ball cannoned off a few players before it went in, but the second betokened a welcome return to form for Johnny Campbell, whose goals had been appearing to dry up.

It was a good victory, and a better one came on the Monday when Sunderland were at Liverpool to play the match that should have taken place on semi-final day. They had spent the Sunday at Southport, having a day off. Everton fans descended en masse to support their city rivals, but they were disappointed to see Sunderland win 3-2 in the pouring rain. It was a tight game with Liverpool playing above themselves, but Wilson, Campbell and Millar (with a rather fortuitous header which reportedly seemed to strike him rather than him striking it) saw Sunderland home. Now only two games remained, whereas Everton had four, but they could both reach the same points total. Goal average seemed to be in favour of Sunderland, but that could quickly change.

Sunderland didn't play another First Division match for three weeks. They played an inconsequential friendly against Clyde on 30 March while Everton were losing 2-0 to Preston in the Lancashire Cup Final, and then 6 April was the England v Scotland international at Goodison Park. Sadly for Sunderland, Everton had gained revenge for their defeat on Saturday in the Lancashire Cup by beating Preston 4-2 in the league five days earlier. This may in part explain Sunderland's antipathy to the Football League's decision to postpone the game on Saturday in favour of the international. The good point was, however, that it gave injured men a chance to recover.

England duly beat Scotland convincingly 3-0 at Goodison with not a single Sunderland player in either side (Scotland operated a home-Scots-only policy, but it is hard to believe that men like Doig and Wilson would not have enhanced their team) and then, on Monday, 8 April, Sunderland beat Dundee in a friendly.

Rather in an atmosphere of anti-climax, Saturday, 13 April effectively secured the league for Sunderland when they won 3-0 at Burnley and Everton went down 3-2 at Derby. It meant that Everton would have had to beat Aston Villa and Sunderland away from home by huge margins, and the *Sunderland Daily Echo* had no qualms about hailing their team as champions for a record third time.

The game at Turf Moor saw Sunderland at their best with McCreadie scoring before half-time, and Gillespie scoring twice in the second half, one of them a rather brilliant header. It was a fine performance from the champions-elect, the only problems being injuries to Wilson and Scott, the men who had perhaps done more than any others to secure the championship.

There remained the visit of Everton. Sunderland had hired Dr Guthrie's pipers from Edinburgh and they duly marched along Bridge Street with thousands of fans in their wake. The Scottish connection with Sunderland could hardly have been more pronounced, and the crowd was a good 20,000 if one allows for people climbing up nearby trees and roofs of houses. McCreadie scored first and 'peal upon peal of popular music proclaimed the glad tidings far and wide that Sunderland were a goal to the good'. After Everton equalised, Campbell settled matters with a 'long oblique shot' to make it 2-1, and Sunderland were the champions. They shared that day of triumph with Aston Villa who won the FA Cup at the Crystal Palace, and St Bernard's who won the Scottish Cup at Ibrox, but for the locals it was Sunderland's day, the players being Doig, McNeill and Gow; Dunlop, McCreadie and Johnston; Gillespie, Harvey, Campbell, Millar and

James Hannah. It was a shame that 'Lalty' Wilson was not playing that day (as indeed it was for Johnny Scott) but the absentees were as much a part of the triumph as anyone. The only pity for their season was that they had not also landed the FA Cup.

4

League Champions 1901/02

IN 1901, the public were informed, came the end of an era. On 22 January Queen Victoria died after nearly 64 years on the throne and therefore began the Edwardian age, although the casual observer might be forgiven for not noticing any huge differences to the Victorian one. There was still the horrendous housing, appalling poverty, dreadful working conditions and the hideous riches of those who did not care about anyone else. There was also an appalling war going on in South Africa, as bloody as it was pointless, and explained away either by the need to protect the interests of the British Empire or the desire to get to the diamonds of South Africa before the Boers did.

The Queen's successor was her son, the Prince of Wales, who now became King Edward VII. It would be a lie to say that everyone was happy about this, for Edward's many indiscretions were well known in gambling, gluttony and particularly womanising. His long-suffering wife Queen Alexandra was Danish and had never really fitted in, being particularly unhappy about the German influence in the British royal family after the Schleswig-Holstein business of the 1860s. Yet she kept herself to herself, unlike her husband who had a string of mistresses whose names – Lily Langtree, Daisy Warwick and Alice Keppel, for example – were well known and indeed the subject of the drawing room gossip of the bourgeoisie and the coarse jokes of the music hall comedians who kept the working classes happy. It was not something that was discouraged either. At least if the working classes were joking about the King's adventures and dalliances, they were not plotting revolution.

And yet there was something likeable about the old goat of a monarch as well. In his 60s and perhaps too old to be assuming the throne, he was nevertheless a far more human character than the 'little vixen' as his mother had frequently been described. He did at least take an interest in his people – or he seemed to – and showed an admirable concern for maintaining European peace. He also had a healthy dislike of his appalling nephew, the Kaiser of Germany.

The prime minister was the Marquess of Salisbury, the title itself perhaps saying a great deal about British political life. He had little opposition, because the

Liberals were at sixes and sevens – between great leaders, William Gladstone having gone and David Lloyd George not yet having risen. The big issue between the two parties was Free Trade, which the Liberals supported, and Protection which was the demesne of the Conservatives. The problem with Protection was that it pushed up prices and made food a lot more expensive. The Establishment was becoming increasingly more worried about a new force called the Labour Party, as bodies like the Fabians and trade unions began to ask pertinent questions.

There were a few changes in social life. Telephones were still rare but gradually becoming less so, and in recent years there had been a positive proliferation of these things called 'horseless carriages' – or cars. Again, they were by no means common and were hideously expensive, nevertheless some doctors aspired to own one, as did a few rich eccentrics. A few houses even had electric lights.

And in football as well, some things were changing. The FA Cup was won by a London-based team called Tottenham Hotspur, the first southern professional club to do so, and the Football League was won for the first time by Liverpool bringing to an end a run of success by Aston Villa. And where were Sunderland in all this? Still there or thereabouts, but they had not yet repeated their great successes of the early 1890s, although they came second in 1901. And of course they now lived in a nice commodious statement called Roker Park, which had replaced the outdated, cramped but still fondly remembered Newcastle Road.

The First Division contained 18 teams. There were still no teams from London and the south, but Sunderland had company in the north-east in Newcastle United who had prospered in their union of East End and West End and were now the Wearsiders' rivals – a state of affairs which was healthy for the finances of both clubs, and indeed for the future of football in the area, for there always has been a symbiosis between Newcastle and Sunderland. They need each other.

As far as Sunderland were concerned, the season opened on the evening of Monday, 2 September. It had been a sobering day with news from South Africa of a Boer attack on a train which killed a number of British soldiers, and an outbreak of smallpox in London (there had earlier been an outbreak of plague – the medieval version – in Glasgow) and what had been a fine day of weather became dull. Nevertheless, a crowd of 14,271 were there to see Sunderland defeat Sheffield United 3-1.

The team was:

Doig, McCombie, Watson, Ferguson, McAllister, Jackson, Common, Hogg, Gemmell, Millar and McLatchie.

That side had three Englishmen in Dickie Jackson, Alf Common and Bobby Hogg.

The other players were Scottish. The only real survivors from the last title-winning team were Ned Doig and Jimmy Millar, but Millar had been to Rangers and had returned. Sheffield United's goalkeeper was the famous 'Fatty' Foulke, always a great character and attraction for spectators, especially for his long kick-outs. United had themselves won the championship in 1898.

Bobby Hogg scored for Sunderland in the first half, and then again late in the second half before Common added a third. The only down side was a rather bad injury to Jimmy Gemmell, but it was generally felt that the season was off to a good start.

Next up were Manchester City; 16,000 attended in good weather and they saw Sunderland consolidate their victory in the first game with another one, the only goal coming from a move involving the two unrelated Hoggs, Billy and Bobby. It was a hard-fought encounter. Billy Hogg was only playing because of the injury to Gemmell, but he certainly availed himself of the opportunity.

It was a solid, if unspectacular start. A defeat is never easy to take, but a defeat in the month of September is often less than a total disaster. It shrinks a few heads, makes everyone concentrate on the next game and generally highlights a few weakness in the play. But the important thing is that it is still September and there is plenty of time to do something about it. It is far from fatal.

Perhaps Sunderland's players were mulling over these philosophical considerations as they returned from Wolverhampton Wanderers on the night of 14 September after a 4-2 defeat at Molineux. Matches that day were played with the flags at half-mast following the death of William McKinley, the US president, early in the morning. He had been shot the week before, and after seeming to recover for a day or two, gangrene set in and, then to the distress of everyone, he passed away. Sunderland started badly with their full-backs clearly over-run by the 'nippy wolves', and at half-time the score was a disastrous 4-1 with even Doig looking out of sorts. Although Doig was able to rally his defence in the second half so that the team could pull one back, it was a chastening experience for Sunderland and the *Sunderland Daily Echo* was quite happy to admit that 'the best side won'. It was also rather a rough game, and Sunderland were advised to watch that sort of thing, but the newspaper added, 'There is nothing to be alarmed about in the defeat.'

The visit of champions Liverpool to Sunderland came next, but that was only as a curtain-raiser to the big game the week after that, namely the visit to St James' Park. A crowd of 15,818 assembled to see Liverpool but the drizzle at the start of the game turned more to 'fully fledged' rain and the spectators did not enjoy the occasion as much as they should have. Liverpool were without the services of Bowen for most of the match, and Sunderland were not really able to capitalise on this advantage in a tame 1-1 draw. Liverpool scored first, but then left-half Dicky Jackson equalised with a shot from distance. It was another disappointment, but still not a disaster for Sunderland.

Even in the early years, the rivalry between Sunderland and Newcastle United was a huge one. United had been in the First Division since 1898, had a bigger stadium than Sunderland, and represented a larger support base. The rivalry was natural and even healthy, and the directors of both clubs were wise enough to do nothing to minimise the 'golden egg'. Yet, even in 1901 there were signs in the local papers that the rivalry, although welcome, was slightly misdirected with the belief gaining ground that as long as Sunderland beat Newcastle or vice versa, nothing else really mattered. It has long been the opinion of this author that the 'Newcastle complex' or 'Sunderland complex' has in fact distorted or hindered the ambitions of both clubs, who really should have done a great deal better than they have.

Be that as it may, nearly 30,000 were at St James' Park that fine September autumn afternoon. There had been a little trouble at a previous encounter on Good Friday the previous season, so the authorities possibly erred on the side of caution according to one version, or acted with undue haste according to another, in deciding to close the pay boxes and the turnstiles at 2.20p,. some 40 minutes before kick-off. The ground had seemed to be full, but on closer inspection there was a certain amount of room, and the result was that quite a few thousand spectators were left outside at the Leazes End in particular, unable to watch the game and relying on the shouts of the crowd.

The game itself was a good one, and the trains back home to Sunderland that night contained quite a few smiling faces for their team, wearing white shirts, had won 1-0. The only goal came from Gemmell, and it was what was known as a 'drooper' – a high shot that deceived the goalkeeper into thinking that the ball was going over the bar, but which in fact sneaked into the net over his head. That was in the first half, and after that Sunderland took control and the wonder was that they did not score more. Doig was seldom troubled, although at one point his ubiquitous cap, which some believed he slept in, fell off and his head was revealed to be bald, to the amusement of some supporters.

Sunderland's team that day was:

Doig, McCombie, Watson, Ferguson,
McAllister, Jackson, Billy Hogg, Bobby
Hogg, Millar, Gemmell and McLatchie

A glance at the evening paper that night showed that Sunderland had concluded September in equal top spot along with Wolves and Everton. Optimism was in the air.

And optimism remained prevalent after Aston Villa visited Roker Park on 5 October. Again it was only a 1-0 win but it was a convincing one. Villa had won the league in 1899 and 1900, but had possibly faded a little over the previous year or so, but they were still one of the giants of the game and 14,385 were present on a windy day to see them. It was the wind that was perhaps the deciding factor, for it was only in the second half with it behind them that Sunderland took command.

The only goal came after a fine movement involving the two Hoggs and Millar, and it was Bobby Hogg who applied the finishing touch. In the first half Andy McCombie had missed a penalty, awarded rather harshly when the ball seemed to hit the Villa man's hand rather than the other way round. Not that it mattered for McCombie hit the bar when he should really have kept the ball low.

Bramall Lane was the next port of call for a game against Sheffield United, who were depleted through injuries and illness, whereas Sunderland had been very lucky so far during the season in managing to keep clear of injuries. A few Sunderland supporters had managed to make the trip and they were rewarded with another 1-0 victory. The *Sunderland Daily Echo* was concerned that the forwards were not scoring enough goals, but 1-0 is enough as long as you defend well. The goal came from Gemmell, who was on the spot to hammer home a badly fisted ball from 'Fatty' Foulke. The veteran goalkeeper, who had defied Sunderland well up to that point, clearly made an error of judgement, and the Wearsiders capitalised on this blunder before once again their defenders were able to close United down. Sunderland, who were now top of the league – if that meant anything at this stage of the season – had completed a double of beating Sheffield United home and away.

In the meantime, relations between the club and the town continued to be good. They were invited by the management of the Avenue Theatre to see a new musical comedy called *Kitty Grey* and were cheered to the echo as they took their seats, then the popularity continued when, on the fine autumn day of 19 October, before a large crowd of 16,946, they ended their sequence of 1-0 wins by beating Nottingham

Forest 4-0 with a hat-trick from Millar and another goal from Gemmell.

It was a quite magnificent performance and the Sunderland crowd left for home in rare good humour, believing that happy days were here again, and that their team could beat anyone, although not every game finished so happily elsewhere. Bolton Wanderers and Wolves ended up in a free fight and a general riot after the referee had awarded Wolves a late penalty which gave them a draw. Some Bolton fans tried to attack the referee Mr Bye who just managed to get to his dressing room, and, upset at his escape, they indulged in a free fight with fists flying indiscriminately at whoever happened to be there – trainers, players, other spectators. It was a shocking scene, and blamed 100 per cent on alcohol, while a few wiser people noticed some soldiers in uniform on leave from South Africa, and wondered whether they were missing the real violence.

At Sunderland, a welcome sign of ambition and determination was seen in the signing of George Prior from St Bernard's, of Edinburgh. He was a centre-forward and clearly this was a response to the feelings expressed that although the team were doing well, the forwards were not scoring enough goals. Sadly Prior never really settled on Wearside, and returned to Scotland at the end of the season, but it did show that the directors were aware of the problem and trying to do something about it.

A temporary rebuff was delivered to Sunderland's ambition on 26 October when they lost at Gigg Lane Bury, who were no mean side having won the FA Cup in 1900 (and they would do so again in 1903) and press reports of this game were all united in describing it as 'fast'. The only goal in front 10,972 at Gigg Lane, on another fine autumnal day, was scored within a minute of the restart after half-time by Monks. Sunderland then pressed hard but could not quite get the goal that they needed to level. McAllister, Jackson and both Hoggs all had hard luck with reasonable chances. As Wolves could only draw that day, Sunderland were still one point ahead of them, but the impressive Bury side were up to third.

It is often said that November is a key month in the league, as conditions start to change. You cannot win the title in November but you can certainly lose it. If you are behind in the table you really have to get going in November and start winning games, and if you are on top you have to stay there. In this context it is difficult to analyse the achievement of Sunderland in November 1901. They played five games, won two, lost two and drew one.

Their first match of the month was two days in and there was no sign of any dismal weather of the kind that we so often associate with November. Rather, it was like the fine, crisp days of September and October and 'Referee' of the *Sunderland Daily Echo* was delighted to see that Sunderland were back wearing their traditional red and white vertical stripes. They had for various reasons (mainly because of a colour clash) been wearing all white for a few games, and it was nice to see them looking like Sunderland again. Whether they played like Sunderland in this game against Blackburn Rovers is a matter of some doubt.

The 14,000 crowd saw an even first half, but then immediately before half-time Sunderland scored twice through Billy Hogg and Millar. This seemed to put them on easy street, but then in a curious reversal of roles from the first half Blackburn suddenly came back by scoring two goals in quick succession and the game was all square. But then when 'Sunderland's chance of being able to win seemed very remote' up stepped Andy McCombie and 'with a shot from a range of about 30 yards, he surprised everybody by landing the ball in the net, it just passing under the crossbar'. The cheering which greeted this feat lasted several minutes, it was reported.

That was a good game, but then, quite inexplicably, the team travelled to Stoke and lost 3-0. The *Sunderland Daily Echo* hinted at complacency when it said that 'the visitors did not seem to realise that they had a stiff task in hand', but it also loyally stated that although the home side deserved their victory, there were not three goals in the game. George Prior was given his debut in place of the injured Millar, but he was not a success, on one occasion missing an open goal.

One would like to think that it was a chastened group of Sunderland players who travelled north after this game, but things took a more serious turn the following week when they went down to fellow title challengers Everton at home. It was 1-1 at half-time, then a defensive collapse leading to the loss of three quick goals and an inability to fight back because of 'the same ragged forward play that characterised last year' meant that Sunderland had now been knocked off their perch, and the Roker Park crowd who had been so exuberant and happy only a short two weeks earlier were suddenly quietened. In tune with the mood of the supporters, night also fell very quickly.

The next game in line was Grimsby Town at Blundell Park, Cleethorpes. The local side were often a source of much admiration for their ability to live with clubs from far larger supporter bases, and indeed they were scrapping away at the bottom of the table. A reasonable crowd of 5,000 fishermen who had recently been embroiled in a prolonged dispute with the owners of the ships turned up and they saw a game which although it once again had an unsatisfactory outcome for Sunderland, nevertheless provided great entertainment. In one of its occasional misprints the *Sunderland Daily Echo* said 'Victory For Sunderland' whereas in fact it was a 3-3 draw. Admittedly, the game finished in a pea-souper of a sea mist which impaired visibility, but a draw it was and Sunderland's shaky title challenge took another hit.

In fact they were probably rather lucky to get away with a point. Grimsby scored twice in the first ten minutes to the distress of the few Sunderland supporters in the ground, but spirits rallied when Billy Hogg pulled one back immediately and then lanky left-back Jimmy Watson, who rejoiced in the name of 'Daddy Long Legs', but had not distinguished himself so far in the match, equalised in the wake of a free kick. The second half was again played at a pace which made everyone forget the miserable, damp conditions, and Sunderland went in front with a headed goal from Gemmell. This should have signalled a win for the Wearsiders but they were notable to add to their lead and suffered when a long-range shot caught Doig unaware. The last ten minutes were played in 'virtual invisibility' but the referee kept going, and the game finished 3-3. This meant that Everton were two points ahead of Sunderland with 13 matches played.

Lowly Small Heath were the next port of call, and Sunderland got back to winning ways with a rewarding victory. It was their first visit to Coventry Road for well over a decade, and it was a great and thrilling game. It also asked questions, however, of the Sunderland defence, with the team 2-0 down and heading for defeat, before a sudden rally with three goals in the latter stages of the game. Millar and McLatchie scored the first two, but the newspapers all seemed to decline to tell posterity who scored the winner, so we must assume it was from a 'ruck' or a 'scrimmage' or a 'stramash' in front of goal. The *Birmingham Mail* did, however, explain that Sunderland 'played more scientific football' than Small Heath, but that 'Doig was at his best – and that is saying something'.

On 7 December, Sunderland had no league game so they split their resources and played three friendlies instead, losing by a surprisingly large margin of 6-1 to St Mirren but beating Scarborough and Prudhoe. Friendly or not, the defeat to St Mirren would have hurt, particularly the Scottish players, and the Saints appeared to have been the first club that Sunderland had played more than one friendly against and not been able to beat, having lost to them on a previous occasion as well.

Difficult opposition appeared on the horizon against The Wednesday the following Saturday. Sunderland were away, but in a neat chiasmus, Sheffield United were at Newcastle and both games ended 1-1. The game at Owlerton was cold and miserable with the pitch in a bad state after heavy storms over the last few days, and a poor crowd of 2,000 was all that turned up. They did not see much to thrill them or even warm them up, but when Sunderland scored through Bobby Hogg after he had picked up a good through ball from Colin McLatchie, things looked good. A late goal from Chapman, however, condemned Sunderland to yet another draw.

The Christmas fixtures were more satisfactory; 7,249 appeared at Roker Park on midwinter's day, 21 December, braving bad weather and rumours of postponements. They were duly rewarded with a game that was dull only as far as the weather conditions were concerned, because Sunderland and Notts County battled to serve up a great match from which it was generally agreed that the home side were lucky to escape with a win and the plucky visitors deserved a draw. Notts scored first when Spencer was able to take advantage of a ball which stuck in the mud between two Sunderland defenders. But the hosts fought back in the second half and were rewarded with goals from Billy Hogg and Gemmell. The standard of football was still a little short of first class, but it was a hard-fought victory of the kind that is so necessary if a team is to win league titles.

155

It was probably Boxing Day at Anfield which swung things for Sunderland. Defending champions Liverpool had not been doing so well in 1901/02 and were the inferior team on Merseyside – something that was as potent a factor there as was the Newcastle/Sunderland factor in the north-east – but they were still good enough to cause Sunderland some apprehension. Anfield was packed with spectators in spite of the bitter wind and the driving rain which sometimes looked like it was turning to sleet.

As often happens in such adverse circumstances, the teams rose to the occasion and served up a terrific match for the huge crowd. The game ebbed to and fro with good chances for both teams, and both goalkeepers frequently in action, and it was not until the very last few minutes that the deadlock was broken when McLatchie picked up a loose ball in midfield and ran on himself and scored. The goal was greeted with cemetery silence by the Anfield crowd but with delight by the small knot of Sunderland's travellers.

Sunderland stayed on in Lancashire because they were at Bolton Wanderers on the Saturday, and their delayed Christmas dinner that night at St Annes was enhanced by the news that Wolverhampton Wanderers had beaten Everton, and that Sunderland were therefore back to the top of the league.

The game on 28 December at Burnden Park was lucky to go ahead – quite a few others didn't that day, such was the wind and rain – but Sunderland probably did well to earn a 0-0 draw against determined opposition.

The condition of the pitch made it difficult for the visitors to indulge in their short passing game, and they had to try passing the ball across the park. Skids were frequent, but the Sunderland defence held out well against the determined Bolton attackers who were better able to deal with condition on their own ground. Yet again Sunderland were heavily dependent on the bravery and agility of Doig, and they were glad to hear the final whistle of 1901.

The final league table of the year showed that there were three teams at the top with 24 points – Aston Villa, Everton and Sunderland – but the Wearsiders had played only 18 games as distinct from the other two who had played 19. There was a long way to go, but Sunderland thus had a slight advantage. The positions at the top of the table were a subject of some discussion in Sunderland households as 1901 gave way to 1902. It was generally agreed that the team of 1901 was a little short of the 'team of all the talents' of the 1890s. It lacked the goalscoring of Johnny Campbell and the sheer drive of Hugh Wilson, for example, but there was still Doig and Millar whose return from Scotland had not always been marked with the sustained success that he had shown before.

The team was solid, perhaps, but not spectacular. Both Hoggs were good players, McLatchie had impressed recently, but Gemmell was inconsistent and there was probably a lack of sparkle in some other areas. But yet, league championships were not always won by 'sparkle'. As important as anything was drive, determination and the ability to win games, to get a victory when a draw would be a fairer result, or to eke out a draw when a defeat seemed inevitable. Did Sunderland have these qualities?

Away from football, the main topic of conversation was still the war in South Africa. Sunderland had had its fair share of casualties of men who had enlisted, and not everyone saw this war as a battle for civilisation against barbarism. There had been heroes like Robert Baden-Powell, Lord Kitchener, Frederick Roberts and that strange adventurer called Winston Churchill, but increasingly people were beginning to ask questions about it. Christmas Day 1901 had seen some heavy British losses at a place called Groenkop, and was it really all worth it? What would be the gain? Would 1902 bring an end to the fighting? More and more people were beginning to ask such questions of the hysterical, jingoistic, unquestioning flag-waving patriotism that was so rampant.

But there was one thing to look forward to in 1902: the coronation of King Edward VII and Queen Alexandra. It had been scheduled for 26 June (although history will tell us that it didn't quite work out like that) because it was considered to be in bad taste to have it in 1901 so soon after the death of the Queen. But very few people in Sunderland knew what a coronation looked like, for the last one had been in 1838 when Sunderland had been a totally different place. One would have to be in one's 70s to have any chance of remembering it, and the average life expectancy in Sunderland in 1902 was well below that. But nevertheless the coronation, whatever it was, was something to look forward to in the summer with promises of extra holidays. But would Sunderland be league champions by that time?

They certainly got off to a good start in 1902. The first edition of the *Sunderland Daily Echo* on 2 January wished everyone a happy new year, gave details about how a potentially horrendous fire at Sunderland's People's Palace on New Year's Eve was put out following prompt action by the theatre staff, and talked about some dreadful batting in Australia by Archie McLaren's team in Melbourne (and the Australian batting was not a lot better either), but the main story was Sunderland's 1-0 win over Derby County on New Year's Day.

The weather was dull but dry, a relief after the constant rain of recent days, and a large holiday crowd of 21,000 were attracted to Roker Park to see Sunderland take on Derby, Steve Bloomer and all. Derby were not without their supporters, who mingled happily with the local crowd. They saw a good game of football which was in some ways typical of Sunderland in 1901/02, very methodical, precise and scientific, but perhaps lacking the flair of previous years. But when Sunderland got the lead towards the end of the first half they knew how to defend it, and they won the two points. The goal itself was a good one from Dickie Jackson when he got a ball from Bobby Hogg about chest high, controlled it, swivelled and scored from about 12 yards. The second half was not without incident but Sunderland remained in control throughout and the final whistle was greeted with a great cheer.

Sunderland, who had spent the new year at their training base at Croft, returned there after being given a few hours to talk to families and friends, for the next game was on 4 January at Manchester City. There the good news continued, and Sunderland, although without Bobby Hogg who had a slight chill, could consider themselves a lot more fortunate than Stoke, who played against Liverpool with only seven men at one point because of an outbreak of food poisoning

Sunderland – League champions 1895

Thomas Hemy's fine painting of Sunderland v Aston Villa at Newcastle Road on a wet day

Hugh 'Lalty' Wilson

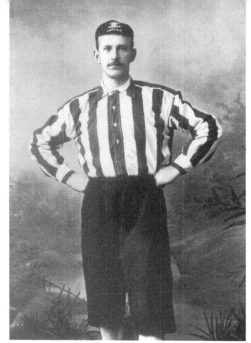

Ned Doig, Sunderland's famous goalkeeper

Johnny Campbell

Jimmy Millar

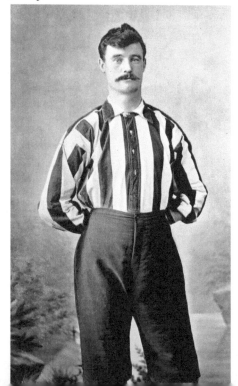

Charlie Buchan, Sunderland and in later years the proprietor of the famous Charles Buchan's Football Monthly

John Cochrane, manager of Sunderland in the 1930s

James Thorpe, who died tragically after a game in 1936

Jimmy Thorpe in action in a game against Tottenham Hotspur at White Hart Lane in 1933

1 May 1937. Queen Elizabeth presents the FA Cup to Raich Carter while King George VI looks on

Raich Carter is carried round Wembley with the FA Cup

Raich Carter as player-manager of Hull on the right alongside a young and rather unhappy looking Don Revie

Roker Park in its heyday

Action from the FA Cup semi-final of 1973 involving Bobby Kerr of Sunderland and Alan Ball of Arsenal

Ian Porterfield (not in the picture) scores the only goal of the game in the 1973 FA Cup Final

Jim Montgomery's famous double save in the 1973 FA Cup Final

Bob Stokoe has just won the Cup for Sunderland

Captain Bobby Kerr with the FA Cup in 1973

The famous statue of Bob Stokoe outside the Stadium of Light.

caused by some fish in the hotel where they were staying. Not surprisingly Liverpool won 7-0.

The game at Hyde Road was played in showery weather before a crowd of 14,000. Sunderland, without playing brilliantly, were always on top of the lowly City side and two goals by Billy Hogg and one by Gemmell were enough to see them home with a degree of ease. Much praise was given to Sunderland's defenders, the lanky Jimmy Watson and the solid Andy McCombie for their part in snuffing out the dangerous Billy Meredith, and 'Looker On' in *Empire News and the Umpire,* although more concerned about the possible relegation of Manchester City, was forced to agree that Sunderland were playing like title contenders.

The feelgood factor continued the following week when Wolverhampton Wanderers visited Roker Park. Captain Matt Ferguson was out and Millar instead took his role. The *Sunderland Daily Echo* was compelled to admit that 'the first half was of a very uninteresting description' for the 13,019 spectators, but in the second half Billy Hogg scored twice. The first was a tap-in, but the second saw him 'dashing in with tremendous speed' to score with 'a high shot'.

It was a somewhat typical victory for Sunderland at this time. The weather was excellent for the time of year and the crowd departed happy with what they had seen. There had been an absence of 'sparkling play' but the goals had been good and well taken, and as a result of their fine play since the turn of the year, Sunderland were four points clear at the top although they had played a game more than Everton, who had been less lucky with the weather than the Wearsiders had been.

Sunderland had no league game on 18 January, playing an ill-attended friendly against old rivals Preston North End, who had fallen on bad times and were now in the Second Division. Maybe one of the reasons for the poor 2,000 crowd on a fine day was the fact that some Sunderland supporters had betaken themselves elsewhere – to nip along and see (and even cheer on!) Newcastle United.

This apparent act of treachery can be explained away by the fact that Newcastle were playing Everton, Sunderland's rivals in the title race. This was Everton's game in hand and they had the chance to reduce the gap to two points, but in a good game Newcastle and Everton played out a 1-1 draw which meant that the Merseysiders were now three points behind with an equal amount of games played. Newcastle had done Sunderland a big favour.

Sunderland's good January continued in the FA Cup. The draw had given them a tricky game at The Wednesday, particularly as it was to be played at their impressive new stadium in the Owlerton district of town, later to become known as Hillsborough.

Sunderland's players, all in 'the pink of condition', got on the train at 4.40pm on the Friday to travel to Leeds where they would stay overnight before moving on to Sheffield. Their supporters took advantage of cheaper rail fares if they travelled overnight, and consequently arrived in Sheffield as early as five or six in the morning where they found a little snow. But it had only been a shower, and as many as 30,096 (the highest attendance of the day) turned up to watch this game between the team who had won the FA Cup in 1896, against the team who were top of the league and considered to be the favourites for both competitions. Not without cause, for it was now five matches since Sunderland had conceded a goal, let alone lost.

That run continued in South Yorkshire. The team was Doig, McCombie, Watson, Ferguson, McAllister, Jackson, Billy Hogg, Bobby Hogg, Millar, Gemmell and McLatchie, and they won 1-0 with a Millar goal early in the first half when a free kick found the forward, who had no hesitation in 'lashing the sphere into the rigging'. Sunderland then defended competently to see themselves into the next round. The result was greeted with great enthusiasm by the fans in the ground and back home where people gathered outside newspaper offices and the Post Office to hear the news. The town of Sheffield had often been looked upon in the past as the 'graveyard of Sunderland', but no longer. Most unusually for a cold winter night, a huge crowd, braving the snow showers, gathered at Sunderland station to welcome the players back and to escort them to their horse-driven cabs which were waiting to take them to their homes.

The fever-pitch excitement and enthusiasm in the town was not exactly calmed down when news came to Sunderland of the draw for the next round – Newcastle at St James' Park on 8 February. An objective analyst would have to favour Sunderland over Newcastle who were at that time struggling to hold a position in the middle of the First Division, but this was the mystical FA Cup which had never so far been any further north than the likes of Sheffield or Bury and was currently in the possession of Tottenham Hotspur. Newcastle United and Sunderland had never actually met in the FA Cup, although Sunderland had beaten Newcastle East End in 1886 but East End protested and won the replayed game. Sunderland, however, beat them the following year.

But the league continued in the meantime; 1 February in the Midlands was a fine, bright day, and the overnight frost had to a large extent disappeared for the game at Perry Barr between Aston Villa and Sunderland. A crowd of 30,000 appeared and it might have been more if Villa had not been knocked out of the FA Cup the previous week, thereby more or less finishing their season. But Sunderland were now attractive visitors wherever they went, and could be sure to draw the crowds.

Once again Sunderland won without losing a goal. The understanding between Doig and his defenders was very pronounced and noticeable to anyone in the crowd, although Watson was out with Jackson playing at left-back. The only goal of the game came when McLatchie took advantage of a slip by Aston Villa goalkeeper George and prodded the ball just past him into an empty net. That was a minute or two before half-time, and the second half saw a titanic struggle as Villa pressed hard, but the Sunderland defence, proud of their record – they were now beginning to be referred to as 'the stone wall' (a deliberate echo of 'Stonewall Jackson' of American Civil War fame) – of not losing a goal, held out. 'Doig was quite at his best,' said the *Sunderland Daily Echo*. And there was more good news when the 'wire' came through that Everton had drawn at Sheffield United, meaning that Sunderland, with only 12 league games left to play, were now four points ahead of the Goodison men with no one else in contention. Aston Villa might have forced themselves back in if they had beaten Sunderland, but they were a point behind Everton and had played two games more.

All this meant that Sunderland could afford to relax a little about the league, but with all due respect to that competition, what was really burning everyone up on the Tyne and the Wear was the FA Cup match. Everyone had made arrangements to travel into Newcastle to see the tie and several 'relief' trains had been booked to supplement the normal services, with everyone going around picking their team and arguing with the 'opposition' about who was going to win. The cynics, as always, said that it would be a draw in the interest of another large gate, but, as it happened, things were taken out of everyone's hands.

Snow fell on Friday, 7 February, but not enough to put the game in peril for the snow stopped that night and in any case the pitch was well protected by straw. The Saturday morning papers of both towns were confident that the game could go ahead. The referee, Mr Lewis of Blackburn, arrived early enough to make a decision by about 1pm if necessary. But the snow returned at about midday and this time it was a real blizzard, so Mr Lewis's decision was a formality.

It was, however, a localised fall of snow, for the other ties all went ahead, albeit in unsatisfactory conditions, and the north-east game was the only one not played. It was a massive disappointment for the whole area, and the feelings of anti-climax were tangible, particular for those who had travelled from as far away as Scotland to see the game and especially when the conditions had taken at least a partial turn for the better early on the Saturday morning.

A bizarre rumour spread that the game was going to be played in Sheffield, if it couldn't be played on Wednesday afternoon at St James' Park. Where that nonsense came from no one could say, but it was immediately and strongly denied. There was more substance about the other rumour that prices were going to be doubled 'to help cover the costs of Saturday's postponement'. This impressed no one, and frankly did not really work, for only 19,700 were able to afford the minimum price of one shilling. There was no organised boycott but many fans simply could not afford one shilling in midweek. If the game had been played with the normal admission prices, it would surely have attracted more than double the attendance that turned up.

There was thus a mixed atmosphere – with perhaps the occasion not getting the support it would have done under normal circumstances. However, it was a fine day for the game with 'pure fresh air and a nip of coldness around'. The crowd assembled and cheered itself up by singing some music hall favourites like 'Two Lovely Black Eyes' and 'Goodbye Dolly Grey', the Boer War favourite about the soldier leaving his lady love for South Africa, perhaps never to return – even though, if one believed the British press, the war would soon be coming to a triumphant conclusion.

The teams were:

Newcastle United: Kingsley, Bennie, Davidson, Caie, Aitken, Carr, Stewart, Orr, Gardner, Peddie, Roberts.

Sunderland: Doig, McCombie, Watson, Ferguson, McAllister, Jackson, Gemmell, Billy Hogg, Bobby Hogg, Millar, McLatchie.

It was generally agreed that Newcastle were the better team, but the manner of the defeat was a painful one for Sunderland with Ronnie Orr scoring from the last kick. For once, Sunderland's legendary defence had let them down, and it was hard to imagine a more painful way of losing a match – to one's local rivals in the last minute of a cup tie – and the Wearsiders and their supporters were distraught. Although Newcastle had had more of the pressing, Sunderland had had their moments in the game as well. But Newcastle wouldn't get much further, for they came up in the next round against Sheffield United who would go on and win the FA Cup.

For Sunderland, although this was a shattering experience, there was no time for self-pity because they had a First Division trip to Nottingham Forest on the following Saturday. It was a game they really had to win to bounce back from their crushing FA Cup defeat, but as often happens in such circumstances, defeats become infectious and one leads to another, simply because players' minds are on the previous results and doubts begin to creep in about how good they are.

This was precisely what happened here. Frankly, Sunderland, normally so well organised and compact, were well beaten by a Forest side who were three men short through injuries. It was 2-0 at half-time and with Sunderland a shambles in defence as the players argued with each other, captain Matt Ferguson was obliged to rearrange the forward line. Bobby Hogg pulled one back midway through the second half, but nothing else happened and long before the end, Sunderland were a beaten side. In theory they had been beaten by Nottingham Forest, but everyone knew that they had been beaten by Newcastle.

The *Sunderland Daily Echo* had no qualms about stating, 'On this afternoon's form, Sunderland would quickly descend from their league pinnacle.' The good news was that Everton lost as well, and although Aston Villa won, and gained on Sunderland, they had played two games more and were still three points behind. So although Sunderland were still in a comfortable place, it was probably a blessing that they had no league game on 22 February, and that their next match was on 1 March. It gave them time to regroup. There is of course nothing wrong with a 'wobble' – which happens to most good teams from time to time – as long as there is a speedy recovery.

March, with better weather and bright spring sunshine, arrived at Ewood Park, and Sunderland survived a second-half barrage to win 1-0, Gemmell having scored in the first half. Once again, Doig was magnificent and it was recognised as an important step on the way to the championship.

And another step came the following week when Stoke were despatched 2-0 at Roker Park. This was on 8 March and on the same day a Football League XI were playing a Scottish Football League XI at St James' Park, something that did little to help the attendance at Roker, and it also meant that Billy Hogg was playing in the English side. While the Football League XI were winning 6-3 with Hogg playing very well, an opportunity was given to John Craggs who took full advantage by scoring two goals, but one of the talking points of the game was when McLatchie scored direct from a corner – a magnificent piece of football, but unfortunately this was not allowed in 1902.

The score therefore remained 2-0 at Roker, but once again a great cheer arose when the wire brought the news that Grimsby Town had beaten Everton and that Sunderland were now six points ahead with only nine games remaining. It was going to take quite a loss of form to lose the title now.

But Sunderland don't always do things the easy way and on the Ides of March, they travelled to Goodison Park and went down 2-0. It was not Sunderland's greatest day, for McLatchie was out injured and then Andy McCombie suffered a terrible ankle injury which effectively finished his season. It was a total accident but he broke a bone which meant that he couldn't stand, let alone play football. It was very sad for the man from Dingwall, but it was far from the end of his career – which would not always bring happiness for Sunderland.

The following week brought better news in the shape of a good 3-1 win over Grimsby. A surprisingly poor crowd of 9,765 attended to see the Mariners on what was a good spring day. Sunderland, who had been badly hit with serious injuries to McLatchie, McCombie and Billy Hogg, had to cobble together a team with Ferguson at full-back and reliable reserves like Jimmy Farquhar, John Craggs and Willie Murray getting their opportunity. They did not let anyone down and Sunderland won 3-1, the highlight of the game being the first career goal scored by Sandy McAllister, the centre-half who had already played nearly 200 games for the club. He was handsomely rewarded with a piano and gold watch for doing so.

This meant that Sunderland were back to being four points ahead, with Everton having played two games more and only having five to play. They needed only another seven points from seven games and duly picked up another two in their Easter fixtures, drawing disappointingly with Small Heath on the Saturday at Roker when they should have won very comfortably and then more honourably in a 0-0 result on Easter Monday at home to Newcastle before a huge crowd of 34,819.

The Small Heath game was played in cold, wintry conditions, which provided some sort of excuse. The Newcastle game, on the other hand, was a closely fought encounter refereed by Mr Boldison of Stockton after Mr Lewis of Blackburn missed his connection at Harrogate, and it provided great entertainment to the crowd, as did the Sunderland Temperance Band who supplied the music. Sunderland, playing in white shirts and black pants, were possibly the better team, but their shooting was a little unsatisfactory.

The Wearsiders were limping rather than charging to the title, but then the awful events of 5 April 1902 intervened into the lives of at least two of the Sunderland players. It was the Scotland v England game at Ibrox that has become known as the first Ibrox disaster when a stand collapsed in the north-west corner of the ground and 26 people fell to their deaths. It happened, the press reported, when a long pass from Andrew Aitken on the right found Bobby Templeton on the left, and as the people swayed to watch the ball, the rotten wood gave way under them. A 'stand' in 1902 often mean just that – where you paid your money, climbed the stairs and stood to watch the game.

Sunderland supplied two players, one for each side – Billy Hogg for England and Ned Doig for Scotland. Incredibly the game continued after the collapse of the stand, and was played to a finish, with the kindly Doig apparently in tears for all the second half as he watched the dead and the injured being carried out. It would affect Doig for the rest of his days, and he was conspicuously absent from the Scotland team when the game was replayed a month later. All in all, Doig would have been better to have stayed with Sunderland that day. He might have made a difference to his team. As it was, on a terrible day of rain and snow, the Wearsiders went down 1-0 to Derby before a crowd of less than 2,000 with both sides sadly depleted by the international.

The full extent of the deaths at Ibrox was not known for several days, and football duly paused to pay its respects. But Sunderland still had a league to win, and on 12 April The Wednesday went to Roker where once again the home side gave a passable impression of a team that did not want to win the league, losing 2-1. Murray scored a good goal for Sunderland before a crowd of 9,300, but there was little else for the spectators to enjoy, and the only thing that saved the team was the fact that Everton slipped up as well. But as the frustrated *Sunderland Daily Echo* said, mustering up as much 'tact' as it could find, this was not exactly championship-winning form. Indeed, Everton, and to a lesser extent Newcastle (who had made a late charge up the table), must have been kicking themselves, for the title had very definitely been there for the winning.

Eventually, on Wednesday, 16 April at home to Bury, Sunderland eased the pressure on their supporters. The game kicked off at 5.30pm to allow more people in, and the club were rewarded with a 10,000 crowd who themselves in turn were rewarded with a 3-0 victory in which Millar, who had been off-colour and off-form for some time, scored a hat-trick. Amazingly, there was a newcomer in the Sunderland ranks. This was Willie Gibson, the Irish international full-back, who was allowed to play at short notice because he was an amateur, and he looked as happy as anyone to be allowed to take part in this joyous occasion as the players all shook hands and waved to the delighted crowd.

It was Sunderland's fourth title, and although they had possibly not been as fluent a team as they had been in other years, and certainly had their problems getting over the line near the end, it was difficult to argue with the fact that they were champions. They were better than anyone else, and although they had their problems on several occasions through the season, there were plenty of good days as well, and the town was rightly proud of them.

They drew one of their remaining league games and won the other two, and were also invited to play in a special competition. It was a complicated arrangement. Rangers had won a trophy called the Glasgow Exhibition Cup in 1901, and to raise funds for the families of the victims of the Ibrox disaster, they put the cup up to be played for by themselves, Celtic, and the top two teams of England, namely Sunderland and Everton. Sunderland were drawn against Celtic at Parkhead on Wednesday, 30 April, and in front of a disappointing crowd of only 4,000 they went down 5-1. It was a rather sad end to what had been a good season for Tom Watson and his men, but it was a low-profile event on Wearside at least, and no one really cared all that much.

Sometimes this tournament is called by historians the British League Cup or the Coronation Cup, but it must not be confused with the other Coronation Cup that took place in 1953 on the occasion of the coronation of Queen Elizabeth II. This one was for

King Edward VII, whose coronation was due to take place on 26 June. Unfortunately it didn't happen for the King developed appendicitis and had to be operated on in what was, in 1902, a very novel and dangerous process. He survived, the coronation eventually took place on 9 August and King Edward VII reigned until his death in 1910.

Usually the playground bullies do eventually beat up the little lads, and the Boer War came to an end on 31 May with victory for the British. It would have to be described as a pyrrhic victory for it came at the cost of an awful lot of lives, and a few justified questions being asked about British society. Why was it, for example, that so many of those who wished to volunteer were classed as unfit on health grounds?

And 1902 was also a great year for cricket. The Australians won the Ashes, but there was the great and famous innings of Gilbert Jessop of Gloucestershire at The Oval who hit what was believed to have been the fastest century ever.

But as far as Sunderland were concerned, there was one very sad postscript to this triumphant season. Captain Matt Ferguson's contribution to the success of the team was sometimes undervalued in the assessments of supporters and journalists. He was never a showy player, but he was always reliable, and in an undemonstrative sort of way, always a good leader who could comfort or cajole as required. He was also a great liaison man between the players and the directors.

After the end of the season, Matt developed a cough. Coughs in winter can always be explained away by colds and flu, but this one at this time of year seemed to be more serious, and one day in late May he collapsed at his house at 4 Duke Street, Monkwearmouth. He was diagnosed by the club doctor as suffering from pleuro-pneumonia, and died at home on 12 June, leaving a widow and three young children. It was as tragic and shocking as it was unexpected. Ferguson was only 26, and had played for Sunderland since 1896 having joined from Bellshill in Lanarkshire, that nursery of so many fine players. The Mere Knolls Cemetery a few days later had never seen such a massive funeral, with most clubs in the region – Newcastle United, Middlesbrough, and the two Sheffield teams – well represented as well as all the Sunderland players and thousands of supporters. To their credit, Sunderland AFC did a great deal to alleviate the distress of Ferguson's widow, who in 1902 would have had no means of support.

5

League Champions 1912/13

1912 WAS the year of the *Titanic*. What happened had definitely shaken a few people who thought that it was unsinkable, and possibly the *Titanic* planted a few thoughts into people's heads that the British Empire itself wasn't necessarily unsinkable either. It was being attacked on two fronts. One was in Ireland. David Lloyd George's successful emasculation of the House of Lords had seemed to open the doors for Irish Home Rule, which should really have been granted about 50 years previously and would have solved a lot of problems if it had been. But now it was the Union Jack wavers who were causing trouble, those who didn't want Home Rule, and who were prepared to turn violent against the country they loved in order to stay with that same country they professed to love so much. And they kept talking about the Pope, whom they seemed to hate so much. It would have been confusing and intractable.

And there were also women. The Suffragist movement was respectable and reasonable, but the Suffragettes were not always. Protests, and green, white and purple sashes and flags were all very well; vandalising paintings, putting objectionable things in post boxes and throwing things at MPs were not. Again, granting women the vote a few decades earlier would have solved the problem, but even the so-called forward-looking Liberals had not seen their way to allowing women to vote. They could teach in schools, they could work in offices using these new and strange things called typewriters, and they could even become doctors, but no, a vote was not a good idea.

The Irish problem was generally confined to Ireland, whereas the women were often looked upon as figures of fun. Generally speaking, there were no other serious problem for the new King George to be worried about. Or were there? Poverty was shocking, health care was virtually non-existent, housing was dreadful and education was limited. Ah, but let these new Fabians and socialists worry about that. Europe was peaceful, although that Kaiser was a funny little fellow, was he not? He insisted on building up a navy because he was jealous of the British one, but he was basically a harmless fool with a withered arm, and the cousin of the King. War between the two countries? Oh good heavens, no!

Some 40 years later, all football-minded boys would look forward to the next edition of the magazine called *Charles Buchan's Football Monthly*. The question naturally asked by precocious children was, 'Who was Charles Buchan?' The answer was usually respectful in the rest of the country and reverential in Sunderland. He was a great centre-forward, apparently, who had played for Sunderland, then served in the war, then turned to coaching and management with Arsenal before publishing his own footballing monthly which claimed to be the best football magazine in the world, and was. Buchan died in 1960 and was greatly mourned, but nowhere more so than on Wearside and particularly among those old enough to remember his apogee in season 1912/13.

Sunderland had last won the First Division in 1902. The intervening ten years had seen a Roker Park team who were good enough to deal with most opponents, but sadly not good enough to cope with the greatest English team of the day, Newcastle United. Newcastle winning three league titles and one FA Cup was hard for the Mackems to take. Sunderland had their successes against them – one of then a 9-1 victory which was as total as it was bizarre – but there was little doubt that the hegemony of the north-east and indeed English football in general had passed along the railway line.

But Newcastle too had peaked by 1911, and it was time, was it not, for a comeback? Sunderland finished eighth in the First Division in 1912 – Blackburn Rovers were the champions – but that was below both Middlesbrough and Newcastle. Newcastle had finished third and had always been considered to be challengers. Sunderland had their moments but lacked consistency and did not always score enough goals.

On this subject, arguments among supporters in the summer of 1912 seemed to centre around Charles Buchan. There were quite a few who did not like him. He suffered from the considerable disadvantage (in some eyes) of being a southerner. He had joined Sunderland from Leyton Orient in March 1911 and had been jeered in a few early games by the more xenophobic of the crowd who thought that all southerners were lazy and feckless. Buchan, still a young man, had retreated back south and was all for giving up the game altogether, but manager Bob Kyle talked him out of it. It was clear that 1912/13 was going to be an important season for Buchan.

The season opened on 7 September, appropriately enough against Newcastle at St James' Park. The game attracted a huge crowd of 56,000 and honour was satisfied on both sides with a 1-1 draw, the goals coming from Albert Shepherd for Newcastle and Jackie Mordue for Sunderland. It was generally agreed that

each team had been on top when they had the benefit
of the breeze, but full time came with neither side
superior. Newcastle still contained quite a few of their
players from the great days in a line-up of Lawrence,
McCracken, Hudspeth, Hay, Low, Veitch, Rutherford,
McTavish, Shepherd, Hibbert and McDonald, while
Sunderland were represented by Scott, Troughear,
Ness, Cuggy, Thomson, Low, Mordue, Buchan,
Richardson, Holley and Martin.

One hopes that the Sunderland fans were happy
with that result, because they were hardly likely to
have had smiles on their faces throughout the rest of
September when they lost four games in a row before
rallying a little with a 2-2 draw against bottom side
Tottenham Hotspur. Two of the defeats were home and
away against champions Blackburn, so excuses could
be made there, but the losses at home to Derby County
and away to Oldham Athletic were harder to explain.
At the end of the month, with Sunderland fourth from
the bottom and with only two points on the board, any
comment about winning the league would have been
met with ridicule and laughter.

Indeed, they had needed more than their fair share
of fortune to earn a point at home to Tottenham. The
crowd of 8,000 had been one of the poorest for a while.
Although Sunderland scored just before and after half-
time through Jackie Mordue and Tommy Hall, they

had incurred the wrath of the home crowd for their 'erratic shooting'. Two points from six games was a very poor yield indeed.

Another defeat followed at Chelsea, but then the skies cleared just as suddenly as they had darkened and the catalyst was a victory over local rivals Middlesbrough. It was a game played in heavy fog, and it was a wonder that the game got finished, but Sunderland suddenly clicked with goals from Hall and Holley before half-time and Low and Mordue in the second half. With the score at 4-0 the referee suddenly stopped play and took the players off because of the fog, although it did not really look any worse than it had been all game. Civil disturbances threatened for the 20,000 crowd at Roker Park did not take kindly to all this, but eventually the referee changed his mind, and led the players back for the remaining few minutes. It was a strange interlude, and no one realised the long-term implications until the end of the season.

But on 12 October, Sunderland at last had their first win of the season. A settled team now emerged of Butler, Gladwin, Milton, Cuggy, Thomson, Low, Mordue, Buchan, Hall, Holley and Martin, and they now all understood each other. Woolwich Arsenal, Notts County, Bradford City and Manchester United were all put to the sword with the 5-1 win on 2 November over Bradford City, the FA Cup winners of

1911, a particularly impressive one. Sunday newspaper *Reynolds's News* stated categorically, 'Sunderland were the most resourceful side seen at Valley Parade this season,' with the right wing of Mordue and Buchan looking particularly good, but it was George Holley who scored four goals (although some sources give one of the goals to Harry Low) that day.

Mid-table respectability now having been obtained, the town became even more animated with the arrival of Manchester United, a club who, since they had changed their name from Newton Heath in 1902, had made quite an impact on the scene, having won the league in 1908 and 1911 and the FA Cup in 1909. They had moved to Old Trafford and were clearly thriving on the huge support that the new city of Manchester gave them, and yet a curious thing happened a couple of months earlier when their successful manager Ernest Mangnall had suddenly hopped across Manchester to become manager of rivals City. But they still had the famous Welsh wizard Billy Meredith, a man who also hopped about Manchester, but spent the bulk of his time with United.

It was quite a remarkable game at Roker Park on 9 November. Tragedy had struck George Holley, whose infant daughter had died (sadly no uncommon phenomenon in 1912), and he was replaced by Walter Tinsley, who was only slightly the inferior of Holley.

But it was the right wing of Mordue and Buchan that impressed 'Will Watch' of the *Northern Echo* who was quite happy to describe them as 'the best in England', even, rather remarkably (even for a more pugilistic age), offering violence to anyone who disagreed with him. 'We'll go into the back yard and settle the difference,' he wrote.

Sunderland, inspired by Mordue and Buchan whom centre-half and captain Charlie Thomson fed relentlessly, won 3-1. Mordue scored with a penalty (he later missed one as well) and the other two goals were scored by Tinsley and Hall, but the whole team was very impressive, and cheered up the 20,000 crowd on what seems to have been a typically dull, sunless November day in the grim north-east.

One or two other strange things happened as well. Mr Adams, the referee, was complimented for the way that he handled a feisty encounter, particularly when Roberts of Manchester United poked two fingers into the face of Buchan 'like a Punch and Judy show' and at one point he had to 'speak to the crowd' at the bottom end when 'some silly fellow' blew a whistle. The culprit was pointed out and apprehended. At the start of the game, both goalkeepers had to be sent back for wearing 'sweaters of unauthorised colour'. We would like to know more about this. It was at this time that goalkeepers were beginning to wear different colours from the rest of their team-mates – usually yellow because so few teams wore yellow – but what outrageous colour were the two goalkeepers wearing on this day?

Two temporary spokes were put into the wheels of the Sunderland 'steam engine' in the month of November by narrow and unlucky defeats at Manchester City and West Bromwich Albion, although they did beat Aston Villa at Roker in a result which would have massive significance at the end of the season, but it was the way that they were playing that was beginning to impress everyone and beginning to remind everyone of the 'team of all the talents' of 20 years previously.

Buchan in particular, wiry and athletic with superb ball control skills, was attracting attention. Those who had persecuted him when he first appeared for his perceived lack of toughness were now 'hanging their heads in shame' according to the local press, and if there were any remaining doubts about how good he and Sunderland were, the events of 7 December 1912 would settle them.

Liverpool were in town, although the dreadful weather limited the attendance to about 9,000 and that was a shame, for they saw a wonderful Sunderland performance as they thrashed the Reds 7-0 in a performance which 'dwarfed all others'. The *Newcastle Daily Chronicle* was compelled to say that Sunderland had not had such a 'romp' since their famous 9-1 defeat of Newcastle in 1908, and it singled out Buchan, who not only scored five goals but was superb throughout. It is also important to stress that Liverpool, although nothing like the outfit that they have become today, were significant opposition, for they had won the league in 1901 and 1906. However, they were simply swept aside and if it hadn't been for their goalkeeper Kenny Campbell, who would go on to be capped for Scotland after the First World War, the score would have been even more overwhelming than 7-0.

'To get a proper idea of the game,' said the *Newcastle Daily Chronicle*, 'one has to imagine, practically speaking, a game of one team shooting at goal, with a forward line continually bewildering the defence, and shooting for goal almost at leisure.' Buchan was singled out as having 'superb artistry' with no one in the Liverpool defence or half-back line able to 'contain him in the least'. Buchan's five goals were supplemented by Mordue and by Harry Martin on the left wing, a man who suffered from possibly being considered the weakest player of the five forwards. But an inferior comparison with the likes of Mordue, Buchan and Holley would never have made anyone a bad player.

The Sunderland supporters stood in the rain and admired all this, staying there long after the game finished, in the rain and the darkness which, in

December, had fallen early, applauding and cheering the performance of their favourites. Yet the season had been inconsistent. September had been an awful month, and a glance at the league table in the evening paper would show that Sunderland had 16 points from 16 games, and were quite clearly a mid-table team. And yet a closer inspection would reveal that the leaders and champions Blackburn were only six points ahead. That was only three games, and there were still 22 to be played. And, of course, just round the corner in the new year was the FA Cup. That was something to be coveted. Newcastle had won it in 1910 – and that still hurt on Wearside.

All these things were discussed by Sunderland supporters as they trudged home through the bleak streets of the town, ill-lit by gaslight and containing several funny-looking fellows whom instinct said it would be better to avoid, and a few ladies plying their unsubtle trade. But there were happier sights as well – street musicians, orange sellers and queues for the theatres and music halls. Business in Sunderland was better than it had been in the past – certainly the shipyards did not lack orders – and although 'prosperity' would have been an exaggeration, poverty, if common and prevalent, was not as all-pervasive as it once was. The Liberal reforms since 1906 had begun to make a slight difference.

There were another five games left in 1912, three of them at Roker Park, but after that 7-0 victory they would not fear anyone. The following Saturday, if anyone in Merseyside had been unimpressed by Sunderland, they would have revised their opinion jolly quickly for the Wearsiders visited Goodison and dished out a 4-0 thrashing to Everton. Sunderland were superior on all fronts with Jimmy Richardson, in at centre-forward for the injured Hall, scoring twice and Mordue and Buchan getting the others. It was a fine, pleasant and crisp December afternoon, and the entertainment was first class, and it was just a shame that of the 20,000 spectators, so few of them were from Sunderland.

But the home fans had another opportunity to see the new Sunderland a week later when Bolton Wanderers turned up at Roker Park. It was midwinter's day, but the 20,000 present saw a rollicking game in which Bolton did little to enhance their reputation as sportsmen. Clearly Buchan was a marked man and was targeted several times by brutal tackles, and although he once had to go off for treatment, he was still there at the end. Sunderland were by no means innocent either and referee Mr Heath was a busy man. The game was played at a fast and furious pace throughout but seemed to be heading for a draw until Buchan, as all good strikers must do when things are not going well, tried a pot shot from 30 yards which sneaked in and released a roar that could have been heard in Newcastle as he once again became the hero of the hour.

But the game was not over yet, and in almost identical circumstances to Buchan's goal, Bolton equalised, and then there was intense drama with time running out and darkness beginning to fall when Sunderland twice claimed loudly for a penalty when Whiteside of Bolton seemed to handle. Mr Heath denied the first claim but conceded the second even though Bolton lost the plot and at one point seemed almost to be about to walk off. But Mr Heath consulted a linesman, awarded the penalty and after an inordinate delay, Mordue sank it.

With the crowd now in even more of a fervour, Stott of Bolton and Sunderland's Martin 'clashed' in circumstances that looked far from accidental and Stott had to go off with a serious facial injury. The game finished 2-1 to Sunderland in 'acriminous circumstances' according to a local newspaper – but we suspect he meant 'acrimonious' – in almost total darkness which did not, however, entirely conceal a few subtle punches being landed. Sunderland had earned another two points but were not likely to exchange Christmas cards with Bolton Wanderers.

'Will Watch' of the *Northern Echo* enjoyed the game but had one major gripe. Sunderland, in order to get a few more supporters into their stand at Roker Park, had reduced the size of the press box and the poor reporter and others had a rather uncomfortable time of it. This was a fair point. It does not do to upset the press. They were, and remain, vital people.

But it was Christmas, a festival much enjoyed in 1912, not least by the football community. Sunderland had a double-header against their old foes in The Wednesday, at Owlerton on Christmas Day and at Roker on Boxing Day. No one wanted to be reminded of what happened a year previously on Boxing Day at Owlerton when Sunderland were hammered 8-0 – a result that called into serious question the probity, commitment and sobriety of their players – but 12 months on everything was a great deal tighter with both teams winning their away fixture. Sunderland won 2-1 in Sheffield thanks to a Mordue penalty and a goal from Holley, but then, to the immense disappointment of an excited crowd 24 hours later, they lost 2-0.

There was some sort of excuse in the fact the game took place on a barely playable pitch – something that limited the attendance considerably – but the real truth was that Wednesday played better than Sunderland did with fine performances from Scotland internationals Dave McLean and Andy Wilson. Watching the pantomime *Cinderella* at the King's Theatre that night was scant consolation for Sunderland's depressed players and supporters, for it had brought to an end a fine run of form.

But all was forgiven on Saturday, 28 December in the last game of the turbulent year that was 1912. The rain had eased from Boxing Day but the pitch was still a quagmire. That did not, however, prevent the two north-eastern giants, Sunderland and Newcastle, serving up a great game to entertain the huge crowd of 34,000. Sunderland won 2-0 with two goals from George Holley, one in each half. The writer 'Will Watch', while continuing his indefatigable complaints about the Roker Park press box, was at a loss to understand how Newcastle had now lost five games in a row, for they played well and might possibly have earned a draw. But Sunderland were that bit more energetic with Frank Cuggy in particular having a great game, and Charlie Buchan a constant menace.

So bragging rights had gone to Sunderland as 1913 dawned. Newcastle now seemed to be out of the league race following their poor run of form, but Sunderland were clearly emerging and climbing. In a crowded top end of the table they were now seventh, only three points below joint leaders The Wednesday and West Bromwich Albion, although they had played a game more. But it was only just past the halfway stage, and a lot remained to be played for. It was now 11 years since they had last won the championship, and in those intervening years Newcastle had won it three times. And of course, as those on Wearside kept being reminded, although Newcastle had only won the FA Cup once, it was still once more than Sunderland. But with men like Mordue, Buchan and Holley in the forward line, and Cuggy and Thomson in the midfield, nothing seemed impossible for the men from Roker Park.

In 1913 Sunderland added consistency to their other qualities. Late 1912 had shown that the talent was there, but in was only as the days began to lengthen again that supporters were able to rely on Sunderland producing the performances on the field. It was not long before fans began to talk about the possibility of a First Division and FA Cup double, achieved only by Preston North End and Aston Villa in 1889 and 1897 respectively. Newcastle had come close in 1905, but no one had achieved it in the 20th century.

The new year opened with Woolwich Arsenal at Roker Park. Woolwich had had a poor season, and in dry but bracing weather which attracted a crowd of about 30,000, Sunderland beat them very easily, 4-1, even without the injured Holley. The goals came from Buchan, Mordue, Cuggy (a great individual goal) and a tap-in from Richardson just at the full time whistle, and once again it was the Mordue/Buchan wing which attracted all the rave reviews.

Heavy flooding in the Midlands meant that Sunderland, who were due to play at Derby County, had no game on Saturday, 4 January, so their next match was in the FA Cup against Clapham Orient, who were rare visitors to the north of England. They were in the Second Division but were struggling, and Sunderland had no problem in beating them 6-0. There was more of a problem with the weather. Many ties did not get started at all, quite a few were abandoned halfway through (including one as near as Newcastle) and the Sunderland match started, by agreement, five minutes early as the weather was obviously closing in. But it was a great day for Jimmy Richardson, who scored four goals.

January concluded with a slightly disappointing 1-1 home draw with Oldham Athletic and a narrow, but valuable, win over Tottenham Hotspur at White Hart Lane. The Oldham game was played on a heavy pitch, and against a very stubborn defence, but the Tottenham match saw Sunderland at their best and earning a great deal of praise from the London papers like *The Referee*, for example. A huge crowd of 40,000 were there to see Sunderland win 2-1 'but if it had been 6-1, none could have said that the home team had not obtained its deserts', wrote the newspaper. Sunderland's play was described as 'strong, fast and clever', but sometimes they were let down by poor shooting. Tottenham scored first but Martin and Low replied to win the day for Sunderland.

This meant that Sunderland's relentless climb up the table continued, and they were now fifth and only three points behind leaders The Wednesday. But it was FA Cup time again. This time there was no easy passage, for Sunderland had been drawn against Manchester City and it will be remembered that City had stopped their winning run in the autumn.

The game at Hyde Road on 1 February was terrifying. The pleasant weather attracted a huge crowd to see two of the form teams of the country in an FA Cup tie, and this included an agreeable amount of 'northern excursionists'. The main problem seemed to lie in Manchester City being too dilatory in closing the turnstiles as the crowd built up. The Hyde Road ground could comfortably house 30,000, but there were 41,000 inside (plus a few who had climbed the wall) when the gates were eventually closed. This action, clearly taken by panicky directors, alienated everyone and left an angry mob outside including some of their own regular supporters who had bought tickets and now were denied admission.

All this was bad enough, but there simply was not enough room for the people inside. Three times the crowd encroached, not because of any ill will or desire to cause trouble, but simply because they were afraid of being crushed to death. It was almost incidental that Sunderland were winning 2-0 with goals from Buchan and Richardson, for the game was simply a farce with the taking of a corner virtually impossible. After the third major invasion of the playing area, referee Mr Adams had had enough and took the players off, effectively abandoning the match with about half an hour to go. Confusion continued for some time before anyone was able to persuade the crowd that the football was over for the day and that they should go home.

Not unnaturally Sunderland claimed the tie. Surprisingly it was not conceded to them, but a replay was ordered with Sunderland being given home advantage, and City were ordered to pay a fine to charity. The same FA meeting also did the draw for the next round, and everyone knew that a home tie against Swindon awaited the winners at Roker Park.

Sunderland had cause to feel hard done by; they had, after all, been well in the lead. But there was no place for self-pity or anger. The game was to be played at Roker Park on the Wednesday afternoon, and the feeling was that as they were well ahead of City in the imperfect conditions of Hyde Road on Saturday, there was no reason why they couldn't do likewise in their far better home environment.

The game was not without crowd problems. Sunderland had doubled their normal prices, claiming that this would deter too large a crowd from turning up. They did not, presumably, expect anyone to believe that specious rubbish, and most people saw it for what it was. It did not really deter anyone for the crowd was given as 24,974 – something that says a great deal about the enthusiasm for the team and the game at the time. The gates were in fact closed, but possibly Sunderland, unlike Manchester City, erred on the side of caution.

There was in fact an accident which might have been serious. About 20 young men, deterred by the high prices but determined nevertheless to see the game, occupied the roof of a coal shed some 30 feet high, outside the ground but which afforded a good view. In spite of numerous warnings from the police they refused to come down, until the roof collapsed under their weight. The casualties were not as bad as first feared with no fatalities, and one broken arm the most serious injury.

The match itself saw a poor first half with the only real incident of note being a penalty miss by Mordue. But the second half saw Sunderland turn it on, adopting their long passing game which had the effect of transferring defence to attack almost instantly with the half-back line of Cuggy, Thomson and Low controlling the centre of the field. Mordue accomplished the much more difficult feat of scoring from a free kick, aided by the modern device of Holley running up to take the kick, then jumping over the ball and allowing Mordue to catch the defence unaware.

Then Holley himself scored. It was from a rebound from a Mordue shot but Holley himself had been involved in the build-up. Once again, Buchan was singled out as the best player on the field and it was difficult to resist that conclusion after the time that he waltzed past about five players and shot – but was denied by a brilliant save by the goalkeeper.

It was a fine occasion for Sunderland, and everyone was now compelled to sit up and take notice. Captain Charlie Thomson proved himself a great diplomat and a great leader. It was his job to deter big-headedness and complacency, but at the same time to foster confidence. He had the respect of all his players and was able to do just that.

The rest of February showed Sunderland at their brilliant best. A windy but dry day on 8 February attracted 20,000 to Roker for the visit of lowly Chelsea. The Londoners really had no answer to the way that Sunderland played. Holley was out again but Hall, who had been disputing the centre-forward position with Richardson, came in at inside-left, and Holley was barely missed as Sunderland romped home 4-0. Leading 2-0 at half-time, and pressing all through the second half, they eventually made it 4-0 at the end, showing great energy when Chelsea ran out of it.

Buchan scored twice, and Richardson and Low once each, but it was once again an obvious team effort. There was a clear dynamism and collective energy about them, as happens with successful teams. Going in to train every day became a pleasure rather than a chore, and hard-bitten professional footballers they may have been, but they nevertheless came to love the club and the supporters, taking a keen pleasure in being able to make so many people happy.

It was the local derby against Middlesbrough that turned the tables in the autumn, and now came the return visit to Ayresome Park on 15 February. Middlesbrough (and indeed Newcastle as well) had been challenging near the top of the table, but as Sunderland had risen, so the Boro had fallen and they were now in the lower half of the table, in spite of having some very good players. This was the day that Sunderland reached the top, admittedly just on goal average, and it was somehow appropriate that they should do so against Boro, the team against whom their run had begun.

And yet it was a rather unsatisfactory state of affairs as well, for both sides were badly depleted. The reason was the international match in Belfast in which Buchan, Cuggy and Mordue along with Middlesbrough goalkeeper Reg Williamson and centre-forward George Elliot were playing for England.

Ireland won 2-1 – Buchan on his international debut, scored England's goal – but there were several strange things about this game.

In the first place, it should by rights have been played in England, but because of the poverty of the Irish association it was agreed to play the game in Belfast to support the Irishmen in troubled times. But there was also an element of politics in all this. Belfast in 1913 was an absolute tinderbox of a city with the Ulstermen resisting Home Rule and being prepared to take up arms in that cause, and it seems that the sending of the English team to Belfast was the FA making a point to the Liberal government that they were sympathising with the Orangemen.

This idea was of course hotly disputed, and the point was made repeatedly that the rescheduling of the game to Belfast meant exposing England's players to unnecessary risk in a country bedevilled by a political dispute which very few people in mainland Britain understood or were bothered about. Terrorism and hostage-taking were not unknown in Ireland in 1913, and a heavy presence of the British Army was necessary to guard the English players, who not unsurprisingly played badly, lost 2-1 and were unashamedly glad to get back home.

Buchan, Mordue and Cuggy would have far rather been at Ayresome Park, but their team-mates managed well without them, beating the equally depleted Boro 2-0. Shorn of the five best players, it was not entirely surprising that only 13,922 were attracted to see the game, which really should have been called off. Bobby Best was given a start on the right wing alongside George Holley while Hall, Richardson and Martin made up the rest of the forward line. Best took advantage of a defensive error to allow Richardson to tap in one of the goals, and the second came when a shot from Martin hit the deputy goalkeeper, rebounded on to the post and then into the net.

In a word, Sunderland were lucky, but it was also an opportunity for some of their lesser-known players to make a name for themselves. Full-backs Charlie Gladwin and Albert Milton both had good games, as did Willie Cringan, a man who would become an inspiring captain for Celtic after the war, with Sunderland doing what they needed to do and winning.

In view of the attention paid to the international in Belfast, not to mention a co-ordinated series of attacks on golf courses by misguided Suffragettes that weekend, it was hardly surprising that Sunderland's topping of the league did not attract major attention. It was only on goal average and they shared the lead on points with Manchester City, Oldham Athletic and The Wednesday who all had 33 from 26 games. Behind them came Aston Villa, Manchester United and Bolton Wanderers with 32 from 26, and Derby were in the picture as well with 30 from 25. It would have to be described as a 'tight' table, but the following week was FA Cup time again with Southern League side Swindon Town paying a rare visit to northern parts.

Often in Sunderland, southerners (particularly those from a more agricultural background like Wiltshire) are perceived as 'soft'. Not Swindon, though, who were given a warm and respectful reception from the 24,895 attendance which did indeed contain a few visitors who were clearly impressed by the large crowd and the noisy and almost tangible expectations of success. It was a shame that, although they won 4-2, this was one of Sunderland's less impressive games, even though they were at full strength with both the *Newcastle Chronicle* and *Sunderland Daily Echo* united in their opinions that the Wearsiders were poor, and even lucky not to have to go to Swindon for a replay.

They scored twice in the early stages, through Buchan and Richardson, and then they made the mistake of easing off and becoming complacent. Charlie Gladwin scored a rare goal with a free kick from just inside the Swindon half which everyone missed and the ball bounced badly to put Sunderland three goals up. Some laughter greeted that goal, but the mood changed markedly in the second half when Swindon scored twice. The first was a good shot and was greeted with a sympathetic cheer; the second was a complete mess in the Sunderland defence with goalkeeper Joe Butler badly at fault and making one of his rare mistakes. This goal was greeted with boos, and Swindon, now scenting blood, piled a little pressure on a panicky Sunderland defence until Richardson eased the pressure by scoring a beauty in which he feigned to shoot one way and deceived the goalkeeper, then tapped the ball gently into the other corner.

And so to the quarter-final. Great was the excitement when it was announced that Sunderland would be at home and their opponents would be the winners of the replay between Newcastle and Liverpool. Phrases like 'fever pitch' and 'bubbling cauldrons of excitement' did not quite cover the atmosphere in the whole north-east on that wet afternoon of Wednesday, 26 February, when before a huge crowd (which included a few Sunderland sympathisers) at St James' Park, Newcastle, albeit unconvincingly and with the aid of a penalty, got the better of the Reds, and all Sunderland seemed to be waiting outside the Post Office, the railway station and newspaper offices for news of what was going on at Derby, where Sunderland were playing the league game that had been postponed early in the new year because of bad weather.

The weather, in all truth, was not a great deal better at the Baseball Ground that day, and only 7,000 turned up to see a strong Sunderland performance which sent them clear at the top of the table, The Wednesday having only drawn on the Monday. Without Thomson and Richardson but well backed up by Hall and Cringan, Sunderland adapted a great deal better to the rotten conditions and the half-empty desolate stadium than Derby did, and two goals from Hall – one very good finish and a penalty – plus one from Buchan made it 3-0 by half-time. This time Sunderland did not make the mistake of switching off in the second half. They should have scored more goals, but 3-0 was a good result.

But the main topic of conversation for the players on the train coming home was Sunderland v Newcastle on 8 March. Everyone was aware that Sunderland had never beaten Newcastle in the FA Cup, but the fact that they were top of the league, and clearly playing a great deal better than their rivals, plus the game being at Roker meant that the Wearsiders had to be the favourites.

A major shock came the way of Sunderland on 1 March. Once again, international commitments played a part, for Mordue, Buchan and Cuggy were in Glasgow playing for the Football League against the Scottish Football League (and they lost 4-1) while Richardson was out injured. It was thus a severely depleted team that went to Notts County and lost 2-1, a result which cost them the leadership of the league. There was another factor as well, however, in that Sunderland allowed themselves far too easily to get involved in the rough stuff that was a factor in the game. Peart of Notts County was 'awarded the long walk' by referee Mr Eccles for a bad foul on Thomson, but Sunderland were no injured innocents, and it was a salutary, but not fatal, experience for the Wearsiders.

The FA Cup tie, however, pushed everything else aside. Oddly enough in the context of the dangerous events at Manchester City a month previously, no arrangements were made to make the game all-ticket, but instead a rather unsettling announcement was made that although the kick-off was scheduled for 3.30pm, the game might start earlier if the gates had to be closed. Prices ranged from one shilling to five shillings and supplementary entertainment was to be provided by the bands of Durham Light Infantry and the Wellesley Boys.

In the event, there were several disappointments. The crowd was surprisingly low at 28,720, although there were several reasons for this. Some people simply could not afford it. There did not seem to be any arrangements for youngsters and a man with three boys, for example, would have had to pay four shillings. There was also the feeling of fear that the ground could not hold the crowd expected and quite a few people stayed away out of apprehension for their own safety or of not being able to see the game in comfort. But there was also a more sinister fear that the match might be fixed to ensure a draw and another big gate at St James' Park on the following Wednesday afternoon, a fear that gained ground when rumours spread that arrangements were already in place for a replay.

While it is hard to imagine players like Mordue and Buchan, or Newcastle's Jimmy Hay and Colin Veitch, going along with this corruption, draws in cup ties were common and usually described tactfully in newspapers in terms of teams 'not wishing to lose the game' and the defences being 'ultra careful'. The conspiracy theorists were given a certain boost when this game finished 0-0 in what was generally agreed even by players of both sides as being a dull encounter.

But the feelings of anti-climax were soon dispersed with the thought of a trip to St James' Park on the Wednesday, even though Newcastle's directors seemed to have made a bad situation worse by doubling entry prices. It was not subtle, but astonishingly 56,717 turned up and many thousands were locked out. It was another draw, but this time at least it was a good game at 2-2 which went to extra time. Sunderland were definitely the better team but could not quite finish it off. All four goals had a touch of the fluke about them, and 1-1 looked like the final score until with three minutes to go, Hay got in the way of a ball that his goalkeeper was going to gather. That looked as if that was that, but then at the other end Gladwin deflected a harmless shot past Butler.

The coin was tossed for the venue for the third game, which would take place on Monday, 17 March, and Newcastle won it. But that was all they won, for, in intermittent rain and sleet, Sunderland at last turned it on and showed the kind of football that everyone knew they were capable of as 49,475 fans saw them win 3-0 with two goals from Mordue (one a penalty) and one from Holley. It was not true to say that Newcastle were never in it, for they had their moments, but the *Newcastle Chronicle* conceded that Sunderland were well worth their place in the semi-finals where Burnley were awaiting them. Newcastle at least had the consolation of having made an awful lot of money.

Before the third game was played, Sunderland had had another tough game at Manchester United on 15 March. Local newspapers in both places told Sunderland to beware the Ides of March, and indeed the recently opened Old Trafford was a difficult ground to visit, but the weather was fine and the Wearsiders eventually won 3-1 having been held at 1-1 at half-time. Thomson was not playing that day for he was in Dublin playing for Scotland (arguably an even more dangerous venue for Scotland than Belfast had been for England), but Buchan with two fine second-half goals, one described by *Reynolds's News* as an 'adroit header', saw Sunderland home.

The ever-changing top of the First Division now had Aston Villa ahead with 38 points from 29 games and Sunderland one point behind, having played the same number of matches. Easter came early in 1913 thus Sunderland, having defeated Newcastle on the Monday of Holy Week (sometimes called Holy Monday), had to play Sheffield United at home on Good Friday, Manchester City at home on Black Saturday and then Sheffield United at Bramall Lane on Easter Monday before Burnley in the FA Cup semi-final at the same venue the following Saturday. Fortunately, this was the time when Sunderland really got into gear, and their three victories over the Easter weekend (1-0, 1-0 and 3-1) meant that the table showed the Wearsiders, with only six games left, were one point ahead of both Aston Villa and Sheffield Wednesday.

The two 1-0 wins proved yet again the old adage that the team that wins the league is not necessarily the team that plays the best football. It is more the team that knows how to win, how to grind out favourable results at difficult grounds, how to score late goals and how to defend leads. Football is not always pretty, but your supporters will forgive you if you win.

The final trip to Bramall Lane was for what would have been Sunderland's first place in the FA Cup Final. Burnley were similarly FA Cup Final virgins, but they were challenging strongly in the Second Division and would be no pushovers. With the game being in Sheffield, a large crowd of 33,586 turned up and Sunderland were well represented with many trains having left from early in the morning.

The result was an anti-climax and a 0-0 draw. Arthur Milton was injured (and would remain so for the rest of the season) but he was immediately replaced by Harry Ness. Otherwise Sunderland were at full strength. The game began in dull conditions, but rain came on at half-time and this, in addition to the amount that had fallen in the previous few days in Sheffield, meant that the pitch became very heavy indeed. *Reynolds's News* was probably spot on when it said that 'the players were palpably tired and play was indifferent'. It was an extremely dull encounter, and everyone was quite happy to settle for a replay.

Elsewhere, Aston Villa beat Oldham 1-0 in the other semi-final, and in the league The Wednesday beat Woolwich Arsenal to return to the top. It was not the best of days for Sunderland.

The replay was a different matter. It was played at St Andrew's, the new home of Birmingham City, on Wednesday, 2 April. The pitch was not nearly as boggy, although the weather was typical of England in April with fine periods of sun alternating with heavy showers. A crowd of 30,000 were there, mainly neutrals, for it was difficult for Sunderland people to get there on a weekday, and they all enjoyed a fast, open game of football which the Mackems just edged as they had that little bit more stamina in the difficult conditions.

Buchan opened the scoring with a header, but then Burnley equalised with a penalty and then scored again before half-time. It was in the second half that Sunderland really took command as Mordue equalised with a penalty and then with ten minutes to go Holley scored what proved to be the winner. There may not have been many Sunderland supporters at the game itself but crowds had gathered back home at various locations, mainly newspaper offices to hear the news, and while Mordue's equaliser was greeted with applause, Holley's winner 'set the town on fire' as everyone rushed to buy the newspaper and then to communicate it to their friends.

And no wonder. Sunderland were now, for the first time, at the Crystal Palace, that magnificent stadium in Sydenham in London where cup finals and internationals were played. Newcastle had played there in 1905, 1906, 1908 and 1911 and lost. They had drawn in 1910 and then won the FA Cup at Goodison, but their lack of success there had seen the ground christened 'The Palace of Doom'. But it had not just been Newcastle who had been hexed there, for Scotland had never won there either. Did the curse apply to all northern clubs? Saturday, 19 April 1913 would supply the answer to that question. The *Daily Mirror* was of the opinion that 'the eggs in most people's baskets will go on Sunderland' – but would they?

But in the meantime, the league season continued with relentless ferocity. Six games remained and Saturday, 5 April saw demanding opposition in West Bromwich Albion. Once again Sunderland were depleted, as this was the day of the England v Scotland international at Stamford Bridge, and Holley was playing for England while Thomson was the captain and mainstay of Scotland. England won 1-0, but both men would have been forgiven if they had asked whenever they came off the field about how Sunderland had done.

They had done very well. In fine weather at Roker Park, some 17,000 had turned up to welcome back and cheer on their heroes after the semi-final triumph, and they saw a good performance from their team.

Any feelings of resentment that Charlie had not been chosen for Scotland immediately disappeared when he won a penalty which Mordue converted, and then he scored with a header to make it 2-0 before half-time. The second half saw the Throstles come more into the game and indeed they scored late on to cause quite a few ripples of apprehension to be felt in the inexperienced Sunderland defence, which lacked the calming influence of Thomson. But with time running out, reserve Walter Tinsley – playing for Holley – scored a third to make Sunderland safe and to send the supporters home happy and relieved.

One can imagine the feelings at Roker Park as everyone awaited news of the other results that day. Rumours spread, but there were very few ways of getting reliable information in the absence of radio and television. It was normally the journalists who were able to get news 'on the wire' from their offices who were able to communicate the results, and pass it on to a crowd who gathered in front of the press box. The news that England had beaten Scotland was greeted with a mixed reception, for Sunderland was as much inclined to Scotland as it was to England, and Middlesbrough 0 Newcastle 0 was treated with indifference, but two results in the First Division were awaited with feelings that were far from ambivalent. The Wednesday 6 Bradford City 0 was heard in stony silence punctuated with a few cries of 'Bradford weren't trying', but a huge cheer greeted Aston Villa 1 Liverpool 3.

Villa had been even more depleted thatn Sunderland by the international, and had now lost ground, but The Wednesday's result strengthened their goal average and kept them one point ahead of Sunderland, but Sunderland had one game in hand, and now awaited the arrival of mid-table Everton at Roker Park on Wednesday.

That same afternoon saw Villa at Middlesbrough, and a draw there seemed to put the Birmingham men out of the race, but at Roker Park in a fine game which saw Sunderland at their best in adverse circumstances the Wearsiders won 3-1 and regained top spot. Albert Milton inadvisedly returned for this match, immediately aggravated his injury and had to retire for a spell before re-appearing on the left wing. No substitutes were allowed in 1913, so Sunderland were more or less reduced to ten men against a good Everton side.

Buchan scored the first goal and then Richardson the second with a delightful shot over the heads of the Everton defence after some good work from Martin, before Holley, who had spent most of the game in the defence doing the work of Milton, scored near the end. Everton had scored a scrappy goal in a scrimmage which was possibly an own goal, but the makeshift

Sunderland defence had reacted very well, and had remained on top.

It was a fine win for Sunderland and restored them to the top, a point ahead of The Wednesday with both teams having four games to play – but three of Sunderland's were away from home, one of them at Villa in the midweek after the two of them had their very important engagement at the Crystal Palace, an occasion for which, incidentally, if one went by what people said, the town of Sunderland was going to empty itself and travel en masse to London.

But Saturday, 12 April came first. It was hardly the easiest of games against Liverpool at Anfield, although the Reds were having a strange season. Sunderland remembered having defeated them 7-0 in early December, but Liverpool had also earned the gratitude of Wearside by beating Aston Villa a week prior to this match. They were also 'under investigation' for 'not trying' in a game against Chelsea on 24 March. They had been cleared by a joint commission of the Football Association and the Football League, but people still wondered.

They might have had more cause to wonder at Anfield. There had been snow overnight – enough to imperil briefly the Scottish Cup Final in Glasgow between Falkirk and Raith Rovers – but the day had turned warm and mild and a healthy crowd of over

25,000 saw a marvellous Sunderland performance. Even without Milton, Cuggy and Holley – three key players but adequately replaced by Ness, Cringan and Tinsley – Sunderland simply ripped Liverpool apart, scoring four before half-time, then another in the second half before the hosts staged a belated rally and the game finished 5-2. Buchan, who clearly liked playing against Liverpool, scored a hat-trick and Richardson scored two.

It was a remarkable game. Sunderland were superb, but there were a few hints in newspapers that Liverpool were making some sort of a point to the management and indeed the authorities by their feckless performance. It could of course have simply been that they were outplayed by Sunderland and any possible complaints from The Wednesday were immediately stifled, for they themselves could only draw at Manchester City.

Sunderland were thus, with three league games left, two points ahead of Wednesday and four in front of Aston Villa. On Monday, 14 April, without kicking a ball they received a tremendous boost, and from a very unlikely source when Newcastle beat The Wednesday 2-1 at Owlerton. Fred Taylor, the club's chairman, immediately sent a note of thanks to Newcastle United and Sunderland now needed only three points from three games.

But the game that really mattered was the one at the Crystal Palace on the following Saturday. Indeed, the whole of the north-east seemed to think of nothing other than how Sunderland were going to do. Plans were made, special trains were laid on, money was saved up and the trip to London (for so many people the only opportunity in their lives to see the capital) was greatly looked forward to. It was far too far away to go by road, and although a few brave eccentrics sailed down, the only really viable way to travel was by rail. Sunderland station on Friday night was therefore a very busy and animated place, even though the weather was not great.

The team left from a thronged Monkwearmouth station at about 10.30am on the Friday after hearing all sorts of best wishes, with dogs wearing red and white jerseys, and people waving flags and blowing horns and bugles. A major doubt surrounded George Holley's fitness, and although he travelled with the party (joining them with Bob Kyle at Sunderland Central) he was honest enough to admit to reporters that he was not sure about his fitness, although there had been a remarkable improvement over the past 24 hours.

In the event, Holley did play, although many believed that he shouldn't have done. It was even suggested that Sunderland should play tactically for a draw without Holley in the hope that he might have been fitter by the Wednesday. The crowd was a massive 121,919, a record which beat the crowd at the final in 1901.

The teams were:

Sunderland: Butler, Gladwin, Ness, Cuggy, Thomson, Low, Mordue, Buchan, Richardson, Holley, Martin.

Aston Villa: Hardy, Lyons, Weston, Barber, Harrop, Leach, Wallace, Halse, Hampton, Stephenson, Bache.

Referee: Mr A. Adams, Nottingham.

It is generally agreed that cup finals seldom produce classic football, and this one was generally agreed to be rather rough with many fouls, and an inordinate amount of time added on at the end which Sunderland, sadly, could not capitalise on and Aston Villa won 1-0. It was the Villans' fifth FA Cup win, equalling the record of Blackburn Rovers.

Sunderland, simply, did not have a good day. They had worked very hard to get there but let themselves down with Holley less than 100 per cent fit, and with Buchan and Mordue never really getting going, they failed to function as well as they could have or as well as their supporters expected them to do. The goal was scored with a header from half-back Tom Barber, a boy from West Stanley in County Durham, while Villa's

Sunderland native Charlie Wallace earned a certain notoriety by missing a penalty. But Wallace had a good game, even though his family were the only happy Mackems that day.

And so everyone trudged home with a tremendous feeling of anti-climax. There was still the league, and there was also the precedent of how Newcastle had in 1905 lost their first FA Cup Final to Aston Villa at the Crystal Palace, but a week later they were champions of England. It was also pointed out that although the FA Cup was the older competition and contained all the drama and romance that the game could offer, nevertheless the Football League was usually won by the best team in England.

In the most supreme of ironies, Sunderland, who needed only a victory and a draw from three matches to win the league, found themselves playing at Aston Lower Grounds against the new FA Cup holders. A huge crowd of 70,000 turned up, for Villa themselves had an outside chance of winning the title, and the FA Cup was (rather provocatively, one feels) shown to the crowd by being paraded round the ground. The large attendance saw a chastened Sunderland team, upset by the FA Cup Final, playing with a great determination not to let themselves down again. Holley was dropped – it was still the opinion of many fans that he should not have been playing at the Crystal Palace – and replaced by Walter Tinsley, and it was appropriate that he scored Sunderland's only goal in a 1-1 draw.

This meant that Sunderland had 50 points from 36 games, as distinct from The Wednesday who had 49 from 37. But Sunderland had a better goal average, and this seemed to mean that Aston Villa's chance had gone for they were four points behind with two games to go. It all meant that if Sunderland won at Bolton Wanderers on Saturday, 26 April, they were the champions.

This duly happened with a 3-1 scoreline and Sunderland were deserved title winners. Mordue with a penalty and then two goals from Richardson were enough to do the job. The only pity was that there were just 13,000 present and very few Sunderland supporters to see them home. Tinsley once again impressed in place of Holley, and everyone remained of the opinion that if Tinsley had been playing in the final, it might have been a different story. In the meantime, Aston Villa continued their association with the north-east by travelling to Newcastle, receiving a great reception and beating the home side 3-2.

Those who missed the game at Bolton had a chance to welcome the team on the following Wednesday for the final game of the season, when Sunderland played Bradford City. The *Newcastle Daily Chronicle* was honest enough to say that the game was 'not a thrilling one' as Sunderland, 'already on holiday', took things very easily against a poor Bradford side. Buchan scored the only goal of the game, and Holley played but more for the purpose of allowing the crowd to clap and cheer him rather than anything else for his contribution to the season, for he was clearly still not fit.

Aston Villa duly finished second, but Sunderland's 54 points constituted a record total and beat the 53 amassed by Newcastle in 1909 and Aston Villa in 1910. Considering their appalling start in September, and that it was 12 October before they achieved their first win, this was nothing short of astonishing, particularly when one considers that their success was achieved in tandem with a long and enervating FA Cup run. But good players abounded in that team, particularly the forward line of Mordue, Buchan, Richardson, Holley and Martin, and the inspiring captaincy of the burly Thomson. Having now won the league five times overall, only once fewer than Aston Villa, they were undeniably one of the best clubs in England, and the 1913 side felt entitled to share the name of the 'team of all the talents' of 20 years earlier.

But as they were greeted and feted that summer at their various appearances at civic receptions and trips to the theatre, one has to hope that the good people of Sunderland enjoyed themselves, and that they did not realise the horrors that were soon to come their way. It was just as well that in 1913, nobody could tell the future.

6

League Champions 1935/36

SUNDERLAND HAD shown a great improvement in 1934/35 when they finished second in the First Division to Arsenal, who had now won the title three years in a row, thereby emulating the feat of Huddersfield Town who had done similarly in the 1920s. There was a connection, and he was called Herbert Chapman, who had started the process with Huddersfield before moving to Arsenal. Chapman had died suddenly in January 1934 but Arsenal kept winning.

A certain amount of optimism could be detected in Sunderland over the summer of 1935. The worst of the dreadful economic depression seemed to be passing, and more and more jobs were becoming available with industry slowly opening up. In the same way as the downward trend is a vicious circle, so too does the upward trend generate more prosperity in that

221

more money is available to buy goods, therefore more factories re-open, therefore even more money is around and so on. It was Keynesian economics, and to us, so obvious, but it seemed to have missed politicians of the early 1930s for so long.

The optimism spread to the football field and the impression grew that Sunderland were at last beginning to get together a good side. It had been a long time since Sunderland had last won the title, in 1913, and it sat ill with the Mackems that things had not been as good as that since the war. There had been reasons for this decline, not least finance, but it hurt that teams like Burnley, Huddersfield Town, Sheffield Wednesday – as they were now called – and worst of all, Newcastle United had managed to become champions.

Sunderland's manager was a man called Johnny Cochrane. He had been with the club since 1928, having previously been in charge of St Mirren. He had had his successes with the Saints, notably the Victory Cup in 1919 (a sort of unofficial version of the Scottish Cup in what was still an unofficial season) and then in 1926, just as the country was bracing itself for the General Strike, he amazed the whole of Scotland by pulling off an amazing Scottish Cup Final victory over a Celtic team which had just won the league, and which included their all-time record goalscorer Jimmy McGrory.

Since arriving on Wearside in 1928, Cochrane had patiently built up a team. Not everyone was totally impressed by him, but he always gave the impression of being hard-working and sincere. It must also be remembered that the 1930s was anything but the era of the 'quick fix' brigade. Managers in that decade, unlike the modern era where an unsuccessful man is given only a limited amount of time and dreads every Monday after a bad Saturday, could think and plan.

The champions of the last three years were in a slightly different category. This was Arsenal. They were not like the northern teams. They symbolised the opulence of London with their plush stadium called Highbury and their supporters who were slightly more sheltered (not entirely, of course) from the recession. They were the team of the Establishment. In the same way, perhaps, that, one was 'meant' to support the National government with all its talk of a 'doctor's remedy' to solve the economic ills, one was perhaps 'meant' to support the team of the Establishment. Sometimes this caused serious problems for Sunderland supporters. In 1932 Arsenal played Newcastle United in the FA Cup Final. Who did the Wearsiders want to win that one?

Arsenal had only recently arrived on the scene thanks to Herbert Chapman. Prior to lifting the FA Cup in 1930 they had not won anything, but having broken through as it were in that famous final against Huddersfield when the Zeppelin was seen overhead, there now seemed to be no stopping them, and it was confidently expected that sooner or later, they would win the First Division and FA Cup double.

By sheer chance, Sunderland's first game of the season was against Arsenal at Highbury on 31 August. Their team was Thorpe, Murray, Shaw, Thomson, Johnston, Hastings, Davis, Carter, Gurney, Gallacher and Connor. The crowd was a huge one reflecting the interest in football at the time, but it was generally agreed that, although Sunderland's inside trio did well, the defence was not up to scratch, and Arsenal, without themselves being any too impressive, won 3-1.

The inside trio was Raich Carter, Bobby Gurney and Patsy Gallacher, who was from Bridge of Weir in Renfrewshire, but the other two were local lads. Carter is generally regarded as one of the best players of all time, a man who had everything – ball control, passing ability, a good shot and the ability to inspire confidence in everyone else. Gurney came from Silksworth in County Durham and played for Sunderland for a remarkable 22 years from 1925 to 1947, and although he then tried his hand at management elsewhere, he never lost his love for the club he had served with such distinction and until his death in 1994 at the advanced aged of 87, he was frequently seen at his beloved

Roker Park. His understanding with Carter was what produced the success for Sunderland.

The inside-left was Patsy Gallacher, who must not be confused with another and older Patsy Gallacher who played for Celtic and was generally regarded as the greatest Celt of them all. The Sunderland man was probably not quite as good as his namesake, but they had a lot in common from their natural ability with body swerves and ball control to their extroverted nature and even a bit of the 'ill-willy' about the pair of them. They did not always take well to the pomposity of officialdom and occasionally needed a bit of strong handling. Sunderland's Gallacher played once for Scotland (Celtic's was an Irishman) and really should have played a great deal more often, but, of course, like so many Anglo-Scots, he was not seen often enough by the Scottish selectors, and at that time they had enough talent to choose from.

The defeat at Arsenal was disappointing, but it was only the first game of the season. Slightly more concerning would have been any reverse on the Wednesday at West Bromwich Albion. Fortunately this was not the case as Sunderland turned on the style to record only their second victory at The Hawthorns since the war, winning 3-1 with 'Argus' of the *Sunderland Daily Echo* stating categorically that Carter 'would have jumped into any England team on this display', adding, 'When occasion demanded, he was back helping his defence – when he went forward he was holding the ball with his body over it and swerving his way round the opposition and taking up either of the inside positions as the occasion warranted.' The introduction of Fred Hall and Jimmy Clark also made a difference. Gallacher scored twice and Carter once in this victory which should, in truth, have been by a lot more.

The 40,000 crowd at Roker Park on Saturday, 7 September 1935 are not likely to have imagined that they were watching the next two champions of the First Division in Sunderland and Manchester City. The home side won 2-0 in a good performance but the *Sunday Sun* was of the opinion that it was only the City goalkeeper who stood between his team and an 'annihilation'. Time and time again he held the Sunderland forwards at bay, and only conceded twice – one to an unlucky own goal, and the other to a header from Bobby Gurney. On the other hand, he saved a penalty from Bert Davis, and such was his determination that he was given a standing ovation by the Sunderland crowd at the end. This was a young man called Frank Swift who would go on to play for England and to become a very respected journalist before meeting his death in the Munich air disaster of 1958.

This was a very good result for the Wearsiders. Sunderland is one of these places where you can instantly tell on a Monday from the demeanour of the citizens how the team had done on the Saturday, and smiles were the order of the day in the shipyards, shops and schools in that fine autumn weather. The prosperity (limited but real) helped people to feel good about themselves as well, and the return visit of West Brom was much looked forward to on the Wednesday night. After that, railway timetables were consulted for the possibility of a few away trips, a rare luxury of the 1930s, but more and more people were now back in work.

The headlines in the *Sunderland Daily Echo* on the Thursday morning said it all, 'Sunderland set 35,000 crowd mad with delight'. While Carter was singled out as the star artist, 'Argus' stated categorically, 'Sunderland gave a general exhibition of football craft and positional play which would be hard to beat anywhere. Every man seemed to know by intuition where a colleague would put the ball and went into the correct position to receive it.' A clear sign of happiness was expressed when even the referee was given credit for having a good game. Funnily enough, in a 6-1 win, centre-forward Gurney seemingly had a poor game, but Carter notched four goals, Davis one and Gallacher the other one, but the half-back line of

Charlie Thomson (the second Scotsman of that name to play for the Wearsiders and not to be confused with Charles Bellamy Thomson of an earlier era), Jimmy Clarke and Alex Hastings was superb throughout.

The league table saw Sunderland as one of four teams one point behind Huddersfield after four games had been played, and they were generally acknowledged to have played the best football of the four. Things were looking up and the whole area was on a high, not least because one of the other challengers was Middlesbrough. Newcastle were in the Second Division to the delight of some Sunderland supporters although the wiser elements saw advantages in having both teams in the same division. Newcastle did not have a game that night, but their players turned up en masse to watch Sunderland. The *Sunderland Daily Echo* could not resist a dig by asking, 'For a lesson in football?'

There followed a weekend in the Midlands as Sunderland stayed in Buxton, playing at Stoke City – as they were now named – on the Saturday and Aston Villa on the holiday Monday. The 2-0 win at Stoke was professional rather than brilliant but Davis and Gallacher got the goals in what was generally described as a poor game, then Carter and Gurney scored in what was a respectable 2-2 draw at Villa Park. Three points out of four for an away weekend was hardly a disaster but 'Argus' remained unconvinced and continued his campaign for the removal of left-winger Jimmy Connor. But Sunderland were second in the league, one behind Huddersfield.

September ended with a very spectacular thrashing of Blackburn Rovers at Roker Park which showed the best side of Sunderland, and then a game at Stamford Bridge which didn't. Gallacher opened the scoring early in the first half but then fell apart in the face of determined opposition from Chelsea and the London men won 3-1. It has long been felt that Sunderland (like Newcastle for that matter) do not play well in the capital and this was a clear case in point. The crowd was a huge one of 65,000 and the Sunderland players seemed to be overawed by it all. They still finished the month only two points behind the leaders, and the general opinion was that the team was improving.

In the meantime, in the world outside of football, things were heating up between Italy and Abyssinia. It is hard to see that as any kind of an 'invasion' or 'war'; it was sheer international and geopolitical bullying. Everyone knew that Italy were about to invade, and all that Abyssinia could generate for itself was sympathy.

October was generally good but there was one awful moment to come, although not before five days into the month when Liverpool visited Roker Park, attracting a reasonable crowd of 30,000. Liverpool had dropped from the standards they set when they won back-to-back First Division titles in 1921/22 and 1922/23. Their performances tended to the mediocre and they were certainly the weaker team of Merseyside, for the 1930s was a great time in the history of Everton. Liverpool were respectably placed in the table nevertheless.

The game ended 2-0 for Sunderland, satisfactorily enough, but the writer from the *Sunday Sun* was critical of the players from both sides for not shooting often enough, being content sometimes to simply pass the ball along the penalty box to each other. Carter, as usual, was exempted from this general criticism. He scored one of the goals, the other being netted by George Goddard, who was playing one of his rare games in the absence through injury of Gurney.

A feature of the team throughout this season was that it was changed remarkably seldom unless through injury. Manager Cochrane clearly believed that he had a good side, and that the players needed to play together week after week as much as possible rather than chopping and changing. He also had to deny repeatedly that he, a Scotsman, showed favouritism to his countrymen, for there were an awful lot.

But no one could really have been prepared for what happened on 12 October when Sunderland were due at bottom side Grimsby Town. It was almost a derby, and many supporters decided to go to Cleethorpes to see the game. The *Sunderland Daily Echo* was arrogantly dismissive of Grimsby, saying that 'the strength of the sides seems to be wide apart' and that Sunderland should actually be top of the table on the Saturday night, if Huddersfield slip up to Middlesbrough.

A crowd of 18,000 at Blundell Park saw an astonishing game as Sunderland's defence, usually so reliable, collapsed totally against a team which simply was prepared to run at them and to take their chances. Up front the much-vaunted forward line of Davis, Carter, Gurney, Gallacher and Connor simply failed to function, and the result earned headlines in even the London newspapers, knocking the Chelsea v Arsenal clash off the back pages. It caused consternation in Sunderland, and immediate reaction among the support was to suspect some sort of corruption.

It was of course the natural knee-jerk reaction to an unexpected and even irrational defeat. To be fair, such things did happen in the 1930s, but there is no evidence (as distinct from gossip) of anything untoward happening here. Indeed, no match-fixing attempt would have been so blatant or so obvious as a 4-0 defeat of one of the challengers by the bottom team. It was quite simply a day on which Sunderland performed badly and Grimsby raised their game to a remarkable extent.

Sometimes, of course, in the grand scheme of things, such events have to happen to bring about an improvement. Certainly from then on, Sunderland learned a lesson and without making any huge changes in formation, the team rallied and lost only one more game in 1935. Clearly the result and the talk about it hurt.

There followed a remarkable and really rather nasty game at Molineux against Wolverhampton Wanderers. Shortly after half-time, Sunderland went into a 4-1 lead with two good goals from Carter and one each from Davis and Connor, looking every inch title challengers and clearly having put the unaccountable Grimsby disaster behind them. The match had been rough, however, and not particularly well refereed by Mr Williams of Bolton, and things took a turn for the worse when Davis foolishly got himself involved in an incident with Richards of Wolves after a throw-in.

Blows were struck and both gentlemen were correctly invited to take the long, lonely walk to an early bath, Davis being lucky to avoid being assaulted by a less than totally bright gentleman from the crowd.

That was bad enough but a far more serious incident occurred when Sunderland goalkeeper Jimmy Thorpe was felled in a collision with a Wolves player. Thorpe, a diabetic, was knocked unconscious and was allowed to lie there while Wolves scored. It was unbelievable, but Thorpe recovered and indeed played well while Wolves piled on the pressure.

This unfortunate happening would seriously affect the health of Thorpe, but more immediately, the referee – under pressure from the hysterical home support – gave a soft penalty. Wolves converted, and might even have equalised near the end. The final whistle brought a relief that Sunderland got the two points but also that no further violence took place.

More civilised was the final game of October when Sunderland, still without Gurney, beat Sheffield Wednesday 5-1 at Roker Park. Wednesday had won the First Division in 1929 and 1930, and had their great day the previous spring when they won the FA Cup by beating West Bromwich Albion 4-2 at Wembley, which had been hosting the finals since 1923. They were looked upon as one of the better teams in English football at this time, and brought a large crowd of supporters with them. It was actually a good day for Sunderland, for not only did they sparkle against their distinguished opponents, but Grimsby once again produced the goods and beat Middlesbrough 1-0. Liverpool beat Huddersfield and Derby County only drew, the net result of which was that the Mackems were able to buy their Saturday night newspaper and relish the sight of their team at the top of the league.

Connor, once pilloried for not being good enough, was the star and the Scotland selector sitting anonymously in the main stand would have been impressed by the way that he ran rings round Joe Nibloe, once of Kilmarnock and Scotland. Alex Hastings at left-half was also under observance by the selector who would have been impressed in that quarter as well. Connor didn't score but laid on the chances for Carter, Davis and Gallacher to do the job.

November is normally a dark, depressing, wet month, and this one was no exception. It is also often the month in which the foundations are laid for a league title challenge. The heavy programme of December and then the bad weather of January and February complicated with the start of the FA Cup present their own challenges, but the basics must be laid in November. Early season form can be unpredictable, but by November things must settle down. Fortunately this happened with Sunderland.

This particular November saw a general election. On 14 November the National government of Stanley Baldwin lost some seats to Labour (who had a lot to make up from their disaster of 1931) but still held a comfortable majority. Sunderland, perhaps surprisingly, voted Liberal National and Conservative in the two-member constituency, but that reflects the rather remarkable recovery from the depression and the feeling that things were now getting better. There was still, however, a fair amount of poverty, and shocking facilities for health and education – something that was as obvious in Sunderland as anywhere else.

The Wearsiders began the month with a 2-2 draw at distant Portsmouth. Very few supporters would have made that trip, one imagines. Len Duns was given a run on the right wing in place of Bert Davis, but the problem was the defence. Two blunders gave Portsmouth their goals, and Carter grabbed an equaliser.

Tommy Morrison replaced Bill Murray at right-back, and that seemed to make a slight difference. Morrison had just recently signed for Sunderland after a career for St Mirren and Liverpool at right-half. Now after a move which amazed everyone, he found himself playing at right-back rather than right-half – and he was good there as well. The weather for the visit to Roker of Preston North End was atrocious, but even so 17,000 turned up to stand in the wind and the rain, and they were rewarded with a 4-2 win over England's first league champions, who were now down on their luck. The scoreline was misleading for Preston's goals were both lucky affairs, and their goalkeeper Holdcroft helped his team avoid a real thrashing.

Young Duns, making his debut on the right wing in front of the Roker crowd, was very impressive and scored twice while Carter and Gurney scored the other two. Carter's goal was a brilliant individual effort, while Preston tried to stem the Sunderland tide by an offside trap which, frankly, they were not very good at. They were sufficiently good at it, however, to cause intense frustration to the crowd. Once again Sunderland were top of the table.

A trip to London came next to play one of the capital's less-fashionable teams, Brentford, at Griffin Park. It is a truism to say that northern teams do not generally do well in London. Not on this occasion, though, because Brentford were simply swept aside by Sunderland, who were described as one of the best teams seen in London during that season. Once again the weather was deplorable, but this did not prevent a large crowd attending to see Sunderland win 5-1. The pitch was heavy, described as 'boggy' in some quarters but this did not stop the Wearsiders, who thus rather destroyed the myth that they could not play on heavy ground. Champions can normally play well in any circumstances and Sunderland asserted their credentials in west London.

Gurney scored first before newcomer Duns managed to evade some hefty challenges to make it 2-0. Then Brentford came back and equalised from what seemed to many journalists to be an offside position. It was hard luck on Sunderland, whose goalkeeper Jimmy

Thorpe once again distinguished himself as Brentford strove to capitalise on their success. The second half, however, was all Sunderland as Gurney, Carter and Gallacher made it five, all goals coming from some fine combination work in the forward line.

The London press, often accused of trying to curry favour with the wealthy clubs of the capital, were fulsome in their praise of the northerners. There was a certain patronising condescension in some remarks well disguised as wondering just how long their good form was going to last, but the general feeling was that this was a fine team with the all-Scottish half-back line of Thomson, Clark and Hastings leading many to wonder why it was that they had never featured as yet to any great extent for Scotland.

The next match was the long-awaited derby at Roker Park between Sunderland and Middlesbrough. In the absence of Newcastle in the Second Division (alongside such distinguished teams as Manchester United and Tottenham Hotspur), the Boro were the closest that Sunderland could get to a derby. They had started the season well, but had fallen away recently, and needed to win to get back into the championship race.

The game attracted a crowd of 50,000 with a large contingent from Middlesbrough in evidence and much banter between the supporters. Sunderland won 2-1 but the manner of their victory was much disputed. Both goals caused some to wonder. One was from a penalty which seemed to be 'ball to hand' rather than 'hand to ball', and the other came from a cross by Duns which seemed to the referee, but not the Boro defenders, to have crossed the line.

The *Sunday Sun* described the game candidly as 'football without frills' and 'not always textbook', and in a desperate attempt not to upset either team's supporters it said that Sunderland were 'not lucky to win' but Middlesbrough were 'unlucky to lose'. Such pieces of sophistry did not disguise the fact that Sunderland were still two points clear at the top of the league with 16 games played and they still had a 100 per cent record at Roker Park.

November came to an end with a difficult trip to Everton, who had won the FA Cup in 1933 and the First Division in 1932. They teemed with talent but were currently struggling a little in the league. Nevertheless, a trip to Goodison Park was always looked upon as a tough assignment, and indeed it was a bogey ground for Sunderland who had not won there since 1927, and it was on that ground that they lost in the FA Cup in 1935.

This time, however, the great Dixie Dean was tamed by Clark, Joe Mercer never really got going, and Sunderland hushed the 40,000 crowd into numbed admiration as Connor, Gurney and Carter scored the three goals which increased their lead at the top to three points, as Huddersfield could only draw 0-0 with Arsenal. Sunderland's 3-0 win over Everton was as good a result as any that season, and if no one believed that they were potential champions, they had to now.

Bolton Wanderers were then put to the sword at Roker Park on 7 December. The crowd was 28,000 which was a good attendance considering the extremely cold weather and the fact that now the final month of the year had arrived, the game had to start at 2pm to guarantee finishing in daylight. Bolton held the home team to 1-1 for a long time, but in the second half, Sunderland went berserk and eventually won 7-2 with Gurney scoring five of the goals. The other two came from Carter and Gallacher, but all of Gurney's goals were the result of excellent teamwork from an accomplished half-back line and forward line. It was the first time that Gurney had scored so many goals, and as all the world loves a goalscorer, he was 'second only to Santa Claus' in popularity on Wearside that Christmas. He had emulated the feat of Charlie Buchan in 1912 of scoring five in a game – and that was certainly good company.

That was a good day for Sunderland in another sense as well, for their rivals all encountered problems and the result was that they were now five points clear of

Derby and Huddersfield. But of course, he is a fool who thinks that the league is won in December, and the next Saturday brought a salutary reminder of that. The visit to Leeds Road, brought a 1-0 defeat to Huddersfield, the goal being scored in the very first minute.

Huddersfield, in an area that one associated more with rugby, both union and league, than football, had a great side in the 1920s under Herbert Chapman, winning the FA Cup in 1922 and the First Division in 1924, 1925 and 1926. They were still a fine side and showed that they were far from out of the race for the 1935/36 championship. They defended successfully against relentless attacks, but oh how the 250 Sunderland supporters, resplendent in their red and white rosettes and woollen hats, groaned when Gallacher missed an open goal late in the second half. Hastings was out that day – his presence was missed – and he was replaced by another Scotsman called Sandy McNab.

It was a lesson, perhaps, in not getting too uppity, but in any case normal service was resumed on 21 December when Sunderland beat Derby 3-1 at Roker. The weather was hard with hoar frost, but Sunderland had taken the precaution of laying down straw on the pitch, and play was possible. Derby were one of the challengers and had a fine side with Scottish internationals like Charlie Napier and Dally Duncan, but there was little doubt that Sunderland were the better team with two goals from Carter and one from Gurney. Several Derby players did not take kindly to this, and had to be lectured by the referee, but Sunderland did not retaliate. This result effectively cancelled out the bad result at Huddersfield and guaranteed that Christmas would be spent with Sunderland at the top of the table.

Christmas was always a big day for football in the 1930s and for many decades afterwards, with fixtures even being scheduled for Christmas Day and Boxing Day. Sunderland's Christmas games were a double-header against Leeds United – away on 25 December and at home the day after. The heavy fog that had enveloped Britain for several days meant that they could not play at Elland Road, but it had eased sufficiently to allow the game at Roker to go ahead.

It was tight, and looked for all the world like a 1-1 draw with visiting goalkeeper McInroy defying Sunderland, who were throwing everything at him as the seconds ticked away remorselessly. But then after a free kick which the exhausted Carter had fired straight at McInroy, the ball rebounded to Gurney who, from a fairly difficult angle, managed to hook it past the goalkeeper and into the net. The *Sunderland Daily Echo* reported scenes of great joy in the stand as a man stood up and kissed his wife – unusual behaviour at a football match in 1935 (and maybe it wasn't his wife!) – but an indication of how much the game and the team were beginning to affect the town.

There remained one match in 1935. It could hardly have been a bigger one, against Arsenal. Since the Gunners had beaten Sunderland on the first day of the season, their form had been inconsistent but many people still felt that they were the main challengers to Sunderland for the title. They were rich, had some great players and still breathed the arrogance that success always brings. They had their legendary full-backs George Male and Eddie Hapgood, and in the forward line Cliff Bastin and Ted Drake, who had recently managed to score seven goals in a game against Aston Villa.

The morning fog eased into something more like mist and eventually evaporated to allow the game to go ahead, and 60,000 were at Roker, including quite a few 'Gooners' on a special train from London. At half-time the score was the rather astonishing Sunderland 4 Arsenal 1. Both sides had netted a penalty – Bastin for Arsenal and Carter for Sunderland with Davis (who had now won his place back from Duns), Gallacher and Carter the scorers of the other goals. But the fun was just beginning. First Drake scored (although some of the press thought it was an own goal), then Bowden made it 4-3 before Connor with a magnificent goal seemed to make things safe for

Sunderland. But then Clark, in an attempt to clear a Bowden shot, could only divert the ball into the net and leave the score at 5-4.

The last few minutes were frantic but Sunderland held out. It was generally agreed to be one of the best matches ever seen at Roker Park, and it was probably the game that loosened Arsenal's grip on the title, which they had held for three years. Sunderland were now seven points clear as they entered 1936, a year that was to bring an awful lot to the world – and not just on Wearside.

It is beyond doubt that 1936 is a 'crowded' year in world history. In Britain, for example, there were three kings and an abdication that was unparalleled in history. A dreadful civil war broke out in Spain with consequences for the whole world and all the while the Nazis in Germany were beginning to give out signals that they were wanting another global war, even when they were (incredibly) allowed to host the Olympic Games. These Games were vulgar, ostentatious and distasteful to the rest of the world, who nevertheless enjoyed the spectacle of the high-profile events being won by Jesse Owens, the black American who did not exactly fit in with Hitler's idea of a 'master race' of Aryan supremacy. And, of course, Sunderland won the league title, which did not go down well in London – nor, indeed, Newcastle.

Sunderland did not have a good January. They lost on New Year's Day, and then distressingly exited the FA Cup, but the month was generally dominated by the illness and death of King George V. There had been worse monarchs in the past, it would have to be said, although like quite a few others he was a dreadful parent. He had been born in 1865, son of the sybaritic Prince of Wales, and he possibly went too far the other way with his strictness and austerity. Nevertheless, he was greatly mourned when he passed on 20 January.

By this time, Sunderland's dream of being the first team in the 20th century to achieve the First Division and FA Cup double was in tatters. The defeat at Roker Park to Aston Villa on New Year's Day was bad enough, but the whole area was thunder-struck when they managed to lose to Port Vale in the FA Cup. The Villa game appalled the huge crowd and the *Sunderland Daily Echo* was compelled to employ words like 'tired' to describe some players who frankly took their lowly opponents far too lightly. Possibly there had been a little too much welcoming of the new year by the Sunderland Scotsmen (new year for a Scotsman in 1936 was usually a bacchanalian experience) but it was simply a dreadful game.

To a certain extent, they redeemed themselves on 4 January by going to Manchester City and picking up a narrow but decisive 1-0 victory. Alex Hastings was back after being out for a few games, and McNab was moved forward to inside-left to cover for the injured Gallacher. Hastings made a huge difference, but it was Carter who got the only goal ten minutes into the second half. In some ways it was the most vital game of the season, for the New Year's Day fiasco had dented confidence, and another defeat might have seen Sunderland on the slippery slope. As it was, a potential slide had been arrested.

But now to the FA Cup. The FA Cup was probably still more important than the league in 1936 with the 'sudden death' aspect of it attracting the fans. Sunderland had never won it – their closest encounter being in 1913 when they went down to Aston Villa in the Crystal Palace final – and what made it all the worse was that Newcastle had now won it three times, the most recent being in 1932. Such things are hard to handle in the north-east.

It would be safe to say that the draw for the FA Cup did not cause too many shivers to run down spines on Wearside. Even when Sunderland drew 2-2 with Port Vale in the first game at Roker (a tie that they should have won and would have done so but for extreme carelessness), it did not really make headline news and the feeling was that it was a temporary blip and that the replay would solve the problem.

To avoid a clash with Stoke City, who had also drawn on the Saturday, the replay was at Vale Park on the afternoon of Monday, 13 January. The pitch was frozen hard but there was nothing unplayable about it. Sunderland were without Clark, Hastings played when he perhaps ought not to have done after an injury in the first match, Jimmy Thorpe in goal had an uncharacteristically poor game, but there was no real excuse to lose 2-0 to a team at the bottom of the Second Division. Perhaps they believed in 'bogeys' and 'jinxes'. The news was greeted with incredulity in Sunderland (and indeed everywhere else) and the Wearsiders became the laughing stock of Britain for a spell, and when the team arrived back home on the Tuesday they were famously greeted with 'stony silence' by the porters and the ticket collectors at Sunderland station.

There were now fears of a total collapse, and clearly Johnny Cochrane had a major problem in rallying his men. Stoke then visited Roker five days later and in a somewhat undistinguished performance, Sunderland won 1-0 through a Sandy McNab goal with the poor crowd more interested in the decline and imminent demise of George V. The monarch duly died within 48 hours and was properly mourned. Little did Sunderland realise that there would soon be another more intimate funeral in the most tragic of circumstances.

Sunderland had a week of enforced leisure on 25 January because it was an FA Cup day (Port Vale lost 4-0 to Grimsby Town), and their next game was on 1 February when Chelsea were at Roker. It was not a pleasant match in any sense. The weather was unpleasant, tackles were hard, a Chelsea player was sent off, but the main talking point was the curious performance of Jimmy Thorpe. Normally very reliable, Thorpe was responsible for all three Chelsea goals in the 3-3 draw. He misjudged a swinging corner for the first, was badly out of position for the second, and the third was the most inexplicable of all when he ran into an opponent and ignored the ball as it entered the net. The crowd stood and gawped at all this. Amazement soon turned to anger, team-mates looked upon Thorpe in bemusement and puzzlement and the press the following day united in condemning him using words like 'atrocious' to describe his goalkeeping. It was openly asked if Thorpe had had any dealings with bookmakers in recent days.

Those who had lambasted Thorpe must have felt very small indeed as the truth emerged. On the Monday it was reported that he was ill and out of the squad for the trip to Leeds in midweek to play a re-arranged game. The *Sunderland Daily Echo* recalled an incident when Sunderland were leading 3-1 and in a goalmouth scrimmage Thorpe received a severe kick over his left eye. It may have been that he was dazed and stunned by that injury, and this would explain his strange performance in the later stages of the game.

All this was true, but there was also the complication that Thorpe was diabetic. Diabetes was not well understood in the 1930s but it was known that it could make some other illnesses and injuries all the more difficult to deal with. Nevertheless, it was confidently believed that Thorpe would recover. But in the meantime, reserve goalkeeper Matt Middleton was chosen to go to Leeds.

Late on Monday night Thorpe's injuries took a more serious turn and he was taken from his Whitburn home to the Monkwearmouth and Southwick Hospital with a high temperature, severe vomiting and delirium. It was on the afternoon of Wednesday, 5 February 1936 that the scarcely believable news broke of his death at the age of 22.

The Sunderland players were in Leeds when they heard the news. They already knew that their projected game at Elland Road had been postponed because of a frozen pitch (presumably it would have been off in any case with the news of Thorpe's death), and the team, rather surprisingly, did not come home but moved to Stockport to prepare for their game against Liverpool on the Saturday.

Thorpe left a widow and a three-year-old son. His father lived in Cleadon and he and his family lived in Whitburn at 134 Millfield Terrace, so he was very much a local boy. Quiet, inoffensive and unpretentious, he also played cricket for Jarrow, and he was well known and well loved. He was buried the following Monday at Jarrow Cemetery. It was one of the biggest funerals ever seen there with Gurney, Middleton, Hastings, Johnston, Shaw and Murray acting as pallbearers.

The inquest held on 14 February criticised the referee for his 'lax' control of the game, and came to the conclusion that Thorpe's death was 'speeded by rough play'. It was scant consolation for anyone that the laws of the game were subsequently changed to prevent players trying to kick the ball when it was in the possession of the goalkeeper. It was one of Sunderland's saddest days.

It is curious how little-known and little-mentioned this is in the annals of the club. It is in total contrast to a similar incident in Scotland less than five years earlier when John Thomson, the Celtic goalkeeper, met his death in a game against Rangers on 5 September. This incident, famous in poetry and song, could not be more widely known and mentioned in Scottish football culture whereas the equally sad case of Jimmy Thorpe is hardly known, even among Sunderland supporters.

The parallels are not exact, of course. Thomson was carried off and died in hospital a few hours later, and the opponents were Rangers. It was a total accident and not even the most rabid of Celtic fanatics said anything other than that. On the other hand, according to the inquest in the Thorpe case, there were people with blood on their hands. It was not an accident, yet the result would not necessarily have been fatal if it had not been for Thorpe's pre-existing condition.

Possibly the comparative lack of fuss made about Thorpe says a great deal about the stoicism and phlegmatic nature of the north-east. Thomson, on the other hand, played in Scotland for a team with many supporters of Irish descent. Both the Scots and the Irish tend to have martyrs in their culture, and Thomson, a brilliant goalkeeper, clearly fitted that bill. But Thorpe too was a brilliant goalkeeper and his loss was a serious blow to the club. When Sunderland duly won the league at the end of the season, Thorpe had played enough games to have received a medal, and one was duly presented to his widow. It still remains a shame that his memory is not better commemorated.

But life must go on. Indeed, the best way of getting over grief is often to do what the deceased would have wanted. In Thorpe's case that meant winning the title. On Saturday, 8 February with Matt

Middleton in goal Sunderland won 3-0 at Liverpool, leading the writer in the *Liverpool Echo* to remark that they were to be compared with the 'team of all the talents' of the 1890s and that their forward line in particular was superb. 'Whatever eulogy I pay the Sunderland side would not be high enough,' the journalist wrote. A crowd of 34,000 were in silent agreement with this assessment as Gurney scored twice and Gallacher once with Middleton not called upon to do very much.

Sunderland now had 41 points and were seven ahead of their nearest challengers, as confidence slowly began to grow among the supporters that the league title was theirs. A week later they were back in Lancashire at Ewood Park, on an FA Cup Saturday, and this game was not given the prominence in the press that it perhaps deserved, but the 1-1 draw at a difficult ground was once again considered a good result. Gurney scored a wonderful goal, and although Sunderland survived a last-minute appeal for a penalty, the draw was considered to be good enough

Grimsby were then at Roker on Wednesday, 19 February, having caused more than a few problems earlier in the season and not only for Sunderland. They were a very unpredictable side and the local press kept on warning Sunderland of the dangers of complacency. In heavy rain which reduced the crowd to little more than 7,000 (it was a working day for most people in any case) it was the diminutive Davis who scored a couple of goals from the right-wing position which he had now won back from Duns. Gurney inevitably scored the other in a 3-1 win. The weather meant that the pitch was heavy, and this game might have gone wrong, but the result was generally greeted with a sigh of relief rather than anything else.

Wolverhampton Wanderers were next up on the Saturday. The weather was colder, but the north-east seemed to have escaped the worst of the snow and ice which caused the postponement of quite a few games elsewhere. As against Grimsby, Sunderland's centre-half was a newcomer from the Midlands called Cecil Hornby. It is a shame that this man did not get more of a chance with the Wearsiders – he played only 12 games – but he was a utility player only deployed when, as in this case, Jimmy Clark and Bert Johnston were injured. He certainly did not let the team down on this occasion.

It was a competent rather than a brilliant performance by Sunderland, whose 30,000 crowd went home satisfied with yet another step towards the title. Carter scored twice and Davis once, and when they were 3-1 up, they decided to contain Wolves rather than try to score more goals. Not everyone approved, but then again championships are won more often by the grinding out of a result rather than spectacular, champagne football.

The following Saturday was 29 February, Leap Year Day, and it was a disappointment as Preston North End beat Sunderland 3-2 at Deepdale. The visitors came up against a nippy forward line which now featured two Scottish brothers called O'Donnell, Frank and Hugh. They had never been a great success with Celtic but were clearly relishing life in Preston and exposed weaknesses in Sunderland's defence to such an extent that the Monday's *Sunderland Daily Echo* was compelled to claim that 'The Defence is Not Up To League Requirements' in a headline. This was a fairly sweeping statement and aimed mainly at full-backs Tommy Morrison and Alec Hall.

It was, however, a little unfair and seems to have been a knee-jerk reaction to what was a disappointing last minute-defeat. But there were other extenuating circumstances as well. There was a suspicion of offside about the second and third goals, and the third one in particular clearly came after 90 minutes had come and gone. In addition, Preston had clearly raised their game. They were a fast-improving side and a little over 21 months later they would meet Sunderland in the FA Cup Final.

In addition, one feels that the critics were not allowing the defence time to recover from the shattering events of earlier in the month, particularly the intimate and close understanding that is required between defenders and goalkeeper. Matt Middleton would prove himself a great stopper. He probably was not quite as good as the late Jimmy Thorpe but he was good enough.

In any case, the league table showed that Sunderland were eight points clear of Huddersfield with 11 games to go. It meant that they could afford to lose four of them before having to worry about any late charge from either Huddersfield or Derby. And although there may have been questions about the defence, no one either in Sunderland or even in London (in the national press) questioned the midfield or the attack with Carter in particular held in great admiration.

Carter was pivotal to Sunderland in 1936. He was articulate, intelligent and quite simply a great player who was so complete in his abilities. He could win the ball in midfield, carry it forward, distribute it and the thing that particularly earned him praise was his willingness to shoot from distance. Naturally such shots do not always work, but the crowd will always forgive a near miss.

Spring, as often, was slow to arrive, but March saw four games, none of which was an outstanding success and one of which was an inexplicable disaster. The first match in March saw the arrival of Everton at Roker

Park, and a good crowd of 20,000 were there to see it. Everton were, of course, one of the big names of English football, although in 1936 they were 'in remission' as it were from winning honours. They had won the FA Cup in 1933 and would win the First Division in 1939, and of course they had as centre-forward that charismatic character Dixie Dean, arguably a little past his best by now, but still a potent goalscorer.

The game was officiated by a curious character called Mr Pinkston, who seemed to have forgotten the elementary precept of refereeing, namely that of keeping a low profile. The crowd comes to see players, not referees, but Mr Pinkston seemed to enjoy giving lectures and warnings to players, sometimes for innocent tackles and all delivered with extravagant hand gestures which singularly failed to impress the supporters or the press.

Sunderland's defence similarly failed to impress anyone in the second half after Hornby had been taken off with an injury. Carter was brought back to help the defence, and he was no defender. Sunderland were three up with goals from Duns, Carter and Gurney but the lead slipped and a point was lost as the game ended 3-3.

It is always disappointing to lose a three-goal lead, and the Roker Park crowd were far from happy with what they had seen, even if there had been extenuating circumstances of the injuries in the defence. On the other hand, there was still a comfortable cushion at the top of the table, and a point against the mighty Everton side of the 1930s was hardly a huge disaster. It was also true, however, that nerves were beginning to play a part in the Sunderland squad. The title had not been won since 1913, some 23 years earlier, and fans were getting anxious.

There were other reasons for anxiety too. That was also the very day that Hitler marched his troops into the demilitarised Rhineland in blatant contravention of the Treaty of Versailles. Opinion was divided on what to do, but history suggests that a strong response at this time from Britain and France might have put the Austrian upstart with the funny moustache and who didn't like Jews in his place. But the western powers dithered. Hitler was not, after all, invading anyone else's country, merely claiming back his own 'like moving furniture about in his own house' as someone fatuously claimed. The lack of response sent out a signal to Hitler, and he was all the more keen to try other things in the future. But surely there couldn't be another war?

A trip to Sheffield Wednesday came next, a city that was close enough for Sunderland supporters to make a day trip to, and a few hundred left by train in the early morning and returned at night. They saw a game which was quiet and slightly disappointing, but the 0-0 draw gave Sunderland another point on the way to the league title, and it did at least quieten some supporters who were calling stridently for changes in the defence. As it happened, Murray and Johnston returned and both played well. Up front Sunderland had genuine bad luck on a couple of occasions, but the 0-0 draw was satisfactory. Derby lost at the same time but Huddersfield won and the gap was now seven points with nine games to go.

But then Sunderland hit a serious wobble. On the day of the spring solstice, 20,000 at Roker Park watched in amazement as relegation-threatened Brentford appeared and comprehensively won 3-1. There were two possible explanations – one was the absence through injury of Carter. That was bad enough but the dubious decision was made to replace him with Cecil Hornby, who was himself possibly not 100 per cent fit and in any case was a defender rather than a forward. The other factor was the obvious and well-publicised appearance of a large contingent of Scottish selectors to watch the Scottish players with a view to selection of the team to play England at Wembley on 4 April. In the event none of the Sunderland Scots was chosen (although Alex Hastings was nominated as a reserve) and the game showed why. But the other side of the coin was that the presence of the Scottish top brass may well have put undue pressure on the players. Ironically, David McCulloch of Brentford was chosen as centre-forward, presumably on the basis of his performance at Roker. But that was in preference to Jimmy McGrory of Celtic who scored 50 league goals that season.

And yet Sunderland were not totally outplayed. Losing 1-0 for a long time, they came back with 15 minutes to go with a good header from Duns and looked for a time after that as if they might have earned at least a draw, but then within the last five minutes 'slackness in the Sunderland defence' allowed McCulloch to score twice and send the crowd home unhappy. To a certain extent, Sunderland were let off the hook when Huddersfield also lost to Stoke, a fellow called Stanley Matthews scoring the only goal of the game.

This was clearly not league-winning form, and worse was to come the following week. We all know that derby games are a law unto themselves. Such is the passion for bragging rights that the 'lesser' team often raises its game, and the 'stronger' team is under more pressure. Such a thing happened at Ayresome Park when Middlesbrough delighted their ecstatic but incredulous supporters by beating Sunderland 6-0.

It reminded the old-timers of the events of 5 December 1908 when Sunderland beat Newcastle 9-1, and then Newcastle went on to win the league. This

258

time it was the other way round, and frankly it defied analysis. Sunderland had no excuse in terms of injuries or player availability, or even the outrageous refereeing of the notorious Mr Fogg of Bolton who added his own piece of vindictiveness to the Sunderland fans who had made the short trip in great numbers.

Sunderland were already 5-0 down when Carter was sent off. It was a shockingly bad decision, and the press were unanimously of the opinion that the referee had simply got it wrong. Carter and Middlesbrough's Brown collided with the ball wedged between the two of them. Carter kicked the ball against Brown, and Brown fell down, hurting his knee on the ground on the way. Mr Fogg saw something deliberate in this, and in spite of impassioned appeals from even some of the Middlesbrough players, the famously sporting and gentlemanly Carter was ordered off. Dignified as always, he went without a word. Davis, less gentlemanly, 'allowing his indignation to overrun his discretion', expressed his opinion to Mr Fogg and joined Carter on the long walk.

Carter was totally innocent and would be exonerated, but this incident couldn't mask an awful performance from Sunderland who were more like relegation candidates than title winners. But yet again, they were lucky in that Huddersfield and Derby continued their self-destruction obsession by dropping points. Derby drew and Huddersfield lost, leaving the Wearsiders six points ahead of the Rams. It was as well that a strong challenger did not emerge, otherwise Sunderland might have been in trouble.

Nevertheless, even without that – which led to the press asking the question 'Why does no one want to win the league?' – tension mounted on Wearside all week until the game against Portsmouth stopped the rot and eased the pressure. It was the day of the England v Scotland international at Wembley, a 1-1 draw, so the Sunderland match took second place in the eyes of the newspapers, but it was a 5-0 win at Roker Park. In the same way as Roker devotees can easily become too depressed after a bad result, they can also forgive immediately after a good performance, and see their team as world beaters. It was the debut of 18-year-old Johnny Mapson in goal to replace the scapegoated Matt Middleton, but he had a very quiet game as Connor (twice), Gallacher, Gurney and Carter (from the penalty spot) made victory very emphatic. Derby lost again to make the margin eight points with six games to go.

Five points would now do it. Conventional wisdom said the league championship would be decided over the Easter weekend, and so it turned out. Sunderland entertained Birmingham City on Good Friday, then travelled to Bolton on Black Saturday and kept travelling to St Andrew's for their return fixture on Easter Monday. Recent form had galvanised the support as 41,000 crowded into Roker on Good Friday, and quite a lot of fans were now talking about going to Bolton or Birmingham over the weekend.

Good Friday was dull and unpleasant with a cold wind blowing from the east, but the large crowd did at least see a victory. It was far from a great game, but at that stage such things were not important. The 2-1 victory was the main thing, even though Sunderland should have scored a lot more. Carter's propensity for shooting from a distance for once let him down with so many shots being caught in the capricious wind and carried over the bar. The two goals came from Patsy Gallacher, one in the early stages of the game and the other which looked, even to the Sunderland newspaper reporters, distinctly offside. Birmingham's goal was a good one from Harris, but supporters were delighted by the 'neat and proper' goalkeeping of young Mapson.

There was little time for celebration for the players who had to travel down to Bolton for the following day's game. By the time they reached the station they heard the further good news that both Derby and Huddersfield had continued their poor form by both drawing. This meant that Huddersfield were now out of it, although Derby could in theory overtake

Sunderland. But five games remained and one win would do it.

It looked as if it might happen at Burnden Park for Carter scored in the first minute. But Sunderland lacked captain Alex Hastings, and were distinctly nervous against a good Bolton team who immediately equalised and then scored a winner in the second half to the immense disappointment of the sizeable travelling support, who had hoped to cheer the champions. It still could have happened for the Wearsiders, but Derby beat Leeds 2-1.

It was a cold Easter Monday, 13 April, at St Andrew's before a miserable crowd of 15,000 when Sunderland eventually did it. It was as if they said 'Enough of this nonsense' and won 7-2. Gallacher was injured, Carter was moved to inside-left and the ever-adaptable Cecil Hornby was brought in at inside-right. Hastings was still out, so the team read Mapson, Morrison, Hall, Thomson, Johnston, McNab, Davis, Hornby, Gurney, Carter and Connor. Leading 3-2 at half-time, including Hornby's first goal for the club, Sunderland turned on the style in the second half and Gurney ended up with four goals, with one each from Carter, Connor and Hornby.

Sadly not a great many Sunderland supporters saw that game, but when the team arrived back in the early evening of the Tuesday the town came to a standstill, as a coach drove them from the station to Roker Park. The trophy was presented after the entertaining 4-3 win over Huddersfield on the Saturday to Hastings, who had still not recovered from his injury and had been unable to play.

The triumph was greatly celebrated and rightly so, for in spite of rather too many wobbles in the latter stage of the season, the play of the team had been something to be proud of with a fine half-back line, and excellent goalscorer in Bobby Gurney and a really outstanding player in Raich Carter.

The celebrations went on for some time. Sunderland's triumph was very popular in Scotland, less so in Newcastle (although it did make a point to the Geordies that there really was no excuse for them languishing halfway up the Second Division), but there was also a strong north v south element here. The London clubs, Arsenal in particular who won the FA Cup that year, were perceived as wealthy, patrician and snobby (the reality was quite different, for London was by no means as affluent as it was portrayed in the north) and it was good that a northern club could break the stranglehold that Arsenal had held over the title for the past three years.

But amid the celebrations there were causes for concern. Unemployment, although clearly receding, was still there (this autumn would see the Jarrow

Crusade), Mussolini had now laid waste to Abyssinia in a despicable piece of bullying, Hitler kept making enough noises to worry even the American press, and, talking about the American press, what were all these rumours about the new King 'having it off' (in that vulgar American phrase) with an American divorcee? The British journalists kept quiet about it – and that too was worrying.

The medals were presented, and how nice it was for one to be given to May Thorpe, the widow of Jimmy, the Sunderland hero who was unable to take part in the celebrations. Yet he was there in spirit. It was just as well that those who celebrated the sixth league championship in 1936 did not know that nearly 100 years later, there has been no cause to repeat the celebrations for a title.

7

FA Cup Winners 1936/37

'UNEASY LIES the head that wears the crown!'
This famous quotation from *Henry IV, Part 2* was
appropriate in at least two contexts in late 1936. In the
first place, in the real sense of the 'crown', there was
a new King on the throne, the third of the year. King
George V had died in January and had been replaced
by King Edward VIII.

Sadly he had been deposed or had decided to
abdicate (depending on one's take) in December
before he had a chance to be crowned, and he had
been replaced by his younger brother King George VI.
George VI certainly was 'uneasy' in that he was never
intended to be King, never wanted to be King and
was never prepared for it. He was shy, stammered a lot
and was totally reliant on his pushy, extrovert, 'pain
in the neck' Scottish wife who for all her faults was
very protective and loving of her husband, and always

managed to say 'No, thank you' when the inevitable offers from other men came her way.

The same could not have been said about Wallis Simpson, the lady friend of King Edward VIII. She was already twice divorced, American, and not in the slightest bit royal. She was clearly unacceptable, but the irony was that sexual relations would not have been a problem. After all, the royal family having mistresses was hardly unusual, and she could have quite easily slipped up the back stairs as countless others had done. The problem was that Edward wanted to make her Queen. This was clearly impossible in 1936 when pompous clerics held sway, and Edward was given a stark choice – the throne or the American lady. He chose love.

The good people of Sunderland whose lifestyles could not have been more different from those of the House of Windsor were as fascinated by this as anyone else. Generally speaking, women tended to be critical of Edward giving everything up for this American who possibly did not merit the term 'whore' in the strictest sense of the word, but was certainly experienced in the ways of the world, whereas men were more sympathetic to the honesty of the King who had on several occasions at least seemed aware of the problems of the unemployed.

It mattered not. By early December, Edward and Wallis had gone (sadly to consort with Hitler on occasion) and the town settled down to the other 'uneasy head that wore the crown', namely Sunderland AFC. Because they were the champions everyone wanted to beat them, but in a very exciting and always interesting title race, Sunderland were at least holding their own, staying very much in the mix, and even after their defeat by Preston North End on 2 January 1937 they were only three points behind leaders Arsenal. Manchester City, who would end up winning the First Division, were ninth. It was a very fascinating chase.

As far as Sunderland were concerned, the problem was inconsistency, and as well as that there was a clear division between form at Roker Park and elsewhere. Eleven games had been played at home and there was a 100 per cent success rate. On the other hand, of the 13 played away, nine had been lost – and this was clearly not the form required if the title was to be retained. On the other hand, it was hardly a problem confined to Sunderland and there was still time to rectify matters, but most supporters were of the opinion that as long as the draw was fair in providing a few home games, this might be the season in which the Wearsiders could have a go at the FA Cup.

There had been a few changes in personnel from the previous season. Local boy George Collin had joined from Derby County in the summer of 1936, and was playing impressively at left-back and on the left wing. Eddie Burbanks had begun to challenge Jimmy Connor for a place. Alex Hastings was still the captain although suffering from injuries and losing out to fellow Scotsman Sandy McNab, and the devastating inside trio of Raich Carter, Bobby Gurney and Patsy Gallacher were still in position.

Other than the soap opera of the abdication crisis in December, which at least provided entertainment (albeit the sniggering, salacious tee-heeing of those who pretended to be shocked), world affairs had taken a serious turn for the worse in that war had returned to Europe. Spain had stayed remarkably aloof from the carnage of the First World War, preferring its own internecine bloodshed which had come to a head in July 1936 when the Spanish Civil War began. It was basically a military coup which went wrong initially and took nearly three years to resolve, and this time although Great Britain and France stayed neutral, the Soviet Union backed up the stricken republic while Germany and Italy muscled in on the side of the right-wing rebels, the basic purpose being the opportunity to try out their weapons, and to give their armies and air forces a rehearsal for the big show that was coming. It was a sinister development.

In such circumstances football often becomes more important, so that people can have something to take their minds off the horror of the approaching cataclysm. The FA Cup started as far as Sunderland were concerned on 16 January 1937. There was a mystique about this competition, now on its third trophy, which had begun in 1872 and had run unbroken (apart from the Great War) since then. It had never been to Sunderland. The closest had been the great season of 1913 when they had lost 1-0 to Aston Villa in a controversial final at Crystal Palace in the same year that they won the First Division. This had deprived Sunderland of an FA Cup and league double, and it still hurt.

What hurt even more was that while Sunderland had never won the trophy, near neighbours Newcastle United had done so on three occasions in 1910, 1924 and as recently as 1932, and they had not been shy about telling everyone about it. The league championship of 1936 had to a certain extent redressed the balance, but Sunderland were still FA Cup virgins.

In the autumn of 1936 Sunderland stayed in the news and registered a fine success in the Charity Shield when they beat Arsenal 2-1 at Roker Park. This was at the end of October and had been Sunderland's first success in this tournament. A month earlier there had been an unofficial British championship game at Celtic Park when the league champions of Scotland and England played each other. Celtic won 3-2, but it had been a close game.

Mid-January is often a somewhat depressing time of year, but the whole of the north-east was lit up with the thought of the FA Cup, even though everyone was travelling south. Sunderland had the longest trip – to Southampton, a distant but still accessible city – while Newcastle were at Preston, Middlesbrough at Wolverhampton Wanderers, and even non-league Spennymoor United, who had done well to qualify, were at West Bromwich Albion. Carlisle United were at Swansea Town – not yet City – and Darlington were at Dartford. There was therefore a dearth of football for the local fan to go and watch, but Sunderland encouraged everyone to go and see their reserves play Middlesbrough reserves and dangled a carrot by saying that the score at Southampton would be announced every half hour, and the reserve match would kick off quarter of an hour later, so everyone would leave Roker knowing the score.

Sunderland's team left on the Friday morning to stay at Bushey in Hertfordshire, accompanied by some supporters. Apparently 400 went – a large away crowd for 1937 – but the majority of them travelled by overnight train to London, then to Southampton. A few went by coach, a particularly tedious form of travel in those pre-motorway days.

Sunderland had shown a sign of ambition by signing Jimmy Gorman from Blackburn Rovers. He was a Liverpudlian who could play at either right-back or right-half, and was rumoured to have cost £7,000. He was not, however, able to play at Southampton because he had not been signed on time.

Formed as a church team in 1885, hence their nickname of the Saints, Southampton played at a ground called The Dell which would not have been familiar to many Sunderland supporters or players. At the time sitting towards the bottom of the Second Division, Southampton had not been without their moments in the FA Cup in the past, reaching the final in 1900 and 1902, and the semi-finals twice in the 1920s. The bookies' favourites for this game were Sunderland to an overwhelming extent, but the Wearsiders and their fans were still haunted by their exit the previous season to Port Vale.

The weather, as often is the case, was considerably milder on the south coast, but it had been no drier, for heavy rain had fallen overnight and the pitch was likely to be a heavy one. In these circumstances, the decision was made that Carter, struggling with an injury obtained in the previous week's draw with Arsenal at Roker, should not be risked, and that his place should be taken by Cecil Hornby. This was a blow for Sunderland and a disappointment to the record crowd of 30,380, an increase of some 2,000 on the previous high, and at least double Southampton's average. It was a record that was likely to stay 'until Sunderland come again' according to an official of the south coast club.

Both teams would normally wear red and white vertical stripes, and in accordance with FA Cup rules, they both had to change – Southampton to pale blue and Sunderland to white. The teams were:

> Southampton: Scriven, Sillett, Roberts, King, Henderson, Kingdon, Summers, Neale, Dunne, Holt, Smallwood.

> Sunderland: Mapson, Hall, Collin, Thomson, Johnston, McNab, Duns, Hornby, Gurney, Gallacher, Connor.

> Referee: Mr Blackhall, Wednesbury.

Mr Blackhall was in fact the third-choice referee. The first had been given another tie because he lived too close to Southampton and the second had called off because of flu, but Mr Blackhall was both neutral and healthy and was generally agreed to have performed well. But there was a certain doubt about the game in the morning. At about sunrise at 8am the pitch was flooded and play would have been impossible. By noon, however, the rain had stopped and a squad of men were out with spikes. This was a success and then parts of the pitch were sprinkled with sand. Things were good enough for Mr Blackhall to sanction play, although conditions were far from ideal. Acting captain Bert Johnston won the toss and chose to play with the watery winter sun behind him and with the benefit of what little wind there was.

There was even some sunlight as the game kicked off, and it was soon very clear that Sunderland meant business. The busiest person on the field was Scriven in the Southampton goal, and Sunderland were two up by half-time. The first goal came within the first five minutes and was the result of a crisp move involving Connor and Gallacher to set up an easy tap-in for Gurney. The second came about midway through the first half and again involved Gallacher, who picked up a ball from Duns and slipped it through to Hornby who hammered home from a distance, giving Scriven no chance. To their credit Southampton fought back but without making any headway, and the half-time whistle sounded with Sunderland well on top.

Twenty minutes into the second half the game looked over when Sunderland scored again. This time it was Gurney who made it and Gallacher who scored with what the *Sunday Sun* described as a 'peach of a shot' which went in just below the bar. Great was the rejoicing among the Sunderland supporters whose accents made their presence obvious, and some of the local support were heard to say that the visitors would go on to win the cup.

But then Southampton fought back. Almost immediately, left-back Collin slipped and allowed Holt to pull one back. That seemed to be a fair consolation for the hard-working Saints, but then with only a few minutes to go, Bert Johnston similarly slipped as he was trying to turn and this allowed 'Ginger' Dunne to pass to Summers, who ran on and put the ball past the advancing Mapson.

This made it 3-2 and the large crowd, who had previously shown signs of heading homewards to escape the intermittent but still fierce showers, came to life again to roar on their favourites to an unlikely draw and a potential trip to Sunderland on the Wednesday. Meanwhile, anxiety began to creep into the raucous northern voices, and they would not have been human if they had not begun to suspect that this might have been another 'fix' for a big gate. But Sunderland's defence rallied and managed to retain their footing for the remaining ten minutes, and there were no further scares or alarms as they finished well on top as deserved winners.

It was a good night for the Sunderland players, and the long journey home for the supporters was made all the sweeter by the news that Preston had defeated Newcastle and that Wolves had hammered Middlesbrough 6-1. It is a sad fact that football fans do enjoy the discomfiture of their local rivals, and in this sense, 16 January 1937 was a good day for Sunderland fans with only Darlington of the north-east teams along with them in the draw on the Monday.

It was the evening edition of Monday's *Sunderland Daily Echo* which trumpeted the news that Sunderland would have to travel again. The good news was that it was the winners of the Blackpool v Luton tie, both of whom were at lower levels, Blackpool doing well in the Second Division and Luton in the Third Division South. Both would eventually be promoted at the end of the season, but it was generally believed that Blackpool would win through.

Naturally Sunderland were represented at the replay at Bloomfield, although the main party were still at Bushey preparing for their league game at Brentford on the Saturday. They were surprised to see Luton emerge winners and impressed by the skill that the Third Division side showed. They were under no illusions. Saturday, 30 January 1937 at Kenilworth Road would be no easy task even though the opposition were two divisions beneath and had no FA Cup pedigree to speak of. They did, however, have a charismatic manager from the north-east and not unknown to Sunderland fans by the name of Ned Liddell. He had been on Sunderland's books away back in 1904 but had never quite broken into that fine Wearside team. The town of Luton itself was not exactly close at hand, but it was nearer than Southampton and quite a few Sunderland supporters felt that they wanted to go there.

The weather was atrocious all over Britain. Sunderland itself had been hit with heavy snow and high winds – the worst storm since 1901, it was claimed – but in Luton, further south and well inland, the conditions were different, although no less severe. There was four inches of frost, it was claimed, and a very thick fog but the game was allowed to go ahead. It was immediately clear from the moment that the first ball was kicked that the conditions were going to be a great leveller, and that the playing ability of so many of the Sunderland men would be no great advantage.

The teams were:

Luton: Dolman, Mackey, Smith, Finlayson, Nelson, Fellowes, Hodge, Sloan, Payne, Roberts, Stevenson.

Sunderland: Mapson, Gorman, Hall, Thomson, Johnston, McNab, Duns, Carter, Gurney, Gallacher, Connor.

Referee: Mr J.H. Whittle, Worcester.

The reporter from the *Sunderland Daily Echo* was concerned that he might not see the end of the game because of fog, but it actually cleared a little as a light breeze sprung up, and Luton, on winning the toss, opted to play with the wind. The crowd was 20,134 with about 400 from the north, and from an early stage, it was clear that Sunderland were finding it very difficult to get going. New signing Jimmy Gorman in particular was finding things difficult, and half-time was reached with Sunderland two goals down. It looked as if a shock exit was on the cards. Roberts of Luton had scored twice (the second looking offside), and Sunderland's forwards never really looked as if they were going to fight back. The score, when relayed back home, was greeted with stunned silence, and everyone began to remember the calamity of Port Vale.

The first 15 minutes of the second half saw much of the same with Sunderland simply not really able to make any impact on the game, but in the meantime, almost imperceptibly, a subtle change was taking place in the weather. The wind had brought some rain and a slight thaw dispersing the mist, and consequently Sunderland were able to get more of a grip, and slowly the half-back line gained control of the midfield.

In the 60th minute they grabbed a goal back. Jimmy Connor crossed from the left, the ball was parried by the goalkeeper out to the other side of the goal where Carter sent it back in for Connor to make the score 2-1, and to breathe new life into Sunderland. The second goal some ten minutes later also saw heavy involvement from Connor, who once again made ground and crossed. Once more the goalkeeper did not save the ball cleanly, and this time it was Len Duns who scored.

After this, Sunderland took control and really should have scored more, but they were also very lucky in the last minute when Payne of Luton missed an open goal from six yards. Matters were adjourned until 2.15pm at Roker Park on the following Wednesday, the early kick-off to allow for the possibility of extra time. The general feeling was that Sunderland had been lucky to get off with a draw, although there had been extenuating circumstances of weather and a tricky pitch. The prevalent view, however, was also that the Third Division team had had their chance and that Sunderland would win comfortably in the replay.

'Argus' in the *Sunderland Daily Echo* pulled no punches, saying that Sunderland were lucky, defensive problems remained and that only Mapson and Johnston saved them from defeat. He indulged in a prolonged moan about the Kenilworth Road press box, 'a long glass fronted cage' which did not afford him a good view of proceedings, but from what he saw, he thought that Luton were a good side and that they were some distance above the Third Division.

The build-up to the replay was encouraged by the better weather that appeared. Sunderland's players arrived back on Sunday, were given three hours to go home, but then they returned to the Roker Hotel for training and getting together. Luton, without some players who were part-time, arrived on the Monday, were seen walking along the beach at Whitburn while manager Ned Liddell talked to all and sundry in his Wearside accent and looked up a few old friends. A huge crowd was expected, and attendance would often involve a few excuses about 'sore backs' and 'grandmother's funerals' at embarrassing interviews the following morning.

Wednesday, 3 February 1937 turned out to be a good day in Sunderland, although there was always the chance of fog. A crowd of 53,200 attended with the Main Stand and the Clock Stand End particularly well patronised and a little swaying on the terracing when things got exciting. It was as if the town had stopped for this replay, and the players responded well to that. They were further encouraged by the state of the pitch which was soft, possibly too soft and inclined to cut up, but nevertheless encouraged Sunderland's close passing style of play.

Sunderland, rather to the surprise of some supporters, kept the same team whereas Luton made one change.

The selections were:

Sunderland: Mapson, Gorman, Hall, Thomson, Johnston, McNab, Duns, Carter, Gurney, Gallacher, Connor.

Luton: Dolman, Mackey, Smith, Finlayson, Nelson, Fellowes, Rich, Sloan, Payne, Roberts, Stephenson.

Referee: Mr J.H. Whittle, Worcester.

Luton won the toss and decided to play with what little wind there was towards the Fulwell End. The game would turn out to be a very unfortunate one for Connor on the left wing, as from the start he was subject to quite a few fouls from the Luton defence who had clearly targeted him as the danger man after his performance in the first match.

It was from one of these fouls that Sunderland took an early lead. Goalkeeper Dolman, who had never been totally convincing at Kenilworth Road, punched a ball that he really should have clutched and it fell to Duns who had the easiest of tasks to put Sunderland one up before some of the latecomers had managed to get into the ground. A minute later, Luton had equalised when with Sunderland's defence unaccountably missing for a long cross, Payne levelled the scores. All this was within the first ten minutes.

But this was a more purposeful Sunderland team and with the full backing of the crowd who were relishing the positive approach, after 17 minutes they took the lead and on this occasion, they held on to it. The goal was a fine one, manufactured in midfield by Gallacher who released Duns. He then made ground and crossed for Gurney, who dummied the ball as defenders crowded in on him and left it for the unmarked Connor to crash home.

Luton fought back, but this time the defence was secure with newcomer Gorman in particular looking well up to the task, and the first half finished with Sunderland playing confidently, the only problem being the fairly obvious injury to Connor. But in 1937, there were no substitutes and Connor simply had to continue.

The second half was just like the first and remained a very open game with both teams having chances, but gradually, as the half wore on, Sunderland's wing-halves Thomson and McNab took more control. It was not, however, until with only three minutes to go that Raich Carter finally settled the issue with a fine drive after a rebound from a Luton defender. The full-time whistle came, and although many of the plaudits were given to Luton, more were given to Sunderland who now knew that they would face Swansea Town – who had needed a replay to get the better of York City – at Roker Park on 20 February.

The one negative point of the game was undeniably the injury to Connor. It certainly looked bad, and Connor was possibly unwise to continue playing, but no one realised just how serious it really was. It effectively ended the career of the likeable Paisley 'buddy' who had followed manager Johnny Cochrane from St Mirren to Sunderland. Like most players he had good games and bad games, but when he was good, he was really very good. It was hard to identify which particular tackle did the damage, but Luton were culpable in that there had been a series of challenges on Connor. If anything good came out of this, it was that it opened the door for Eddie Burbanks.

In the meantime, it was probably true to say that Sunderland were slowly slipping out of the First Division title race. It was still very open but Sunderland were now ninth after a trip to Goodison Park, admittedly with an injury-weakened side, where they lost 3-0 to Everton and Dixie Dean. Charlton Athletic of all teams were at the top of the table with Brentford, Portsmouth and Middlesbrough not far away. And the eventual winners, Manchester City, were still well below them.

But Sunderland had not given up and before they played Swansea they registered two good home league victories – against Bolton Wanderers on Wednesday, 10 February and Huddersfield Town three days later. The game against Bolton ended in a convincing 3-0 scoreline played in front of a poor crowd (because it was a working day) but the visit of Huddersfield was a far tighter affair with the Yorkshiremen possibly a little unlucky not to get a point in a tight 3-2 win for Sunderland. The crowd of 24,000, however, left happy, feeling that their league challenge had been resurrected and looking forward to the visit of Swansea, who had that day lost at home to Doncaster Rovers and who were closer to the bottom of the Second Division than they were to the top.

The game against Swansea did go down well with 'Mirror' of the *Sunday Sun*. Clearly in a curmudgeonly, grumpy mood, he even moaned about the size of the crowd, yet 48,500 to see a First Division v Second Division game on a windy day does not seem to be outrageously bad. The quality of the game he was similarly unimpressed with, calling it 'the poorest and the most lacklustre Cup tie I have seen for several seasons' and referring to 'the non-constructive wrecking tactics of the Welsh side'. He suggested that the Swansea attitude was that we cannot beat Sunderland, so we will just do what we can to make things difficult, on the grounds that we might just be able to get a replay.

'Mirror' clearly did not have a good experience at Roker Park that day, but Sunderland and the crowd did, and the only really important thing was that the Wearsiders walked off the pitch at the end, knowing that they were in the last eight of the FA Cup.

The teams were:

Sunderland: Mapston, Gorman, Hall, Thomson, Clark, McNab, Duns, Carter, Gurney, Gallacher, Burbanks.

Swansea: Moore, Lawrence, Caldwell, Harris, Leyland, Lloyd, Lewis, Warner, Brain, Williams, Lowry.

Referee: Mr A. Taylor, Wigan.

Swansea played with the strong wind in the first half but did not make a great deal of the advantage, and at half-time the game was still goalless. The second half was all Sunderland and once they scored their first goal, it was more or less all over. The goal was described unfairly as 'scrappy', but in fact it was a good striker's goal by Gurney, who managed to get the ball past the central defender and the goalkeeper from a cross by Gallacher. That was in the 52nd minute. Half an hour of constant Sunderland pressure followed until a brilliant diving header from Duns following a Burbanks corner. That more or less finished the game, and in the last minute Sunderland scored a third goal. It was an own goal when Caldwell tried to put a Burbanks cross out for a corner and diverted the ball into the net. On the run of play the final score should have been a great deal more than 3-0, but no one really bothered too much about that.

The evening papers (or the radio, an increasingly common phenomenon on Wearside in the late 1930s) told supporters that Sunderland would be joined by Arsenal, Preston, West Brom, Millwall, Manchester City and the winners of the replays between Grimsby Town and Wolves, and Everton and Tottenham Hotspur. There was nothing there that was impossible, it was felt, and a genuine air of optimism was around.

The draw was made at lunchtime on the Monday and Sunderland were drawn away to the winners of Grimsby v Wolves. The other ties were West Brom v Arsenal, Millwall v Manchester City and Tottenham or Everton v Preston. The opponents turned out to be Wolves, and although no one minimised the dangers involved, the general feeling was that it could have been worse. Molineux was a fine pitch to play on and Sunderland often did well there. They had met Wolves twice before in the FA Cup, losing in 1905 and winning in 1891.

Wolves had a good FA Cup pedigree, and indeed they were looked upon with a certain amount of affection for their winning of the trophy in 1908 when they beat Newcastle United in the final at the Crystal Palace during the glory years of the Geordies. It was a remarkable final won 3-1 by Wolves, who were halfway up the Second Division at the time, and all the goals were scored by men whose names began with the letter H – Hedley, Hunt and Harrison for Wolves and Howie for Newcastle. (Billy Harrison's wife had also presented him with triplets that very morning.) The result was greeted with undisguised joy on Wearside, for the noisy neighbours were becoming just a little too overbearing. Wolves had also won the FA Cup in 1893 and by now were in the First Division but had not yet crossed Sunderland's path, being due to do so both home and away at the Easter weekend.

Before the quarter-final Sunderland had two league games, one of them of crucial importance to north-eastern bragging rights and not without significance either for the title race. This was a re-arranged fixture against Middlesbrough at Roker on Wednesday, 24 February which was won decisively, 4-1, with a hat-trick from Carter. This fired up the supporters but the flames were soon doused when they went to West Brom on the Saturday for a game that was rich in goals and good football, but Sunderland came off second best. Scoring four goals away from home was good especially when done by four different men – Gurney, Duns, Carter and Burbanks – but the loss of six goals simply had to lead to serious questions being asked about the defence.

This result meant that Sunderland, who could have been within touching distance, were still five points off leaders Charlton. Retaining the league title was not 100 per cent out of the question but the team that was now making the most progress was Manchester City. But such matters were put on the back burner until such time as the quarter-final was dealt with. Surprisingly, in spite of losing six goals in the West Midlands, the announcement was made that the defence was to stay the same against Wolves.

The team had gone to their headquarters at Bushey for a couple of days before the game at Molineux, and oddly and ironically enough they were joined there by Preston who were preparing for their game against Tottenham Hotspur. But poor Johnny Cochrane was indisposed. A soaking on the golf course led to a cold and a recurrence of an old chest complaint, while it was reported that Wolves were treating their players to a brine bath.

All this stuff was eagerly devoured in the newspapers and more than 1,000 fans were preparing to make the trip from the Wear to the Midlands, while those who attended the Sunderland A v Washington game at Roker were, as was now the custom, promised an update every 15 minutes, with that game kicking off at 3.15pm so that it would finish with everyone knowing the score in both matches.

The weather on 6 March was acceptable but the ground was described, with a touch of hyperbole one feels, as a 'sea of mud'. A crowd of 57,751 assembled (and paid a combined £4,278) with the Sunderland directors all wearing red carnations and Sir Walter

Raine, the chairman, wearing a club-coloured scarf, and many red and white rosettes spotted in the crowd. Community singing was heard including the national anthem, a few First World War favourites, and 'Pennies from Heaven' (the 1936 hit by Bing Crosby), but the *Sunderland Daily Echo* marked sardonically that there was no 'Blaydon Races' because Wolves had 'apparently never heard of it'.

This crowd, huge though it was and a record for Molineux, was incredibly not the highest attendance of the day as 64,815 were nearby at The Hawthorns to see West Brom v Arsenal, while Spurs v Preston attracted a barely believable 71,013 to White Hart Lane, such was the passion for football, particularly the FA Cup, in the late 1930s. The economic depression had now clearly gone, money was around and the product was worth going to. There was in addition another dynamic at work, the notion that it was possibly a good idea to enjoy life as and when one could. It did not take a genius to work out that the international situation was deteriorating badly, with daily reports of what was happening in Spain a potent reminder of what could soon happen to the rest of the world.

The teams were:

Wolves: Gold, Morris, Taylor, Wharton, Cullis, Gardiner, Smalley, Galley, Clayton, Jones, Ashall.

Sunderland: Mapson, Gorman, Hall, Thomson, Johnston, McNab, Duns, Carter, Gurney, Gallacher, Burbank.

Referee: Mr G. Twist, Lancashire.

Mr Twist, inevitably called 'Oliver' by the fans, had a good game, and he needed to for there were times when life became a little feisty. He denied Sunderland what seemed to be a clear penalty and had to take the names of Clayton and Johnston, but deserved credit for keeping a lid on things.

It is not often that a team which earns a draw and a replay suddenly finds itself the favourites for the tournament but that was precisely what happened here. The reason for this was the other ties. In each of the three of them, the team that one would not have expected to win did so. West Brom beat Arsenal ('the Throstles are Chirping' said the press), Preston won at Tottenham and most amazing of all, Millwall of the Third Division South beat the strong-going Manchester City. Sunderland and Wolves drew 1-1 and the impetus was now with the Wearsiders. Or was it?

Wolves scored first towards the end of the first half after a little hesitation from centre-half Bert Johnston, and after half-time a little anxiety could be detected in the ranks of the Sunderland team and supporters, but the players stuck manfully to their job, and in the 70th minute they earned their equaliser. It was scored by the young Newcastle lad Len (sometimes called Leslie) Duns, who had begun to impress on the right wing. His goal was described as 'the goal of a veteran scored by a youth' as he cut in from the right with the ball and scored just as three defenders converged on him.

Sunderland now piled on the pressure. Duns had another chance, a strong claim for a penalty was denied when Gallacher was brought down inside the box, and one or two other efforts were saved by Gold in the Wolves goal. For Sunderland, Sandy McNab at left-half was immense as indeed were Gallacher and Carter, and they were unlucky not to earn a win. But the cynics looked at the huge crowd and reflected that there were compensations in the draw. The cynicism was hardly dispelled when it emerged that arrangements for the replay were already in place.

The Monday draw for the semi-final gave Sunderland the additional boost of the news that they were to play Millwall at Hillsborough if they beat Wolves in the replay. An unchanged team was announced for the replay, which was to kick off at 3pm, but the doors were to be opened at 1pm and season ticket holders had to claim their seats by 2.15. There was almost an assumption – a dangerous one – that Sunderland, who had admittedly played very well at Molineux, were already through to the semi-final with newspapers like the *Daily Herald*, *Daily Express* and *The*

Times all expressing admiration of how well they had performed. In the meantime, the King's Theatre had obtained a film (with sound) of the game at Molineux and had invited the players to a private showing before releasing it to the public.

But the 'big bad wolf' still had to be beaten, and as excitement reached fever pitch in Sunderland, Wolves quietly slipped into town. People talked about superstitions around wearing lucky coats and rosettes, and great was the speculation about how the pitch would play. No one ever knew what the ground conditions or the weather would be like in March, usually the most unpredictable meteorological month of the year. The final would be played at Wembley on 1 May that year – and it was tantalisingly close.

The attendance given was 61,796. Snow had fallen in the morning, but was melting in the watery sunlight of reluctant spring. This actually had a positive effect on the attendance for in the shipbuilding industry with labour on a quasi-casual, piece-work basis, some of the dockers could not work and went to the football instead. Other firms bowed to realism and made arrangements with their workers to re-arrange shifts, and basically all roads led to Roker Park. A few hundred visitors had arrived from the Midlands but they were hardly noticed in the sea of red and white favours, and the decision to lock the gates at shortly after 2.30pm was a wise one.

Sunderland kept the same team as in the first match, but Wolves made a few changes. The line-ups were:

Sunderland: Mapson, Gorman, Hall, Thomson, Johnston, McNab, Duns, Carter, Gurney, Gallacher, Burbanks.

Wolves: Gold, Morris, Taylor, Smalley, Cullis, Gardiner, Jones, Galley, Clayton, Thompson, Ashall.

The referee was once again George Twist, and when he blew his whistle, the weather had changed for the better with all the snow melted. Wolves opted to play into the Fulwell End. The first half kept the huge crowd on their toes, but there was too much tension in the air to allow classy football, and the opening 45 minutes finished goalless with neither side able to claim any advantage.

The second half was much the same with Sunderland having the balance of play but unable to convert the pressure into goals. Tension increased, and then with about five minutes to go the huge crowd were hushed into silence when Gorman, who had already made a few errors, was caught out of position and Galley tried a cross-cum-shot which deceived Mapson.

All now looked bleak for Sunderland, and some of the huge crowd at least thought that the cause was lost and that they were fated never to see Wembley. A few people were seen to be trickling towards the exits as Sunderland's pressure became more and more desperate. A header by Carte was punched out by Gold, then the goalkeeper saved another header from Duns, before with virtually the last kick of the ball, Thomson found Gurney on the edge of the box with his back to the goal. Gurney then proved just what a great player he was by swivelling and shooting low past Gold. It was afterwards claimed that the roar of relief was heard in Newcastle and even in Scotland, and that ships in the North Sea stopped, thinking it was the outbreak of war. That was hyperbole, but the relief could not have been more noticeable. The crowd, which had gone silent, suddenly came to life again as total strangers hugged each other in the sheer joy of the occasion.

But there was still extra time to be faced. Normally extra time was slow and leaden-paced with two exhausted teams able to produce little in the way of exciting football and basically playing out time for another replay a few days later, in the days before penalty shoot-outs. This game was an exception, for Sunderland, now buoyed by their late equaliser, found new energy and after four minutes went ahead when Duns scored after a corner taken by Eddie Burbanks. This might well have killed Wolves off if Sunderland had been able to hold on to their lead just a little longer, but once again Gorman was beaten to the ball, Ashall managed to send it across to Thompson and to a 'public library' silence at Roker Park (other than the Wolves fans) the Midlanders were back on level terms.

At this point exhaustion took over, and both sides more or less went through the motions. Although Gold was by some distance the busier keeper, Sunderland were unable to take advantage of their midfield superiority and convert it into goals. Wolves centre-half Stan Cullis, who would one day be a very successful manager of the club, was outstanding against Carter and Gurney, but everyone was happy when Mr Twist called it a day. Sunderland had had 80 per cent of the play but could not force a win.

The third game of this wearying tie was scheduled for the neutral venue of Hillsborough on Monday, 15 March. Sunderland had a league match at Portsmouth on the Saturday, and for this game their directors made a decision which split the support. They dropped five players – Hall, Johnston, McNab, Carter and Gallacher. Some, they claimed, were injured, but others quite clearly weren't and they were being kept for the replay. Sunderland's weakened team played quite well but lost 3-2 (their first defeat to Portsmouth for a long time) and this result probably saw them kiss goodbye to their chances of winning the title. Whether one agreed with their decision or not, there were no further injuries and the team that ran out at

Hillsborough was the same as the one that finished the replay at Roker Park.

Wolves actually beat Chelsea at Stamford Bridge that day, and were not without their backers in the press on the Monday morning. Sunderland, who had stayed in London after their game at Portsmouth, travelled through a lot of bad weather with wind, sleet and snow and found Hillsborough to be a heavy ground on which silky football would have been difficult. The teams were:

> Sunderland: Mapson, Hall, Gorman, Thomson, Johnston, McNab, Duns, Carter, Gurney, Gallacher, Burbanks.

> Wolves: Gold, Morris, Taylor, Smalley, Cullis, Gardiner, Westcott, Jones, Clayton, Thompson, Ashall.

> Referee: Mr G. Twist, Lancashire.

The conditions, although very muddy, seemed to be better for Sunderland. They ran out very comfortable 4-0 winners with goals from Gurney, Carter, Gallacher (the latter two coming in the vital period just before half-time) and Charlie Thomson's late penalty. The *Sunderland Daily Echo* told that strains of 'Blaydon Races' were heard – a song that was more traditionally associated with Newcastle, but with one or two subtle changes of words and geographical terms it was adopted by Sunderland fans as well. Everyone left the ground wondering why it had taken them so long to book their spot against Millwall, the first Third Division team to have reached the FA Cup semi-finals.

The trains going home that night contained quite a few very happy but now impoverished supporters, some of whom, having pushed their luck by taking a day off the previous Wednesday, now faced dire consequences for having done the same again on the Monday. Not that it mattered, however, compared with the fact that the team were now 'a step nearer their ambition' as 'Argus' in the *Sunderland Daily Echo* put it. The same 'Argus', having been very critical, sometimes unfairly so, in the past about some players – his treatment of Gorman in particular sometimes bordered on persecution – now trumpeted what a fine team Sunderland had, and how they stood on the verge of their first FA Cup Final since 1913, they were now going to Wembley for the first time and how with a side with players like Carter, Gurney and Gallacher up front and a fine goalkeeper like Johnny Mapson, it was difficult to see a team like Millwall beating them.

Millwall, sixth in the Third Division South, did not seem to be a major threat to Sunderland's ambitions. But, contrary to popular belief, situated in a heavily populated area of south-east London, they did not lack support, and they were on a high following their recent and rather amazing defeat of Manchester City in the quarter-final. City were destined to win the First Division that season, but frankly that had not looked very likely at The Den that day when Dave Mangnall had scored the two goals for Millwall to put Charlie Hewitt's men into the semi-final.

As far as Sunderland were concerned, the title now became something of an irrelevance to their FA Cup ambitions. It was still mathematically possible to repeat their triumph of 1936, but realistically it was not likely to happen. Players were given a rest now and again, new moves were tried out, there was a fairly obvious desire to avoid injuries, and the team at Wolverhampton on Easter Monday was not far off the reserve side. Sunderland's form was not actually all that bad with two wins and a draw in five games, but what really mattered was 10 April at Leeds Road, Huddersfield, the day of the semi-final against Millwall whose results and form were now watched with unprecedented interest on Wearside.

The outside world continued to be ominous. Everyone was looking forward to the coronation of King George VI in May, but the elephant in the room that would simply not go away was Hitler and Nazi Germany. Already Spain was being devastated in a war of appalling brutality, and everyone was aware that the last time Sunderland reached the FA Cup Final in 1913, a war followed soon after. Something similar seemed to be happening here.

The *Sunderland Daily Echo* on Friday, 9 April reported that an aeroplane had flown from Tokyo to London in 94 hours, a remarkable achievement, but an aeroplane seemed to be about the only method of transport not being deployed to convey Wearsiders to Huddersfield on the Saturday. Special trains were leaving from as early as 6am, buses were being used as well and, a sign of the times, information appeared in the newspaper about where you could park your car. There were also advertisements from fans looking for car owners and offering to pay half the petrol for a lift. Car ownership was still out of the question for most working-class families, but it was within the pocket of the emerging and growing middle class in the increasing prosperity of the late 1930s. It was no longer the province of the eccentric and the over-wealthy upper classes.

Sunderland's chairman Sir Walter Raine would not be there as he was still recovering in a Newcastle nursing home from a major operation, but his wife would be present sporting a rosette of red and white carnations, as indeed would manager Johnny Cochrane. Sir Walter, however, would follow the game with great interest, although surprisingly there does not seem to have been any 'live' commentary on the radio, the only football programme being *Sporting Sketches* where Tom Cragg would give an eye-witness account at 6.50pm of what he had seen at Huddersfield.

The team were staying at Harrogate overnight, and would be attending the theatre on the Friday. Sunderland station was a busy place that Friday morning with loads of well-wishers seeing everyone off and shaking hands with Raich Carter and Bobby Gurney in particular, for they were the players who would surely score the goals that would send Sunderland to Wembley.

Millwall had received a boost with the news that Dave Mangnall, their centre-forward, had returned from injury, but Sunderland were without their excellent red-haired left-half Sandy McNab. He would be missed but there was an excellent deputy handy in Alex Hastings, who had been replaced as captain by McNab.

The teams were:

Sunderland: Mapson, Gorman, Hall, Thomson, Johnston, Hastings, Duns, Carter, Gurney, Gallacher, Burbanks.

Millwall: Yuill, E. Smith, Inns, Brolly, Wellbanks, Forsyth, Thomas, Burditt, Mangnall, McCarthy, J. Smith.

Referee: Mr G. Davies, Lancashire.

A crowd of 62,813 were there, with Sunderland supporters possibly making up 40,000 of them, and they saw a surprisingly even game for teams who were two divisions apart. There was no problem with the weather, but the pitch was almost barren of grass. It made for a good surface though, and the players were able to get a good grip with their studs.

Rather to the surprise of most of the crowd, it was Millwall who scored first and a rather brilliant goal it was as well from their star striker Mangnall. A long ball from Inns found McCarthy, who headed on to Mangnall who 'pulled the ball down and in the same movement put it into the net'. The smartness of Mangnall's action had the Sunderland defence 'well beaten'.

Sunderland's reply on the half-hour mark was something rather brilliant from Gurney. Yuill in the Millwall goal saved from Carter and was able to push the ball to out the right. It looked to be going for a corner but Gurney chased and managed to screw the ball into the net from an angle that looked well nigh impossible. The roar that greeted the goal was loud and lasted for minutes with some people gawping in astonishment. Half-time was reached with the score 1-1, but Sunderland were by far the better team, even though Millwall were furious about a penalty that they felt they should have got.

It was more of the same in the second half except a little more so, and the winning goal came from Gallacher when he headed in a Thomson free kick. It was not a particularly fierce header but the ball bounced at just the wrong time for Yuill, and the goal was enough to win the tie for Sunderland. Millwall tried hard but Sunderland were just that little bit faster to the ball, the Londoners' only chances coming when Johnston cleared off the line with Mapson beaten, and when the ball later dropped on to the crossbar before Gorman got it away.

In the other semi-final played at Highbury, Preston beat West Brom 4-1 to set up an exciting final on 1 May. Nothing else really mattered in Sunderland until then. The league title had been given up, and even Raich Carter's international appearance for England v Scotland was usually cloaked in sentences like 'I hope he doesn't get hurt'. That was on 17 April and Scotland's 2-1 win at Hampden was watched by 149,415, then a week later the Scottish Cup Final between Celtic and Aberdeen was watched by 147,365 – these are the official figures but the general feeling was that there were an awful lot more in both cases, such was the popularity of football in 1937.

Plans for the coronation to be held on 12 May were going ahead, and frequently in those days one would see demonstrations and invitations to young men to join the International Brigades to go to Spain to fight 'against the rising Fascist tide'. The reasons for all this became apparent on Monday, 26 April when Hitler's Condor Legion fighting on the Fascist side completely obliterated the inoffensive Basque town of Guernica in a chilling demonstration to the whole world of just what German aerial power could do. It had its effect at Munich in 1938 when Britain and France were bullied into giving away most of Czechoslovakia.

But in Sunderland, the FA Cup was the thing. Tickets were not easy to come by, but those who could go made their plans. It would be the first time that so many of the Sunderland supporters had ever been to London, let alone Wembley, and the excitement was tangible. League form had been dismal. There was a win over Liverpool, but there were also a couple of awful away defeats at Grimsby and Leeds, which would in normal circumstances have hurt deeply, but no one seemed worried. The important thing was that everyone was to be kept fit for Wembley.

The *Sunderland Daily Echo* of Tuesday, 27 April, which also reported the horrendous bombing of Guernica, also revealed that there would be 24 special trains running from the north-east, a couple of which were very early on the Saturday morning but most were on the Friday night. There were various warnings about counterfeit tickets, but the main story that would have attracted Sunderland fans was the marriage of Raich Carter to Rose Marsh in Derby with Bobby Gurney as the best man. The honeymoon, however, would have to wait until after the final.

Wednesday's newspapers also reported that Sunderland, who were staying at Bushey, had more or less made up their mind that Alex Hastings would be the unlucky man to drop out in favour of Sandy McNab, and that they had won the toss for the lucky dressing room number one which apparently had housed all the winners since 1923. The Thursday had nothing new except a fictitious story – of the type that is frequently concocted in FA Cup Final week – of Johnny Cochrane being offered a job at Tottenham Hotspur for the following season, and Friday was totally dedicated to stories like the 'Ha'way' train (as in Ha'way the Lads) leaving Sunderland with fans on board, and how the *Sunderland Football Echo* would be printed on pink paper if the Wearsiders won, and would be available in London on Saturday night for celebrating fans.

With such hysteria going on, it must have been a relief to get away to Wembley. One set of players got a less-than-happy send-off, however – those of Celtic. They had won the Scottish Cup the previous week, and as a reward they were taken to the FA Cup Final. This necessitated the overnight sleeper train from Glasgow

Central Station, and playing their irrelevant league game at Motherwell on the Friday night before departure. They had possibly been celebrating too much and lost 8-0 to Motherwell, their record league defeat. Admittedly their goalkeeper was injured and so was another defender, but they were still a chastened lot when they arrived in London on the morning of the final.

Celtic probably would have been supporting Preston, because the two O'Donnell brothers, Frank and Hugh, had recently played for them, but on the other hand it would have been difficult for anyone of the Celtic persuasion not to support a team which had a man called Patsy Gallacher in it. But there was no lack of Scotsmen on the park – five for Sunderland and seven for Preston, and both managers, Johnny Cochrane and Tommy Muirhead, were from north of the border as well. Two of the Preston players would go on to become famous managers – Bill Shankly and Andy Beattie. Shankly, of course, became the legendary boss of Liverpool in the 1960s and 1970s, whereas Beattie was the first Scotland national team manager, who earned a certain notoriety for resigning in the middle of the World Cup of 1954, claiming that he was not being allowed to do his job because of people at the SFA interfering all the time.

The preliminaries at Wembley were almost as nerve-wracking as the game itself with all the community

singing of 'Abide With Me' and other favourites, and
then the appearance of the King at his first final as
the monarch. Unlike some others, George VI was a
genuine football fan and had, apparently, been looking
forward to attending this game for a few weeks. He
had with him King Faroukh of Egypt, a man reputed
among other things to have had the largest collection
of pornography in the world.

Of all things, there was a bus strike in London
that day, something that might have caused a few
problems for the fans, but they all seemed to get there
in time and the stadium looked a resplendent sight.
The teams were:

> Sunderland: Mapson, Gorman, Hall,
> Thomson, Johnston, McNab, Duns, Carter,
> Gurney, Gallacher, Burbanks.

> Preston: Burns, Gallimore, Beattie, Shankly,
> Tremelling, Milne, Dougal, Beresford, Frank
> O'Donnell, Fagan, Hugh O'Donnell.

> Referee: Mr R.G. Rudd, London.

It was the classic 'game of two halves'. Frank O'Donnell
scored for Preston just before half-time to give them
a deserved lead, but then Sunderland gradually took
control and scored their three goals with precision and
accuracy. They were on level terms when Carter headed
a ball out to Burbanks, who crossed for Gurney to head

home from close range after 51 minutes. The next 20 minutes saw Sunderland gradually attain supremacy and in the 72nd minute Carter, having miskicked just previously, collected a ball from Gurney then flashed a low drive past the Preston goalkeeper in a lovely piece of clinical finishing. About ten minutes later, after good work from Gurney and Carter, the ball came to Eddie Burbanks, who scored with a lovely shot from the edge of the box.

There was now no doubt. Sunderland had won the FA Cup, and Colin Veitch, hero of Newcastle United 30 years earlier, and by this point writing for the *Sunday Sun* was fulsome in his praise, 'It has been weary waiting for directors, players and supporters, but it was a glorious victory when it came.' As often happens, there was the air of unreality (and often the real fear that it has all been a dream and that we are about to wake up) as Carter collected the trophy from the Queen, who apparently asked him how his new wife was. He was then carried shoulder-high by his players.

It was a popular triumph and the press were universal in saying that Sunderland deserved their victory for their second-half performance. They were such a superb team. The wing-halves were often the key men in any team and here Sunderland excelled with Charlie Thomson and Sandy McNab. The forward line had no weaknesses in it with Carter one of the best players in the world on his day, and although there had been a few criticisms of the full-backs, they both played well at Wembley. A special word was saved for young goalkeeper Johnny Mapson, who celebrated his 20th birthday the day after the final and who had taken over the position in such dreadful circumstances following Jimmy Thorpe's death.

Chairman Sir Walter Raine was still ill and unable to attend but Alderman Fred Taylor, one of the directors, sitting next to the Queen in the directors' box, had to apologise for getting too emotional when Sunderland scored, but the Queen replied that he was so animated that he was scoring more goals than the players.

The new Mrs Carter had not seen much of her husband since the wedding, and had a job finding him after the game until someone took her to Broadcasting House where he was being interviewed. It was only then that she and 'Rate', as she called him, were reunited. London was described as a 'splash of red and white' and fans sang and danced until well into the night. Street dancing, 'the likes of which had not been seen since the Armistice', was reported in Sunderland as well.

The players arrived back home on the Monday night, having been greeted in Newcastle ('Even the ranks of Tuscany could scarce forbear to cheer') by the mayor and his wife, and the trophy was taken to

Roker Park to be paraded there. These scenes were unparalleled in local history, and winning the FA Cup was celebrated with even more intensity and fervour than the league championship the previous year.

Naturally Sunderland talked about nothing else for the rest of the summer with even the following week's coronation taking second place. It was naturally hoped that this might lead to more sustained success on Wearside but sadly it did not. The 1937/38 and 1938/39 seasons were disappointments, and then the war came along. The 1950s were characterised by plenty of good players like Len Shackleton and Charlie Fleming but no great team. Sunderland were no strangers to relegation, either, and their great rivals Newcastle, after a purple patch in the FA Cup in the early 1950s, shared in the mediocrity which spread relentlessly and remorselessly over the region, with everyone talking nostalgically about '37'. It was only after the digits of 37 reversed to 73 that things changed, and even then only temporarily.

8

FA Cup Winners 1972/73

THE FIRST few months of 1973 have been well documented and relentlessly devoured by Sunderland fans since that heady peiod. There can be very few who cannot tell you about Ian Porterfield's goal, Jim Montgomery's double save and Bob Stokoe's trilby hat, and no doubt there will be those who watched the game on TV who will try to tell you that they were there at Wembley that day. As the years pass, they have more chance of getting away with lies like that. And they can be readily forgiven, for by 1973 the miracle of television (and the intense coverage of the FA Cup Final on both BBC and ITV) meant that everyone was part of the experience.

The year must be seen in its context. Since the Second World War (there is little point in denying it) the history of Sunderland had been miserably disappointing. There had been great players – Len

Shackleton was undeniably the best, but there had been many others whose names one could reel off – and many great matches, but the crucial point was that nothing had been won to add to the triumphs of 1936 and 1937, now many years in the past. A major war had taken place, the National Health Service had been established, there was a welfare state, everyone now had a television and many working men had cars – but Sunderland supporters had had little to cheer about with even the unthinkable fate of relegation happening on more than one occasion.

And of course there was Newcastle United. However, much as one hears comments like 'I don't care about them' and 'They are nothing to do with us', the fact remains that the fortunes of Newcastle are followed with equal passion on the Wear as they are on the Tyne – with of course the obvious difference that the Mackems want to see Newcastle defeated.

Most of the time they got their wish, but Newcastle won the FA Cup on three occasions in 1951, 1952 and 1955. These triumphs went down like a lead balloon in Sunderland, and no one ever believed the 'it's good for the area' sort of vacuous nonsense that local politicians and newspaper columnists were forced to come away with. Newcastle had their disasters and relegations as well, but in 1969 they had actually won a European trophy. This was the Inter-Cities Fairs' Cup, and although Sunderland supporters were not slow to point out that it was not the European Cup which Celtic and Manchester United had now won, it was nevertheless a great triumph for the Geordies – and a constant source of massive pain for Sunderland.

It was hardly a coincidence, given the tangible depression on Wearside, that the year after Newcastle's European triumph saw Sunderland's second relegation in 1970, and frankly since then in spite of what the newspapers of the time insisted on calling 'loads of bubble and squeak' or as the vulgar put it 'piss and wind', the Mackems had not really looked like getting back to the top flight with only a few things to make life happier for them, like for example Newcastle's exit from the FA Cup in 1972 to Hereford United, something that was celebrated with inordinate, vicarious happiness on the streets of Sunderland.

But for Sunderland the word 'doldrums' didn't even begin to cover the depression. When Bob Stokoe took over in November 1972, the team were fourth from the bottom of the Second Division and heading inexorably towards the hell of another relegation. Although we are talking about professional footballers and managers who (apparently) cared about little other than money, there was nevertheless an element of the local hero returning to save the sinking ship in all this, and

Stokoe's appointment was greeted with not exactly joy and ecstasy, but a certain amount of anticipation and interest. Some were disappointed that Sunderland had not gone for the controversial, unlovable, familiar but also undeniably successful Brian Clough.

Born in 1930 in Mickley, near Prudhoe, Stokoe had impeccable north-east credentials for the job. Originally a Sunderland supporter, he had played most of his career for Newcastle, his famous moment being the 1955 FA Cup Final when he was part of the half-back line alongside Jimmy Scoular and Tommy Casey which played such a large part in beating Manchester City, for whom a man called Don Revie played. Stokoe's impressive Newcastle past was largely forgiven by the Mackems who were more interested in his managerial career with a variety of clubs, most recently Blackpool, who had won a competition called the Anglo-Italian Cup. This tournament has long ago been relegated to its deserved obscurity but it was at least something for a Blackpool team who had never really got over the departure of the great Stanley Matthews. Stokoe was happy enough at Blackpool, but when the call came for him to return to the north-east, he could not resist it. Like so many other people who have gone south, he always looked out for the results of Sunderland and Newcastle first when he put on the television or got his Saturday night newspaper.

When appointed prime minister in 1940, Winston Churchill knew what his task was. Another prime minister, William Gladstone, was said to have been chopping down a tree when he received his invitation. He allegedly put down his axe and said, 'My mission is to pacify Ireland.' Stokoe's mission was quite simply to save Sunderland from relegation. If anyone had talked about the FA Cup, it would have been along the lines of 'a good cup run would be nice' or 'always a chance of the big money if we could draw someone like Manchester United'. The ambitions would be no more than that.

In general terms, the town of Sunderland was not doing as well as other parts of the United Kingdom. There had certainly been a general improvement in everything since 1945 but the economic boom of the 1960s had been less pronounced in the north-east than elsewhere. Inflation was a problem, and the early 1970s saw a Conservative government generally picking fights with the unions under the guise of fighting inflation, while the real problem was caused by people who called themselves the 'gnomes of Zürich' and who organised runs on the pound when they felt like it in order to make more money for themselves.

Stokoe understood all this, but his immediate concern was the rescue of Sunderland, which he succeeded in doing. He actually had two triumphs in

1973. One was the FA Cup, and the other was the way that he not only saved the team from relegation, he effectively rocketed them up the table to such an extent that it was widely stated that if he had been with Sunderland all season, the team might have challenged for the title.

And how did he do that? He did it simply through strength of character and maximising what is now called 'new manager bounce'. Symbolically, he changed the strip so that the team wore traditional black pants rather than the more snazzy white ones, but he also managed to motivate a few players who had seemed to be less than totally committed to the somewhat dictatorial, brash and unbending ideas of Alan Brown. It took time. There were still a few bad results in late 1972 and there was a flu epidemic to cope with as well, but gradually points began to be picked up in tandem with the FA Cup run, the support began to get more animated, and at a comparatively early stage, relegation ceased to be an issue.

Normally a cup run can have an adverse effect on league form with players often accused of not trying in league games lest they miss out on cup ties and big bonuses. This did not happen under Stokoe. The players soon recognised a man of their own stamp, and the supporters did too. One occasionally heard ignorance from the terraces about Stokoe being a 'Geordie bastard' – but then again one must never expect too much intellect from some supporters – although this soon stopped in the wake of some good results.

The third round of the FA Cup sent Sunderland to Notts County. County were managed by Jimmy Sirrell who had started his career playing for Celtic as long ago as 1946. He was not the most dynamic of managers – indeed he seemed far too nice for the job – but he had done well for Notts, who were now a respectable Third Division team. As Notts had home advantage, this was a good draw for them against a poorly placed Second Division side.

The game was played on 13 January. The weather was dull and cold, but the pitch was playable and 15,142 attended – far more than the Meadow Lane average and clearly supplemented by a fair amount of Sunderland supporters who perhaps realised that if they wanted to watch their team in an FA Cup game, they would be as well to take every chance that they could.

The teams were:

Notts County: Brown, Brindley, Worthington, Masson, Needham, Stubbs, Nixon, Bradd, Randall, Mann, Carter.

Sunderland: Montgomery, Malone, Bolton, Tones, Watson, Ashurst (McGiven), Horswill, Kerr, Hughes, Porterfield, Tueart.

It was generally agreed that Sunderland were lucky to get off with a 1-1 draw, which earned them a replay at Roker on the Wednesday night. Notts County, who took an early lead, should have scored a few more before Dave Watson earned a late equaliser with a header at the near post from a free kick. Goalkeeper Jim Montgomery made one spectacular save and quite a few reasonable ones, and Notts had reason to feel hard done by as far as Lady Luck was concerned.

There were, of course, those who would claim that a draw and a lucrative replay was what the game was all about in any case, but in truth, even if County had won, it would not have been the greatest of shocks, nor would it have attracted a great deal of attention other than on Wearside. Sunderland were paying the price of mediocrity, that of being ignored by the rest of the country. The big talking point would have been the defeat of Manchester United, going down 1-0 at Wolverhampton Wanderers, while locally Newcastle won but Middlesbrough bit the dust.

But it was all eyes on Roker Park on Tuesday, 16 January for the replay, and a large crowd of 30,033 turned up, taking advantage of a cold but reasonable night for mid-January. The start of the year was by no means a bad winter, and was also something of a lull on the industrial front. There were miners' strikes in 1972 and 1974, but the winter of 1972 and into 1973 saw nothing other than sabre rattling, albeit an awful lot of it. The crowd was Sunderland's largest for some time and showed two things. One was that the club had a huge potential and latent support, and the other was that they were now beginning to be prepared to show a little trust in Stokoe. He was worth a go, at least, it was felt.

Stokoe made a few changes from the first match, mainly positional, but Jackie Ashurst was out and the team read Montgomery, Malone, Bolton, Horswill, Watson, Tones, Kerr, McGiven, Hughes, Porterfield and Tueart, while County remained unchanged. The 'Roker Roar' was heard for the first time in a while that night, but the game was a dour battle with, if anything, County the better team until half-time with an excellent performance from Don Masson, the man who in later years would become the hero of Scotland in 1977 as the team reached the Argentina World Cup – and then the villain in 1978 when they got there.

But the second half changed all that. It was as if Sunderland took inspiration from the frenzied cries of those wearing the red and white scarves, and they gained control. One of Stokoe's positional switches, described by one journalist as 'thoughtful' – 'inspired' might have been a better word – was the moving of Watson to the forward line, and it was he who broke the deadlock. Ian Porterfield made it by a neat bit of play in the midfield, then captain Bobby Kerr dummied the ball and allowed it to run on to Watson, who was able to angle it across the goalkeeper to put Sunderland 1-0 up.

This fine goal released a certain amount of joy (if not yet delirium) behind the goals and in the stands, but there was still a long time to go yet, and although Sunderland were by now clearly the better team, tension grew as they failed to finish off a stubborn County who, admittedly, didn't look as if they were likely to get an equaliser – but of course you never know in cup football. Time was passing and Sunderland looked in command until with only minutes left Dennis Tueart (Newcastle-born, but no more committed Sunderland player was in existence) managed to lob a ball over the head of the advancing goalkeeper after a neat bit of play on the left.

This late goal sealed the tie and triggered off one of these tiresome pitch invasions which so characterised football in that ugly decade of the 1970s. Yet in some ways it was great to see the enthusiasm of so many young fans. They had never really had very much in their lives to cheer them up, and although a triumph over a team a division below them was hardly a glorious occasion, it was nevertheless a step in the right direction and it gave them something to be happy about. Walking back into town that night with scarves held high was an experience that quite a few of these youngsters would never forget, and the jibes about Stokoe's Newcastle past began to steadily diminish from that point. Reaching the fourth round was at least something.

The following night, in a tie which had been postponed on Saturday, Reading beat Doncaster Rovers 2-0. It was a fixture that had been followed with some interest on Wearside, for it meant the return to Sunderland of Charlie Hurley, one of the club's all-time greats. It had been such a pity that so many of his years with Sunderland coincided with them being in the wilderness of the Second Division. He was now the manager of Reading.

Reading were a Fourth Division side, and it was clear that Hurley would have a lot to do there. Possibly too close to London for their own good, Reading had never been one of the more successful clubs in English football, although they had in the past been in the Second Division, their best season being 1927 when they also reached the FA Cup semi-final. Inevitably in the north, like quite a lot of southern teams, Reading were perceived as being 'soft' and 'effeminate'. Anyone who knew Hurley, however, would have had no doubts that he would have toughened them up.

The Reading game was scheduled for 3 February, and in the meantime, with confidence visibly rising around Roker Park, Sunderland drew at Swindon

Town and beat Millwall at home. This was clearly good enough to get the team well away from the relegation zone, and the word 'relegation' was heard less and less for the rest of the season.

Stokoe's ambition was also seen when Sunderland at last signed Billy Hughes's brother John from Crystal Palace. Sadly it did not work out, but it did send out the signal that the Wearsiders meant business. John had been one of the great Celtic side of the last decade, and stories that Sunderland (and Newcastle) were making bids for him were a common leitmotif of the late 1960s, particularly when he could not always be guaranteed a place in that talented Hoops team. His problem was inconsistency, but on his day he could be a world-beater, and Sunderland fans had seen how good he was in a pre-season friendly at Roker Park in August 1965.

At last John had joined Billy at Roker, but the problem was that he was now an injury problem and his knee gave way on his debut against Millwall, and he never played again. It was a brave effort, though, and it possibly made Billy all the more determined.

A crowd of 33,913 were at Roker Park for the fourth round. There cannot have been many times that Reading had played in front of such an attendance, and it was a bizarre scene with the great reception given to the opposition manager, the scale of which astonished the press. Hurley had indeed been a hero on Wearside,

but even he was staggered by the adulation that he got.
The teams were:

> Sunderland: Montgomery, Malone, Guthrie,
> Horswill, Watson, Young, Hughes, Kerr
> (Ashurst), Porterfield, Lathan, Tueart.

> Reading: Death, Dixon, Youlden, B.
> Wagstaff, Hulme, T. Wagstaff (Butler),
> Cummings, Hunt, Bell, Chappell, Habbin.

Whether it was because of the tremendous reception
accorded to Hurley, no one could say, but Sunderland
seemed overawed by the occasion, and early in the first
half Reading took the lead to the undisguised delight
of their small knot of supporters paying a very rare
visit to the north-east. It was Chappell who scored,
and in spite of determined efforts from the home side,
Sunderland did not equalise until near half-time when
Steve Death didn't handle a cross ball cleanly and
Dennis Tueart was on hand to score what was really a
rather scrappy goal.

But if the Reading goalkeeper made an error there,
he made up for it in the rest of the game. His name
was a gift for the newspaper reporters who could say
things like 'only Death robbed Sunderland' or 'face to
face with Death' and on many occasions in the second
half at that Roker End of the ground, Death defied
Sunderland with great saves from Tueart, Porterfield

and Kerr, some that even elicited a reluctant round of applause from the home support. Like most good goalkeepers as well, he had his fair share of luck in the shape of Sunderland hitting the post and the bar, and being denied by an offside decision late in the game.

Stokoe had shuffled his team around but to no effect, and the large crowd were becoming despondent during the second half until they heard the news that Newcastle were going out of the FA Cup to Luton Town. Radio coverage of games was nowhere like as comprehensive as it is now, but a few score flashes were given now and again, and that result cheered everyone up. But nothing happened to change things at Roker, and the demeanour of Hurley and his Reading men at the end showed just how delighted they were to have earned a draw and to be able to take this tie to Elm Park on the Wednesday night.

The *Sunday Mirror* underneath its rather predictable headline of 'Reading In At The Death' naturally bestowed praise on Death, but while quoting Stokoe about how surprised he was to see how well a Fourth Division side like Reading played, it was also very optimistic that in the replay, Sunderland would be too good for the Royals.

So it turned out. Sunderland won 3-1 at a canter before a crowd of 19,793 which surprisingly contained quite a few visiting supporters on a cold winter night so far from home. Many were London-based, but it still said a lot for them. By this time both teams knew that the winner would be going to either Liverpool or Manchester City (it was Manchester City, as it turned out) in the next round, so there was a great deal of money at stake.

Stokoe was not a man you could keep out of the news for very long. He appointed Arthur Cox as his assistant around this time, and then amazed the support by bringing back Ritchie Pitt to the side. Pitt and he did not see eye-to-eye. Indeed, their falling-out had been spectacularly unsubtle, but suddenly Pitt found himself in the centre of defence. The idea apparently had been to cup tie Pitt so that he couldn't be played against Sunderland by anyone who decided to buy him (Arsenal were said to be interested), but somehow or other, Pitt and Stokoe made it up and without either of them necessarily developing any great affection for the other. Nevertheless, they established a *modus vivendi*; Pitt stayed and played well.

The teams were:

Reading: Death, Dixon, Youlden, Carnaby
(Butler), Hulme, B. Wagstaff, Cumming,
Chappell, Bell, Hunt, Habbin.

Sunderland: Montgomery, Malone, Guthrie,
Horswill, Pitt, Young, Hughes, Kerr,
Watson, Porterfield, Tueart.

Once again the ploy of playing Watson as a forward worked a treat, and it really was a rather easy stroll. Watson, Tueart and Kerr had all scored before half-time – and there should have been more goals – before Reading scored a consolation goal with a penalty in the second half but far too late to challenge Sunderland's lead. The sporting home crowd gave Sunderland some applause, and Hurley – through gritted teeth – wished them all the best, but as it was his old club, the teeth were not all that fiercely gritted. The radio told everyone that Manchester City had beaten Liverpool, and so it was now a visit to Maine Road at the end of the month.

So far so good for Sunderland, but wins over Notts County and Reading were not likely to set the heather on fire. Manchester City would change all that though. They had in recent years emerged to become a top-class side. For too long they had played second fiddle to the charismatic Manchester United, but in three successive years they had won the First Division in 1968, the FA Cup in 1969 and then in 1970 in addition to the League Cup, they had won the European Cup Winners' Cup. Much of this success had come from Joe Mercer, but now his assistant, Malcolm Allison, outspoken, brash and not always likeable, was in charge. They were still a great team, and indeed having defeated Liverpool they were now quoted, along with Arsenal and Leeds United as the favourites for the FA

Cup, a perception enhanced in the eyes of the press by their having been given a home draw against Second Division Sunderland.

Stokoe had once again dipped into the transfer market and come up with a forward: Vic Halom from Luton Town. It was an inspired transfer. Halom scored his first goal in the psychologically significant 4-0 win over a poor Middlesbrough side on 17 February and almost immediately the fans took to him. The win over the Boro was seen by many supporters as a great thing – the usual hyperbolic reaction to a local derby victory followed, and phrases were heard about how Sunderland would 'not disgrace themselves' against Manchester City.

Stokoe took the squad to Blackpool for some intensive training. He was aware that he still had work to do with some of his players who were struggling to cope with him, and he was also aware, having seen both the good and the bad side of this at Newcastle, that team spirit and everyone getting on with each other was so important. Nor was it easy to keep people happy. Transfers always meant that someone would lose his place in the team. And yet it was so vital to keep the fringe players happy. You never knew when you were likely to need them.

The weather on 24 February in Manchester was a factor. It had been frosty, the pitch was hard and had been sanded in places, but the sun was out and it was pleasant enough, if a little cold on this early spring day. Surprisingly, a few miles away on the other side of the city, Manchester United's home game in the First Division was called off, and the result was that the Sunderland support, already impressively large and the biggest away following for some time, was supplemented by some other fans wearing red and white scarves that day. A huge crowd of 54,478, by some distance the highest of the day, assembled at Maine Road.

The teams were:

> Manchester City: Corrigan, Book, Donachie, Doyle (Mellor), Booth, Jeffries, Summerbee, Bell, Marsh, Lee, Towers.

> Sunderland: Montgomery, Malone, Guthrie, Horswill, Watson, Pitt, Hughes, Kerr, Halom, Porterfield, Tueart.

The game was a cracker and full of talking points and incidents with one good goal and one scrappy goal for each side. The other ties on that day were all settled quietly with the expected team winning in most cases, and therefore the Maine Road fixture won the most attention in the media.

When Tony Towers of Manchester City scored from the edge of the box on 15 minutes with a fine, crisp drive, things seemed to be going as planned and as expected. But then one of these irrational things happened when Joe Corrigan and Willie Donachie presented Sunderland's Micky Horswill with a goal. Corrigan took a goal kick and slipped it to Donachie. In 1973, the ball had to travel outside the penalty box before it came into play, and Donachie touched it before it left the area. Rightly the referee ordered a retake, and astonishingly, Corrigan did the same thing again. Horswill, now alert as to what was going to happen, nipped in past Donachie and scored. It was an astonishing piece of folly by Manchester City, but full marks were due to Horswill and no one on Wearside complained.

The second half saw a great Sunderland goal from Billy Hughes after he ran the length of the City half down the left and seemed to have lost the ball to a determined challenge from a defender, but he suddenly cut inside, shot and scored. It was a great individual goal of the kind that John had often scored for Celtic, and Sunderland were now, with time slipping away, 2-1 up and on the brink of a major upset.

That they didn't finish the job was due to a very controversial late equaliser. A Mike Summerbee corner was punched into his own net by Jim Montgomery, when he appeared to have been impeded by the ever-controversial Rodney Marsh. Later in the game, Sunderland received a boost when Tony Towers was sent off after a clash with Horswill. Horswill was rather lucky not to escape a similar fate for his part in this somewhat undignified scuffle, but Sunderland did not quite have the energy to capitalise on their one-man advantage.

It was heartbreaking, but Sunderland fans were reconciled by the thought that they would have settled for a replay at Roker at the start of the game anyway. Back home the decision was taken that the replay was to be all-ticket and with commendable speed (which did little to dispel the 'conspiracy theory' that it was all 'meant'), tickets went on sale on the Sunday morning for the Tuesday night. Queues apparently formed from early in the morning, and some Sunderland supporters allegedly came off their buses and trains and went straight to Roker to join the queue.

The official attendance for the replay was 51,872, but most people were in agreement that the real figure was far more than that. There were always ways of getting in unofficially to matches by bribing gate checkers, climbing walls and printing counterfeit tickets, and these methods were all employed to gain entrance that night. By the time the teams came out on Tuesday, 27 February, everyone knew that Luton at home was the reward.

This game more or less had the stage to itself apart from the odd league fixture, and it enjoyed loads of media coverage. Some journalists from the national daily newspapers who had never been to Roker before were genuinely amazed at the passion in what was still, in spite of some dreadful performances in the past, a football area.

Manchester City were worried. They were slightly under-represented as far as support was concerned for the threat of a rail strike deterred quite a few who feared that they might be trapped in the north-east overnight, and although their players had loads of experience at all levels, they had seldom encountered anything quite as intense as all this. They were still the favourites, though, and Allison – 'Big Mal' – was not slow to say how they were going to win the FA Cup that season. If anything, that intensified Sunderland's passion.

Stokoe was able to field an unchanged team, while City were without the talented Summerbee, suspended for previous indiscretions and replaced by Ian Mellor, while, ironically enough, Towers – who had been sent off in the first match – was able, under the regulations of 1973, to play.

It was a totally thrilling occasion for a Sunderland fan, the best game at Roker for many years, reminiscent of the great days of the immediate post-war years, and on this occasion, with added drama caused by the floodlights, the cold night and the presence of TV cameras which ensured that the highlights could be watched when one got home. Many players on both sides commented on the sheer level of noise engendered by the passionate home support. They lifted their side to almost unbelievable levels that night.

Sunderland started off playing towards the Fulwell End, and on 15 minutes they went ahead thanks to a magnificently developed goal involving several players and finished off from the edge of the box by Halom, while you would have thought had been with Sunderland all his life from the way he had settled in. Hughes then put Sunderland 2-0 up with a fine goal after his first effort had been blocked, something that showed the never-say-die spirit of the player and of the club.

It was astonishing stuff, but there was always the fear that City would fight back, a fear that was intensified early in the second half when Francis Lee pulled one back. City now pressed and pressed, but Sunderland defended manfully with a few fine saves from Montgomery and a little luck now and again, until the visitors were caught out with too many men forward, and Tueart broke down the right and fired the ball across. It was parried to Hughes, who finished the job and gave Sunderland their best result for a very long time.

Full time came and so did delirium. Tears on the terraces were no uncommon phenomenon. It took a long

time for the euphoria to disperse – there were 39,000 at
Roker the Saturday after to see the league game against
Oxford United, for example – and this was the night
that really made the country sit up and take notice.
There was an element of the patronising in some of the
press comments, such as 'Sunderland take a great deal of
credit, and we wish them well, but ...' and 'Sunderland
– and Luton for that matter – have done the Second
Division proud', but generally speaking it was agreed
that Manchester City had been well beaten by the better
side. No one as yet thought realistically that Sunderland
could go all the way, but there was certainly a more than
reasonable expectation that they could beat Luton and
get as far as the semi-final. This was untold riches in
comparison with the dreadful days of recent years.

The quarter-finals were played on 17 March with
53,181 at Roker Park, and although it was the only all-
Second Division tie, it was the best attended of them
all. That said a great deal about where Sunderland
should have been and how much they had been
betrayed by generations of dreadful stewardship and
management. Much was made on Wearside about how
the only time Sunderland had won the FA Cup was
1937, and if you reversed these numbers it would be
73, but no one really thought that they were going to
win it this time around. Nevertheless, an indication
that Sunderland were now being taken seriously was

shown when the BBC decided to send its *Match of the Day* cameras to Roker Park.

Luton were about the same standard as Sunderland and would finish halfway up the Second Division. The Hatters, as they were called, were managed by Harry Haslam, who had made a difference to them since his arrival in 1972. They had no great FA Cup pedigree although they had contested the 1959 final, losing to Nottingham Forest in what was unfairly labelled as one of the 'less fashionable' finals of recent years. For this tie they appeared in an orange strip, brought a reasonable support with them and made no bones about saying that a trip to Kenilworth Road for a replay would be an acceptable outcome. However tempting that might have been for financial reasons, it would have no attraction for Sunderland. The semi-finals were now within sight, and the atmosphere within the town ever since the Manchester City game had been quite something with very few conversations about anything other than football.

The teams were:

Sunderland: Montgomery, Malone, Guthrie, Horswill, Watson, Pitt, Kerr, Hughes, Halom, Porterfield, Tueart.

Luton: Barber, John Ryan, Thomson, Shanks, Garner, Moore, Jimmy Ryan, Anderson, Busby, Hindson, Aston (Hales).

Of Sunderland's nine games to win the FA Cup of 1973, this one was possibly the least interesting of them all. They were always the better team in the first half but just couldn't apply the finishing touch. Luton's desire for a replay couldn't have been more obvious in their apparent lack of ambition. Montgomery had been presented with a gold watch before the game because he had broken the club's all-time appearances record, and seldom could he have had such an easy game.

Sunderland's two goals were good ones, however, both coming from corners on the left. The first, early in the second half, was taken by Bobby Kerr and found the head of Dave Watson. The second came as time was running out when Billy Hughes found the head of Ritchie Pitt, who headed the ball down to Ron Guthrie to finish the job with a goal that was so rare as to be a collector's item as far as he was concerned.

That was good enough, and as the players trooped off they were in the semi-finals for the first time for nearly 20 years, this time along with Wolves, Leeds United and the winners of Chelsea and Arsenal who had drawn at Stamford Bridge. The town was naturally jubilant, and much was the discussion about who they wanted or did not want. It was generally agreed that they did not want Leeds, and probably Wolves would have been the preferred opponents, but in the event it would be the winners of Chelsea veersus Arsenal at

Hillsborough. It turned out to be Arsenal, who beat Chelsea 2-1 at Highbury on the Wednesday night.

Arsenal were a team who had, for all their wealth, underperformed until 1971 when they suddenly came good and won the double. They were also the beaten finalists in the 1972 FA Cup Final and this time around, like Leeds, they felt that they had an outside chance of the double. They tended not to be well liked by other teams for their opulence and even arrogance on occasion, but they were always a force to be reckoned with. Stokoe was quite happy with them as opponents, for he felt that they had a few defensive weaknesses.

The fact that the game was at Hillsborough was looked upon as a positive as well, for it was a good ground and not too far away for the supporters. Certainly the fans were well enough motivated, even though realistically and on form, one would have had to have fancied the Gunners. But it was the FA Cup and anything could happen.

Second Division form continued to be good with three wins and a draw between the quarter and the semi-finals. However much Stokoe kept saying that there was still a relegation battle going on, it was clear that this was pure rhetoric and the reality was totally different. Sunderland were steadily climbing up the table, playing the fixtures which had been piling up because of bad weather, the cup run and the flu epidemic at Christmas.

But Stokoe and Ritchie Pitt fell out again. It was kept away from the public and the press at the time, but it all happened when Sunderland won at Preston North End a couple of days after they reached the semi-final. It was an odd time for the two to pick a fight with each other, but clearly the strain had been telling on the pair of them. Lance Hardy's excellent book *Stokoe, Sunderland and '73* gave Pitt's version of what happened. Pitt claimed that Stokoe picked on him through mistaken identity for Preston scoring a consolation goal, shouted at him, the player knocked a few tea cups off a table in the dressing room, and the manager summoned him to his office the following day to tell him that he didn't like him and that he was wanting rid of him.

Strong stuff, but almost literally a storm in a tea cup. Pitt retained his place in the side up to the FA Cup Final, and if intemperate words had been spoken, they were quickly forgotten. It does not appear that the pair exchanged Christmas cards with each other in subsequent years, but both men emerged with a great deal of credit for managing to swallow their pride and to establish a way of working with each other. One is not compelled to like everyone that one works with, but there are times when it is expedient to minimise personality clashes and to learn how to get along. Clearly both realised that they were on to a good thing with each other – Stokoe aware that Pitt was a fine defender whom he needed, and Pitt knowing that Stokoe represented his best chance of ever winning an FA Cup Final.

Meanwhile, Arsenal won two games and lost one, thus staying in the First Division championship race, but they had major injury problems. Frank McLintock, the man who had more or less carried Arsenal at centre-half, had been ruled out with a hamstring problem. Hamstring injuries take their own time to heal up, and McLintock's was a bad one. Up front a similar problem emerged in that centre-forward John Radford was ruled out with a knee injury.

All this was bad enough, but Arsenal still had enough good players to cope with these fundamental problems, it was felt. After all, Sunderland were a Second Division team as the press kept telling everyone, and Arsenal had, only two years earlier, won the double. But a major dilemma presented itself to manager Bertie Mee when injury problems began to threaten another central defender in Jeff Blockley, who suffered from a thigh strain but had seemed to recover. Mee then had the problem of deciding whether he was sufficiently match fit for a vigorous semi-final. Otherwise he would have to go for a less experienced player in the centre of the defence. In the end Mee took a gamble on Blockley, and it was probably the wrong decision.

It was announced officially that there was a colour clash and, it being a semi-final, both teams would be obliged to change. In the event Sunderland wore white and Arsenal yellow. This seems a shame because although both teams usually wore red, there was surely a world of difference between red and white vertical jerseys with black shorts on the one hand and red with white sleeves and white shorts on the other. The decision that both had to change meant that neither set of supporters had the opportunity to see their favourites in their familiar and traditional strip.

As far as Sunderland were concerned, tickets were sold very quickly. The capacity of Hillsborough was 55,000, so the Wearsiders were given an allocation of 22,000. Around 4,000 were offered to season ticket holders while a ballot was held for those who could prove attendance at the league games against Carlisle United and Bristol City. Not unnaturally, both of these mundane fixtures were played in front of large crowds – a good thing in itself and much appreciated by the players – and it was a fair way of settling the ticket problem, although inevitably there were squeals of unhappiness from those who did not get a ticket. Trains, buses and cars would leave Sunderland from a very early hour on 7 April.

In the meantime the players had left town for a base at the Peak District town of Buxton in Derbyshire. There should have been a game against Queens Park Rangers on Monday, 2 April but a blizzard put paid to that one, to the relief of Stokoe and Sunderland. They stayed in the luxurious Palace Hotel, already well known to Stokoe for Newcastle had been known to use that haunt in his playing days.

The emphasis was on relaxation and companionship. Snow, a common phenomenon in these parts – on 1 June 1975 it would stop a cricket match – was enough to knock out any football games, but the players were able to go for gentle runs, play golf and enjoy games of snooker well away from querulous wives and demanding children. Unlike many managers, Stokoe did not have a huge problem about his players enjoying the occasional drink either, although one or two had to be warned not to overdo it.

Naturally the game was discussed, and tactics decided upon, but the players approached the Saturday relaxed and confident. It was no great surprise to find that the morning newspapers all predicted a win for the Gunners, even with their injury problems, and indeed it was confidently stated that the final on 5 May would be a repeat of the 1972 occasion between Arsenal and Leeds, for the Yorkshire side were looking equally good against Wolverhampton Wanderers. The opinions of journalists are usually easily dealt with, but the words of Malcolm Macdonald of Newcastle were less well received, when he decided to play to the gallery with a few ill-chosen words about Sunderland's prospects.

Sunderland had had a few well-hidden injury worries, but Stokoe was able to announce more or less the team that he wanted. Arsenal, as expected, were without McLintock and Radford, although the latter was announced as substitute and indeed came on to play a part in the game. Mee had decided to gamble on the fitness of Blockley. The teams were:

Sunderland: Montgomery, Malone, Guthrie, Horswill, Watson, Pitt, Kerr, Hughes, Halom, Porterfield, Tueart.

Arsenal: Wilson, Rice, McNab, Storey, Blockley (Radford), Simpson, Armstrong, Ball, George, Kennedy, Kelly.

The weather was dry but the temperature was more like January than April with a swirling, icy blast. Sunderland attacked the Kop end of the ground where all their supporters were, and it was soon obvious that they were making a lot more noise than their Arsenal equivalents, largely because their men were playing with verve and enthusiasm.

Sunderland were under a great deal less pressure than Arsenal were. They were expected to lose, and if they did, everyone would still congratulate Stokoe for a job well done and wish him all the best. Arsenal, on the other hand, had to deliver. Their supporters had enjoyed a major taste of the good life in 1971, but no further success had followed, and supporters had noted with dismay that Tottenham Hotspur had won the League Cup a month earlier by beating Norwich City 1-0. In theory this really had nothing to do with Arsenal, but in fact it hurt deeply in the same way as Sunderland supporters would not have enjoyed Newcastle winning a trophy.

As Sunderland went on the attack, it was soon apparent that Arsenal's gamble on the fitness of Blockley had failed, for he was ponderous. He even appeared to lack confidence, something that is often a sign of a player being unable to trust his body to do things without bringing further pain. Already Sunderland had come close on several occasions through Micky Horswill in particular, before they went ahead when Blockley seemed in two minds about whether to clear a long ball or pass it back to his goalkeeper. In the event, he was hideously short with a pass back and in nipped the alert Halom to beat Bob Wilson with a slight miskick which was nevertheless good enough to enter the net.

There was an element of self-destruction on Arsenal's part about that goal, but there was little doubt that Sunderland deserved the lead, and although the Londoners had one or two half-chances, with one particularly good save from Montgomery, half-time was reached with the Wearsiders on top and still 1-0 up. The half-time score was greeted with a certain amount of surprise in the nation's living rooms and at other matches, and it was now apparent that Arsenal were going to have to raise their game.

The radio commentator was certainly of that persuasion, but one got the impression that he felt it was only a matter of time before the Gunners equalised and then got on top – although it did not work out like that. Blockley was replaced. It was a questionable decision, for only one substitute was available in 1973 and the new introduction was Radford, an attacker who was himself struggling with injury.

About quarter of an hour into the second half, the listening nation was stunned when Sunderland went further ahead. A throw-in on the right was taken by Kerr and headed on by Tueart to Hughes, who glanced it towards the goal and Wilson could only palm the ball into the net.

The exuberant celebrations of the fans from the north had to be tempered by the realisation that, although Wembley had now appeared on the horizon, it was still a long and dangerous path. And yet the midfield of Horswill and Pitt were holding well, Tueart and Porterfield were still looking productive and there was little to worry about at the back.

But you never know in football. The game became a little feisty and both Dicky Malone and Charlie Guthrie got themselves involved in incidents that they would have been better off out of. But the minutes were slowly, all too slowly, ticking away and confidence was growing with some of the Arsenal players beginning to argue among themselves, a clear sign that things were not going well for them.

Less than five minutes remained when Arsenal pulled one back. It was a shot from Charlie George, their hero of 1971, but it had an element of luck about it, for Montgomery got a hand to the ball but could not stop it from trickling over the line to the horror of the massed ranks of Mackems behind the goal.

One only really understands the meaning of the word 'pressure' in these circumstances. From the veterans of Wembley of 1937 to the youngsters who probably did not really know where Wembley was ('somewhere in London'), anxiety pervaded the Sunderland ranks – and it was not mere anxiety, it was that heart-stopping, stomach-trembling, gut-tying-itself-in-knots sort of agony that only a football supporter in these circumstances can understand. But with quite a few lifelong atheists vowing that they would go to church the following morning, suddenly, just as Arsenal were about to take a corner, the referee blew his whistle, pointed to the dressing room and Sunderland just went mad.

From Maine Road came news that Leeds had beaten Wolves 1-0 through a Billy Bremner goal, but there was still an air of unreality about it all. There were all the tears on the park, and the players and Stokoe waving to the fans, but there was still something that was hard to accept. Arsenal had been defeated, and only Leeds stood between Sunderland and the FA Cup, yet as recently as Christmas the Wearsiders had been reckoning with the possibility of Third Division football for 1973/74. It was barely credible.

But everyone pinched themselves and no, they were not dreaming. The trains and buses home that night were a curious mixture of drunken singing and bemused, exhausted faces. There was still an awful lot to take in.

One is ignoring the truth if one says that the north-east does not have a persecution complex about the rest of the country. But if anyone felt that the nation wanted Arsenal to beat Sunderland in the semi-final, that could certainly not be said about the final. Leeds were not well liked, to put it mildly. Very few people outside of Leeds itself could put in a good word for them, and even the solidarity of Yorkshire (a county which had an even more pronounced 'us against the world' complex than the north-east does) was severely put to the test when called upon to defend the Whites. When Celtic defeated them in the European Cup semi-final of 1970 there was as much rejoicing in England as there was in Scotland, and even Rangers fans were not entirely unhappy.

'Dirty Leeds' was now almost a cliché. Billy Bremner rejoiced in nicknames like 'the Scottish terrier' and Norman Hunter was not called 'Bites Yer Legs' for nothing. Behind them all was manager Don Revie, a totally ruthless man who had once, according to *Stokoe, Sunderland and '73*, offered Stokoe (when manager of Bury) a bribe to 'take it easy' in a relegation battle. The two men were not friends.

And yet there was more to Leeds than that. They had won the League Cup in 1968, the First Division in 1969 and the FA Cup in 1972 with quite a few near misses too. And as well as the 'raw meat' brigade they also had some fine players like Johnny Giles, Allan Clarke and Eddie Gray, and Revie, to his credit, was a fine tactician. And it has to be admitted that a lot of the negative feelings about the men from Elland Road were because of sheer jealousy and prejudice. Quite a lot, however, wasn't.

Whatever one's feelings about Leeds, it was hard to see past them in the final. Sunderland had done very well, it was generally agreed, in beating Manchester

City and Arsenal, but Leeds were different altogether, and the Wearsiders couldn't do it three times in a row, could they? The final was scheduled for 5 May, and both teams had a month to prepare for it.

Sunderland's games were comparatively innocuous and basically irrelevant, but Leeds had other fish to fry. Sunderland, astonishingly, played eight times between 7 April and the final. They won five, lost two and drew one (but who was counting?), something that showed that they were in good form and attuning themselves nicely for the final, the important point being not to get hurt. There were protests about the amount of fixtures, but the Football League was obdurate, and as Sunderland were so many matches in arrears they were in no position to argue anyway.

All this caused no little angst including the predictable 'the world's against us' and 'if it had been Arsenal or Manchester United, it would have been different', but it paled into insignificance in comparison with the two other major issues – how to get a ticket, and whose TV you were going to watch it on if you didn't – as the town was subject to more media scrutiny in terms of newspaper articles and TV documentaries than ever before. Sales of red and white scarves soared, and stock which had lain unsold for years suddenly disappeared.

An allocation of 20,000 tickets was never going to be enough and it all depended on a ballot of those who had been to some of the irrelevant league games. Naturally the newspapers were full of sob stories of those who had been regulars during all the bad years (and God knows, there had been plenty of them) but couldn't get a ticket for this one. But there was always the consolation of watching the final on TV – not exactly a fate worse than death.

Leeds, on the other hand, could not afford to worry about the final on its own. They too had a fixture pile-up in the First Division. Their form was indifferent to put it mildly and they finally conceded the title to Liverpool at Anfield on Easter Monday, but their hopes had been dwindling for some time. They had more success in the European Cup Winners' Cup. They beat Hajduk Split 1-0 on 11 April at Elland Road and drew 0-0 in Yugoslavia in the second leg of the semi-final. It almost goes without saying that they were 'feisty' encounters. Allan Clarke was sent off in one of them, but it meant that Leeds were in the final to play AC Milan some 11 days after Wembley.

Sunderland stayed at the Selsdon Park Hotel, a location made famous – or infamous – by being the home for various conferences of the Conservative Party in the past, while Leeds stayed at Hendon. There were the predictable wars of words with various players of other teams seeming to go out of their way to annoy Sunderland and their fans by telling them just how good Leeds were, and how well Sunderland had done to get this far, but. It was all very annoying but also very predictable and it made for good television.

London was wet on Saturday, 5 May, punctuated by the occasional ray of sunshine, and pundits continued to make fools of themselves by saying how much the conditions would affect the game, but on one thing, they remained universally adamant – that Leeds would win. It was annoying, but it did have the effect of making areas like suburban London, the West Country and Lancashire adopt an unusual passion for Sunderland, the underdogs. Back home, the town was like a ghost town in a western, and one wonders what the feelings were in Newcastle. It was difficult to support Sunderland, but on the other hand, Bob Stokoe was a deserved hero of the Tyne as well – and feelings about Leeds were no less visceral in Newcastle than elsewhere. In Scotland, if you were not obsessed about the Celtic v Rangers Scottish Cup Final then there was no problem. You wanted Sunderland to win. Billy Bremner was Scottish but he was no hero.

The Duke of Kent was the statutory member of the royal family. Not a few of the fans wondered who he was, but he was dignified as he shook hands with everyone, and seemed to be interested in the game. It was, however, with some relief that the match actually got started, and everyone could watch the football.

The teams were:

Sunderland: Montgomery, Malone, Guthrie, Horswill, Watson, Pitt, Kerr, Hughes, Halom, Porterfield, Tueart.

Leeds: Harvey, Reaney, Cherry, Bremner, Madeley, Hunter, Lorimer, Clarke, Jones, Giles, Gray (Yorath).

Referee: Mr K. Burns, Stourbridge.

Sunderland's heroes of the FA Cup Final are well known. The goal scored by Ian Porterfield and the astonishing double save by Jim Montgomery can be watched ad infinitum on YouTube. The Montgomery save never fails to amaze, and it was probably the point at which Leeds realised that they were not going to win. It is probably not true that football is controlled by some fate, destiny or god, but there are times on the field when one realises that one is not going to win this particular game. 'The heads went down' is possibly one of the most horrible clichés of them all, but that certainly happened to Leeds at Wembley that day.

The reverse was not true, however. Those on the terraces and back home who said 'I knew we were going to do it' were, frankly, liars. One is far more inclined to believe the stories of the supporters who hid under beds and in garden sheds for the last few minutes, and were only summoned out by the roar that swept the whole town when Mr Burns blew for time up. A few fans have been honest enough to admit to what can be tactfully described as 'toilet accidents', but presumably the smell did nothing to diminish the wholesale hugging and kissing that went on, even among strangers in the streets.

Porterfield, Montgomery and Stokoe himself all had their moments of glory, but tribute must also be paid to other members of the team. Malone, for example, was meant to be annihilated by Gray. He wasn't. The central defence of Watson and Pitt was going to be overrun by Clarke, Mick Jones and Peter Lorimer. But none of those prolific goalscorers found the net that day. The midfield was meant to be dominated by Bremner, the 'red-haired terrier' from Stirling. But Sunderland's midfield put 'the wee Scottish bastard' (as he was universally described) in his place.

The celebrations have been well described. They went on for days, weeks and months with tea intervals at local cricket matches often prolonged as opponents entertained each other with their own recollections while the umpires were impatient to get the games re-started. The next few football and cricket seasons were dominated by conversation about this final, and anyone in any social gathering with any Sunderland connection can still be guaranteed to try to bring 1973 into the conversation. It was the year of Watergate,

Edward Heath, inflation, the Yom Kippur war, miners'
problems – but it was also the year that Sunderland
won the FA Cup.

It has not happened since, and it is now such a long
time in the past.